THE AVIATION PIONEERS OF MCCOOK FIELD

Candid Interviews with American Aeronautical Visionaries of the 1920s

Jerry Koszyk

Foreword by
Jonna Doolittle Hoppes, with
James H. "Jimmy" Doolittle III

Copyright © 2022 by Jerry Koszyk

Library of Congress Control Number: 2021942726

All rights reserved. No part of this work may be reproduced or used in any form or by any means—graphic, electronic, or mechanical, including photocopying or information storage and retrieval systems—without written permission from the publisher.

The scanning, uploading, and distribution of this book or any part thereof via the Internet or any other means without the permission of the publisher is illegal and punishable by law. Please purchase only authorized editions and do not participate in or encourage the electronic piracy of copyrighted materials.

"Schiffer Military" and the arrow logo are trademarks of Schiffer Publishing, Ltd.

Designed by Christopher Bower
Cover design by Danielle Farmer
Type set in Dejanire Headline heading font/text font Industry Inc

ISBN: 978-0-7643-6352-8
Printed in Serbia

Published by Schiffer Publishing, Ltd.
4880 Lower Valley Road
Atglen, PA 19310
Phone: (610) 593-1777; Fax: (610) 593-2002
Email: Info@schifferbooks.com
Web: www.schifferbooks.com

For our complete selection of fine books on this and related subjects, please visit our website at www.schifferbooks.com. You may also write for a free catalog.

Schiffer Publishing's titles are available at special discounts for bulk purchases for sales promotions or premiums. Special editions, including personalized covers, corporate imprints, and excerpts, can be created in large quantities for special needs. For more information, contact the publisher.

We are always looking for people to write books on new and related subjects. If you have an idea for a book, please contact us at proposals@schifferbooks.com.

DEDICATION

This book is a tribute to all those with aeronautical vision during the last century, who toiled and risked their lives to make aviation one of the safest modes of transportation and, consequently, a travel option enjoyed by everyone today. Current pilots and passengers owe much to these pioneers, and I for one openly express my gratitude.

EPIGRAPH

I truly believe it almost was magical, that in one place there came together all of these talented, ingenious people who had the place, the enthusiasm, and the background to do some miraculous things.

—Darlene Gerhardt, looking back on her years at McCook Field

CONTENTS

Foreword | By Jonna Doolittle Hoppes, with James H. "Jimmy" Doolittle III 6
Preface 8
Acknowledgments 10
McCook Field Timeline 12
Chapter 1 | George E. A. Hallett 15
Chapter 2 | Albert Francis Hegenberger 22
Chapter 3 | Thomas Harriman 27
Chapter 4 | Harry Anton Johnson 31
Chapter 5 | Leigh Wade 33
Chapter 6 | J. Parker Van Zandt 40
Chapter 7 | James H. Doolittle 44
Chapter 8 | Harold R. Harris 55
Chapter 9 | Howard Calhoun Davidson 67
Chapter 10 | Hester Christiansen 72
Chapter 11 | Alan Morse 75
Chapter 12 | Darlene E. Gerhardt 77
Chapter 13 | Louis Hagemeyer 84
Chapter 14 | Franklin O. Carroll 89
Chapter 15 | Oakley Kelly 93
Chapter 16 | George C. Kenney 98
Chapter 17 | Reuben H. Fleet 101
Chapter 18 | John A. Macready 104
Chapter 19 | Jean Alfred Roche 111
Chapter 20 | Alexander N. P. de Seversky 118
Chapter 21 | Albert William Stevens 123
Chapter 22 | Insights from the Interviews 126
Chapter 23 | The Planes and Parachutes of McCook Field 134
Chapter 24 | Life at McCook Field 181
Epilogue 185
Bibliography 186
Index 188

FOREWORD

BY JONNA DOOLITTLE HOPPES, WITH JAMES H. "JIMMY" DOOLITTLE III

I'm not sure anyone alive today can remember a world without airplanes. But just over a hundred years ago, aviation was a fledgling science and very few people had seen, much less flown in, one of those flying machines. Between the years 1917 and 1927, US aeronautical research and development was concentrated at McCook Field, a small military airfield in Dayton, Ohio, where commercial, civilian, aerobatic, and military aviation merged. Here some of the greatest minds converged to establish the United States as a competitive player in international aviation. We owe a great deal to those early pioneers—the pilots, engineers, mechanics, photographers, managers, and even clerks.

My cousin James H. Doolittle III and I collaborated on this foreword. Jimmy, a third-generation military test pilot and mechanical engineering grad of Texas A&M, spent about twenty of his thirty years on USAF active duty in military flight test operations—twice as a member of the US Air Force Test Pilot School (USAFTPS) flight instructor staff and as commandant of that great school. He also flew more than two hundred missions as a Douglas A-1 Skyraider pilot in Southeast Asia during the Vietnam War. Jimmy has a keen appreciation for those involved in developing airframes, both in the early years and modern times. His experience makes him uniquely suited to understand the importance of McCook Field and the individuals who worked there. Like Gramps, he knows his life depends on engineers and mechanics.

Our grandfather's love of aviation began with the 1910 Aviation Meet in Dominguez Hills, California. In 1917, with the onset of World War I, he enlisted in the Army Signal Corps as a flying cadet and ended up in San Diego as a flight instructor. According to Gramps, his assignment to the Air Service Engineering School at McCook Field in 1922 was one of the milestones of his career. In those early days, engineers felt pilots were all a little crazy, and pilots were convinced that engineers were not thoroughly acquainted with the pilot's viewpoint. From a philosophical point of view, Gramps felt that it would be good to have engineers and pilots understand one another better. It seemed desirable to marry these two capabilities in one person. He wanted to be that person.

One of the individuals who facilitated that marriage between pilots and engineers was Col. Thurman H. Bane, who was a pilot with an engineering degree, a rarity in those days. As an administrator of McCook for a number of years, Bane deserves credit for the development of much of the philosophy behind the work at McCook Field. According to Gramps, Bane never received adequate recognition for his many contributions to aeronautics in that early McCook Field era.

Although best known for his military exploits, Gramps was proudest of his accomplishments in the science of aviation. It was much easier to get him to talk about his days at McCook Field and the calculated risks they'd taken to advance flight. We never witnessed

Foreword

our granddad talking about his days at McCook without displaying an immense and enthusiastic grin on his face. He considered McCook Field "pilot heaven" because of the variety of planes and the number of interesting experimental work going on all the time.

His ties to McCook Field predated and postdated his assignments there. He consulted McCook engineers about fuel tank modifications and obtained a turn-bank indicator (an instrument being tested at the field) for his coast-to-coast flight in under twenty-four hours. He was allowed the unprecedented opportunity to use all their aircraft for any test work he wanted to do while earning his master's degree and doctorate from MIT. When he concluded his studies, he returned to McCook as chief of the flight test section. He said, "It was the opportunity I had hoped for, the chance to be both pilot and engineer. I could alternate between drawing board and cockpit, recommend innovations, draw them up, and then try them out."

Gramps believed that all his air victories, military successes, and scientific discoveries were the direct result of a team and that every member of that team contributed an essential part to the overall success. Many of those team members were his colleagues at McCook Field and many of their pictures hung on the wall in the hallway in his home in Santa Monica, a virtual who's who of aviation.

Jimmy and I are absolutely around-the-bend crazy about aviation history and preserving firsthand accounts. We personally owe Jerry Koszyk a debt of gratitude for capturing, preserving, and now sharing those firsthand accounts from McCook Field, which morphed via Wright Field into the Air Force Flight Test Center at Edwards AFB, the premier military flight test organization. Earlier works have ignored the importance of McCook Field in the evolution of aviation. Many of the stories captured by Koszyk would be lost without his hard work.

That's what makes this book so important. We learn the unique perspective of those who were there during the infant days of American aviation. Aviation today owes them so much.

PREFACE

McCook Field looking west along North Keowee Street toward the Great Miami River. *Army Air Service photo from the American Aviation Historical Society archives*

It's the summer of 1976. Armed with a map of Dayton, Ohio, and in possession of some fifty-year-old aerial photographs, I find myself driving west along Keowee Street. I'm looking for evidence that a place called McCook Field once existed. The facility figured prominently in the early days of aviation research and development. To the south is a low-cost housing project. To the north are single- and multi-family homes. Lining Keowee are the usual twentieth-century commercial buildings—a KFC eatery, a Shell gas station.

Then I see it—a marquee announcing "McCook Shopping Center." Tenants are a drugstore, a movie theater, small shops, and a bowling alley called "McCook Bowl." I park and walk into the bowling alley, hoping to find the neighborhood resident who doubles as the local historian. Every neighborhood has one. A woman in her forties standing at the counter listens to my request and points nearby to a man in his sixties. "He has lived here forever," she says.

After introducing myself to the man, he immediately excites me. "Yes," he says, "I remember McCook Field very well. I used to play ball there all the time." He goes on to tell me that the very area where we are standing was once part of McCook Field.

I excitedly ask him where the hangars were located in relation to the bowling alley. He looks puzzled. "Hangars? What hangars?" Well, I say, beginning to feel some puzzlement myself, "You know, the hangars where the planes were housed."

The man then drains the last of my excitement, confidently assuring me that hangars were never part of McCook Field. "There weren't any airplanes at McCook. It was a baseball field! I don't recall any airplanes *ever* being here. You, sir, must have this place mixed up with another one."

Sign that marked McCook Field in 1977. *Photo by author*

Once a place of stellar aeronautical achievement, McCook Field no longer exists, not even in the memories of longtime residents.

It did exist, though. In the last century—to be exact, in December 1917. The facility opened that month on the north edge of Dayton, Ohio. On the grounds of the facility were large, wide-doored hangars that housed bona fide airplanes and a few flying contraptions. Nearby were busy mechanical shops, a wind-tunnel building, classroom units, and related structures, including an administrator's home. Adjacent to the campus of buildings was an open field with a short runway. The facility's official name was the Air Service Engineering Division, but the place was dubbed McCook Field and, almost by default, became a center of aeronautical innovation.

Over the next ten years, McCook Field distinguished itself with the kind of work that has led some aviation historians to declare it "The Cradle of Modern Aviation," a sobriquet of distinction that it manifestly deserves. At McCook, celebrated pilots, engineering and mechanical whizzes, and steadfast administrators parlayed genius and courage into significant aviation advancement. They worked under the tutelage of the Aviation Section of the US Signal Corps, which was the precursor of the US Army Air Service and today's Air Force. Their assignment was simple: develop and build next-generation airplanes capable of performing military missions and otherwise advancing the state of the art of this new thing called aviation.

It sometimes was a struggle. Private-sector aviation companies chafed at the government-sponsored competition. Myopic members of Congress saw little military value in aircraft because "The War to End All Wars" already had been fought and won. And, as in all-new technological undertakings, triumphs only slightly edged out disasters. McCook Field was equivalent in energy and inventiveness to Silicon Valley, with McCook personnel introducing transformational aeronautical technology.

The heart of this book is interviews with some primary personalities of the McCook saga. Their recollections of what transpired at McCook remind us all of what can happen when true believers and visionaries are given license to pursue their ideas. Personal accounts of life at McCook Field show again how talented people can do extraordinary things just by showing up, day after day.

ACKNOWLEDGMENTS

This book was a personal project that consumed many years of my life, and I couldn't have completed it without encouragement and help along the way.

My interest always has been in the development of an aircraft, rather than stories about its subsequent performance, whether in combat or commerce. I am a longtime pilot and experienced cross-country flier, but it is a plane's design and engineering that fascinate me.

In 1975, I lived in Indianapolis and was then, as now, an avid reader of aviation history. On many days away from my job as an air traffic controller at the Indianapolis Air Route Traffic Control Center (ARTCC), I would travel down the road to the National Museum of the United States Air Force, just north of Dayton, Ohio. There, as I pored over material in the museum's library, I kept coming across one name: McCook Field. As was my habit, I decided to buy a book about this place called McCook and learn more.

So, I asked the museum's curator, Shelby Wickam, where I might find and purchase such a publication. He responded that no book about McCook Field had yet been written and suggested that I do so. I had a good laugh at that. I was an amateur aviation researcher, after all, not a professional writer. However, over the next couple of weeks, I quit laughing at the prospect of writing such a book and started thinking, *Why not?*

That was in 1975, forty-seven years ago, an inordinately long time to spend on the research phase of a writing project. So, what happened between then and now? Life, mostly. My marriage ended. (No, not as a consequence of my obsession with McCook.) My career was upended when air traffic controllers struck in 1981 and President Reagan promptly struck back. As the years went by, my book project was shelved, taken down from the shelf, dusted off, and restarted—then reshelved as the dailiness of living pressed in on me.

It is not as though I did nothing during those years, however. My research seemed unending, with days spent at the Smithsonian Libraries and the National Archives (back when you could just walk in and search through boxes). I traveled across the country for interviews with some of the principal characters in the McCook story. They included Harold Harris, Leigh Wade, James Doolittle, Bessie Louise Bane, the widow of Thurman Bane (longtime commanding officer of McCook), J. Parker Van Zandt, George Hallett, Albert Hegenberger, and less heralded engineers and workers who recalled their days at McCook.

One of the unheralded veterans of McCook became my walking book of knowledge: Darlene Gerhardt. She was there as a secretary in 1921 and still was there when it closed. She dated some of the pilots, eventually married a flyboy and engineer of significant note, and completely absorbed the McCook experience. Interviewing her was better than opening a trove of documents because I could ask her follow-up questions.

I spent many days at Darlene's Dayton apartment as she pulled out box after box of McCook papers and photographs. Her former husband was McCook engineer William Frederick Gerhardt. You may recall seeing old film of Gerhardt as he tried to get his fragile, seven-wing craft airborne through pedal power. In a YouTube film clip of one such attempt (https://www.youtube.com/watch?v=TsywnRpRDUM), his "Cycleplane's" wings uneremoniously collapse. You probably laughed at the ridiculousness of it, but the Gerhardts didn't laugh. They had put every cent they had into what they hoped would be the first man-powered aircraft. By the way, what you don't see in that film clip is the machine towing the pedaled craft. It was driven by none other than James Doolittle. McCook was a community, and Darlene Gerhardt sometimes babysat the Doolittles' two sons.

During the course of my research, I received much direction and encouragement from noted aviation author Walter J. Boyne, then director of the National Air and Space Museum of the Smithsonian Institution.

I also am indebted to the late George Goddard, whom I first met in the mid-1970s. In 1969, he had published a book, *Overview: A Lifelong Adventure in Aerial Photography*, which recounted his exploits. I visited him at his home several times, and he graciously let me copy tapes of his interviews with McCook figures I couldn't reach. Some had died by the time I'd begun my research.

The copied Goddard interviews were conversations with John A. Macready, Jean A. Roche, Alexander P. de Seversky, Oakley Kelly, Louis Hagemeyer, Frank Carroll, George Kenney, and Reuben Fleet. Goddard's daughter Diane Goddard Gergh has also graciously given me permission to include those eight interviews in this book. I thank her for allowing me to include them. General Goddard was inducted into the National Aviation Hall of Fame in 1976 and died in 1987, at the age of ninety-eight.

This book is properly illustrated with photos of people and planes. For that, I am indebted to the American Aviation Historical Society. The society's managing editor, Hayden Hamilton, with whom I spoke, provided excellent-quality photos to supplement my own.

My inability to complete this project in a timely way subtly haunts me. People who took the time to tell me their story did so with the expectation that I would tell future generations about the place called McCook Field and its role in aviation history. Famed world traveler and journalist Lowell Thomas was excited about the project, for example, and agreed to write a foreword for the book. However, he passed on before I could hand him a manuscript.

With the publication of the book, I finally am keeping my part of the bargain, assisted by Giles Lambertson, a writer and friend. We also created a screenplay together, titled *This Field Is Small*, a cinematic telling that dramatically weaves together some of the exciting moments that characterized the McCook Field experience.

While I am disappointed the project has taken this long to wrap up, I am pleased it finally is complete. These pioneers of the last century and their accomplishments deserve to be widely remembered. This book is my contribution to remembering them.

MCCOOK FIELD TIMELINE

1917

April | US involvement in World War I officially begins.

July | Congress sets funding for military aviation at $640 million, up from $600,000 in 1916.

October | The US Army Signal Corps authorizes the establishment of McCook Field on 200 acres just north of downtown Dayton, Ohio. It is designated for the Aviation Engineering Section and is named after one of "the Fighting McCooks," fifteen members of a Civil War family that previously owned the land.

December | First arrival of personnel to the partially completed facility.

1918

Throughout the year | The McCook Armament Branch develops the Nelson gun control, a synchronizing machine gun that fires through a propeller. This was in response to a corresponding German invention. Lt. Frank S. Patterson—for whom Wright-Patterson Air Force Base is partly named—was killed near McCook while testing this gun system. Later in the year, Albert Hegenberger combines a turn indicator with a bank indicator.

1919

April | The first backpack, nonstatic parachute jump is made by Leslie Irvin. (*Note*: The Irvin parachute company is still in business as of 2020, producing parachutes and seatbelts under the name Airborne Systems.) In 1926. Maj. E. L. Hoffman of McCook receives the Collier trophy for the development of this lifesaving device.

September | Maj. Rudolph "Shorty" Schroeder sets an altitude record of 28,268 feet while carrying a passenger.

October | First reversible-pitch propeller is developed.

November | The Air Service Engineering School opens. The lead instructor is Edwin E. Aldrin, father of future astronaut Edwin Eugene "Buzz" Aldrin Jr. Today, the school is called the Air Force Institute of Technology and is located at Wright-Patterson Air Force Base.

1920

February | Official altitude record of 33,113 feet set by Maj. Rudolph "Shorty" Schroeder.

April | First flight of an ambulance aircraft, a modified DH-4.

McCook Field Timeline

1921

The Gen. Billy Mitchell bombing demonstrations of captured German naval ships are carried out off the Virginia coastline. Many McCook Field personnel participate. Technology developed at McCook Field is utilized.	Summer
The first pressurized cockpit is developed.	June
The first crop-dusting by aircraft occurs, a system developed at McCook.	August
Altitude record of 34,508 feet is set by Lt. John Macready in a supercharged LePere aircraft	September

1922

Record parachute jump of 24,200 feet is accomplished by Lt. Albert W. Stevens.	June
Extensive night-flying tests by Lt. Donald Bruner lead to the development of landing lights.	July
The Sperry airway beacon is tested at McCook for a Dayton-to-Columbus route.	August
A backpack parachute is deployed in a true emergency and saves the life of Lt. Harold R. Harris.	October
The first "flight" of the de Bothezat helicopter, piloted by Thurman Bane, McCook's commanding officer.	December

1923

The first all-metal aircraft is tested. A sensitive type of altimeter is developed by the engineering division. Albert Hegenberger helps develop the earth inductor compass, later used for long-distance flights, including a 1924 around-the-world flight and the 1927 Lindbergh flight from New York to Paris.	Throughout the year
First successful cloud-seeding occurs.	January
First nonstop flight coast to coast is completed, a McCook Field project, by Lts. Oakley Kelly and John Macready.	May
A model airway is established between McCook Field and Columbus, Ohio. On this route, McCook aviators experiment with night navigation equipment. The research later benefits the US Postal Service in its night-flying operations.	Summer
The Barling Bomber, the world's largest, undergoes testing at McCook.	August
The first Dayton, Ohio, air show is held for a crowd estimated at sixty thousand.	September
The first flight of the "Cycleplane" occurs, a pedaled craft designed and built by W. F. Gerhardt and E. L. Pratt.	July

McCook Field Timeline

1924

March | James Doolittle conducts a flight to prove the efficacy of wind tunnel stress tests, an aeronautical design and testing breakthrough.

April–September | First around-the-world flight in four two-seat Douglas Cruisers, a McCook project. McCook pilots Leigh Wade, Erik Nelson, and mechanic Jack Harding participate. The flight gains worldwide aviation fame for Donald Douglas and his three-year-old Douglas Aircraft Company.

June | Lt. Russell L. Maughan completes a "dawn to dusk" flight, the first crossing of the North American continent during daylight.

October | International Air Races are held in Dayton. McCook personnel help plan and promote the event.

1925

July | First radio beacon developed for a Department of Commerce airmail aircraft.

November | First night aerial photograph by McCook Field Lt. George Goddard in demonstration near Rochester, New York.

1926

Throughout the year | The "Air Service" is changed to the "Army Air Corps."

January | Record altitude of 38,704 feet set by Lt. John Macready.

April | Ground is broken for Wright Field as a replacement for McCook Field.

August | Eugene Hoy Barksdale, for whom Barksdale Air Force Base is named, is killed during a test flight.

1927

May | First outside loop completed above McCook Field by James Doolittle.

June | First nonstop flight of *"the Bird of Paradise"* from US mainland (Oakland, California) to Honolulu, Hawaii, completed by Lts. Lester Maitland and Albert Hegenberger. This is a McCook Field project, and each man receives a Mackay Trophy in 1927.

October | Wright Field formally dedicated with Orville Wright in attendance. (*Note*: Wilbur had died of typhoid fever in 1912. Orville would die in 1948 of natural causes.) Dismantling of McCook Field begins.

CHAPTER 1
GEORGE E. A. HALLETT

INTERVIEWED MAY 1978
Upon leaving McCook Field, Maj. George E. A. Hallett was hired by Charles Kettering, an inventor and director of research at General Motors. Hallett went on to, among other things, oversee the development of twelve- and sixteen-cylinder GM diesel motors used extensively in railroad engines and submarines. He eventually retired to a home in his native California, where he died in 1982.

Q: Were you in the service before World War 1?

A: No. Before we got into World War I, I had gone to work at North Island (in San Diego Bay) as an aviation mechanic, and I had been told to make mechanical troubleshooters for the field. And then the commanding officer told me to prepare lessons for lectures and so on for the highest-ranking mechanics and make better mechanics, better troubleshooters, out of them. I had never heard a lecture in my life. I had never gone to high school, you know, and . . .

Q: Wait a minute. You never went to high school?

A: No. So, I wrote out a course and taught it to classes of about twelve enlisted men. I developed my own method of teaching them about how to shoot trouble. I was told to write down what my course was, so it could be copied. And I did. It was a book that they published by the millions and used very widely within the service during World War I.

Due to the great need for more mechanics, we had an enormous buildup to do, since we were so darned small to start with. I was to go east and revise five of the big northern flying fields into mechanic schools for the winter of 1917–18, when they couldn't teach primary flying and the fields were given up at the end of the summer. I went to Washington to interview about 270 men I had helped select. I interviewed each for about ten minutes, picked out seventy of them, and split them into five groups for the five flying schools.

I went around to the schools. I was still a civilian—a young, skinny civilian. I had a letter dictated by me and signed by H. H. Arnold, who was running the Air Service at the time. All of that enabled me to turn those darned flying schools inside out, and that's just what I had to do to make them into mechanic schools for that winter.

I believe we trained about ten thousand mechanics in that short time. I had run classes for officers as well as enlisted men at North Island. My commanding officer at McCook Field was one of my students, and H. H. Arnold had known me very well. That helped me immensely, of course, There were high-ranking army people with experience in aviation who had confidence in me. So, things moved right along.

In June 1918, I was notified that I had been commissioned a major. They had to give me that much rank to pay me enough money. I already had reached the maximum pay level for Civil Service. I had to earn enough money to support my family and so on. Then I was sent to Wilbur Wright Field (Riverside, Ohio), where we had a little organization that checked on the stuff that aircraft builders were putting out. We checked out, for instance, the DH-4 and the SE-5, and the first experimental Martin bomber. I could tell you stories about that one.

At the end of the year, my chief assistant, George J. Meade, and I moved into Dayton. Meade later was chief engineer for Pratt & Whitney Aircraft. We lived in the little Miami Hotel there and planned in detail the complete revision of the Air Service's existing power-plant section, which hadn't done very much. I got busy.

The man who had been running the section, J. G. Vincent, was one of the developers of the Liberty engine. I asked him about experiments they had been making with a General Electric turbocompressor. They mounted a Liberty engine on a truck and took it on top of Pike's Peak, 14,000 feet or so and got only slight gains in performance—nothing very promising.

I asked Vincent for his opinion of the turbosupercharger. He said, "Oh, you'll never get a net gain with that." Well, I considered what he said, but then I chose that type over two or three others, chose that type to work on some more. We made enough progress that in a few years we were the only ones still developing it. The French, Germans, British, and Italians all had been working on it to some extent but gave up because they weren't getting much from it.

Q: So, Vincent did not believe that there was a future in the turbosupercharger?

A: Yes, at that time. That's a fact. We had our troubles developing it. We melted blades off that turbo. Finally, one of my engineers, E. T. Jones—I had him in charge of that part of the work and he also was my first assistant—he got the idea of taking the turbine out from behind the big centrifugal blow, which shoved all the air away from it, and putting it out on the side of the fuselage, where the forward slipstream would cool it. No one had thought of that.

Q: I had heard they had a problem, that they had to move it. E. T. Jones was the one who had the idea?

A: Yes. I liked that idea and OK'd work on it right away. Then we had to develop a better intercooler and several other things we had to lick before we could go ahead and really begin to get results. We had excellent test pilots right from the beginning, and they helped us out a great deal.

I flew the Lepere plane, a French design built by Packard with a Liberty engine and a turbo compressor. I took it up to about 20,000 feet. I planned on oversupercharging it, experimenting with it. While oversupercharging, I happened to collapse the float chamber, the float in the carburetor, one of the two carburetors—I don't recall just which. So, I had sheets of flame coming out of the exhaust on the right side but nothing abnormal on the left. I hastened to study the diagram and get the fuel shut off as fast as I could. In the meantime, the flames were licking down the side of the fuselage, which might have easily ignited. It was covered with plywood, as I remember. Then I enjoyed the glide down from 20,000 feet to the field, which looked the size of a postage stamp at first.

Q: I take it you were a rated pilot?

A: Yes, I was. But I've never done anything exceptional in flying except flying for my own satisfaction to test every change in the engine, every installation change that was worthwhile.

Q: Was this the same Lepere airplane used by John A. Macready? (*Note*: Macready was a famed military test pilot at McCook Field, whose specialty was high-altitude record attempts and long-distance flights.)

A: That's right, and Macready was the one who OK'd my flying it. He was in charge of the plane. Macready gave me part of my flight training, my aerobatics and so on. He knew I could handle it. In respect to the supercharger, let me point out that when World War II started, we were the only country that had an active turbosupercharger, one that was ready for production. I had Jones write the NACA.

> *I had him ask at NACA what they thought of jet propulsion. We had some ideas. In response, they got out a little report and said jet propulsion was far too inefficient a means of propulsion to be of any interest. That's what it amounted to. And they were right. That's the funny part.*

Q: Excuse me. NACA here is the National Advisory Committee for Aeronautics, the predecessor of NASA, the National Aeronautics and Space Administration...

A: That's right. I had him ask at NACA what they thought of jet propulsion. We had some ideas. In response, they got out a little report and said jet propulsion was far too inefficient a means of propulsion to be of any interest. That's what it amounted to. And they were right. That's the funny part. Jet propulsion isn't any good, even now, much below 300 miles an hour and we had no way to fly anywhere that fast. Nor any way to land at the necessary landing speeds if we had been able to fly that fast.

Anyhow, we went ahead. We didn't have any variable pitch propeller, so we had to put on propellers that were overloaded turning at eleven hundred rpm instead of fourteen hundred, so they wouldn't overspeed and burst at the higher altitudes. That's the way Macready and Harris made their altitude flights. (*Note*: Then-lieutenant, later general, Harold Harris was a longtime McCook Field test pilot.)

Q: You must have done some work with Shorty Schroeder. (*Note*: the 6-foot, 4-inch Rudolph William "Shorty" Schroeder was one of the first test pilots at McCook and set several altitude records. In 1940, he became a vice president at United Airlines.)

A: Oh, yes. Shorty was an old friend. He was a wonderful flier, no question about that. Wonderful flier and a fine fellow. He did a lot of work for us. He also was a good mechanic and was able to help us a lot on the earliest flights. He flew the earliest flights on the turbosupercharger. We made a lot of progress during that time. In later years, long after I was out of the service, something happened to Shorty, and he got an idea that he invented just about everything. He had his troubles and so on. But Shorty was a real good friend.

Q: What year did you go to McCook and then leave McCook?

A: I went to McCook, took charge of the power-plant section, in December 1918, certainly by January 1919. I left in December 1922. I left the same day as Maj. Reuben Fleet.

Q: Now, Reuben Fleet, there's an interesting man.

A: Oh, yes, indeed. He was wonderful. Without Fleet, we could not have done much at McCook Field. He was the contracting officer and was the one who found ways for us to place orders for exceptional stuff that we couldn't have gotten ordinarily. But Fleet would find a way to get them. He took his chances, too. Very honest, but nevertheless, it took a lot of doing.

Q: There is something about McCook's administrator, Thurman Bane, that I don't quite understand. (*Note*: Colonel Bane was commanding officer of McCook from 1918 until he retired in 1922 at the age of thirty-eight. He died at the age of forty-seven. According to an interview with his widow Bessie Louise in 1978, he died of a misdiagnosed brain tumor.) Bane resigned his commission in 1922 or 1923 when he was just at the center of his career. He was extremely well liked. You could not find anybody who would say anything bad about him. I don't understand why he resigned. He seemed to be the right man for the job at the right time and yet he left.

A: Well, I know he was not appreciated in all quarters in Washington. They had a great deal of trouble with him, and I think that's probably why he left. That would be my bet. Bane was an awfully good man.

Q: Anyway, other than the turbosupercharger, what were some of the other projects you worked on?

A: Well, we started the development of better air-cooled cylinders. Up to that time, there had been nothing but cast-iron air-cooled cylinders. The Anzani even clung to the cast-iron cylinders for years to come. The Anzani was from a French motor designer. Anyway, we had to redesign it, rearrange the cylinder as well as go to aluminum, six sections of special aluminum alloys. We used different testing methods, different cooling methods, and some added inventions like the mercury-sodium-cooled valve before we began to get "brake mean-effective pressure." In other words, before we could get performance out of an air-cooled cylinder comparable to what we could do with a fluid-cooled cylinder and get the same economy to power. That was fundamentally important.

(*Note*: In the early days of aviation, engine cooling was the big nut to crack. It was not unusual for engines to fail from overheating. Since 1911, the most prestigious award for advancement in aviation has been the Collier Trophy. In 1927, the trophy was *not* awarded to Charles Lindbergh for his solo nonstop flight from New York to Paris. Rather, the award went to Charles L. Lawrance for a design that produced the Wright Whirlwind engine, which powered Lindbergh's "*Spirit of St. Louis*" on its thirty-three-hour flight—without overheating.)

Around that time, I had some personal ideas. One was about a four-cylinder heads design, aluminum heads, with quite different air flow around them—just ideas of mine I thought might cool. None of them yielded much gain, not enough to be worthwhile. Then I had an idea about cooling exhaust valves. I knew the limitations of the so-called mercury cooling valve, which we played with a little bit. I came along with one filled with copper to conduct the heat from the hot head up to the stem where it might get dissipated into the air stream.

Then I had another idea that I thought was good. I wanted to use the exhaust gas velocity to suck air down through the exhaust valve stem and out the edge of the seat, drawing enough air to cool it. I thought it was a pretty good idea. I learned it did function that way, and it did help cool the valve, though not enough to make the grade. About that time, I found that a man named George Westinghouse had, about fifty years before, developed the very same idea. Even his patent sketches looked somewhat like mine. His was for a big stationary gas engine. I guess they never used it either.

Then, in about 1920, we imported Sam Heron, an English engineer from Farnborough. He was a wonderful engineer. He brought what knowledge of air-cooled engines he had from England. Adding it to what he had, we really began to get fine results. From then on, we went to town. Heron invented the sodium-cooled valve, which had this hollow valve that became liquid and slushed back and forth, carrying the heat from the head to the stem. That overcame the troubles of the mercury-cooled valve that worked on the same principle. The mercury-cooled valve had to be sort of "tined," if you know what I mean, so the mercury would stick to the surface inside the valve. That didn't last under high-temperature operation. The sodium had no such trouble and didn't etch away the steel at high temperatures the way the mercury did.

That solution still is a success and still is used widely, in the truck industry as well as the aircraft industry. Finally, we developed the air-cooled cylinders that truly became the foundation for all the good air-cooled engines built in this country and copied in foreign countries. We built up the industry in the US and led the world for a short time in the air-cooled engine industry.

Q: I have heard of an engine controversy in the 1920s and 1930s. There were those that were pro-air-cooled and those that were pro-water-cooled. Where did you stand?

A: Well, we had no fixed stand one way or another. There were advantages in each type, for certain applications. I had thought that the light air-cooled engines in radial form would be better for fighter planes. The airplane designers backed me up 100 percent. Then the time came when the small high-speed V-12-type engine would beat that a lot because of the low head resistance. That came in as we got higher airplane speed. And we had variable pitch propellers by that time and other things that helped out immensely. There were reasons to change back and forth between the types of engines, not whims, but very solid reasons. So, we changed back and forth on that.

Q: You barely mentioned something earlier. You accomplished all you did, without ever going to high school. I think that is more than just mentionable.

A: I was one of the few mechanics who always was interested in how an engine could be made better. Every time I fixed little troubles on an existing engine, I tried to think of how to avoid such troubles in the future by redesigning the engine. That's one thing that helped me. The other thing was that I read a lot. I'd taken correspondence courses, ICS courses, but I'd never completed a course. I bought all the books, studied them, and memorized them. That was a great help to me. As soon as I got to McCook Field, I began to have immense educational advantages working with the craftsmen who were there, with the facilities we had and so on.

Q: When did you first get involved in aviation—what year and where?

A: Two San Diego fliers had built planes from seeing photographs of them and were flying them down at Imperial Beach. That's on the south end of our bay. I used to go down there on weekends and watch them trying to fly these things and help them sometimes with their engines. Half the time, of course, they never got off the ground. If they did, they'd make a straight flight. They had about a half mile there to do it in. If they got real cocky, they'd try to make a turn, and that's when they would crash a wing.

One pilot had an air-cooled car engine, a Cameron car engine, in it and that lost power, probably from poor cooling. The other was a six-cylinder, two-cycle Elberge engine, either that or another make. I can't recall what that one was. One of the men was B. F. Roerig. He had the two-cycle engine, and the other was Charley Walsh and he had a three-cylinder Elberge engine. Walsh went on and did some exhibition flying.

Other than that, I had no connection with aviation. Then, in 1910, Charles K. Hamilton came around and flew a Curtiss pusher plane over Coronado Polo Grounds and had a forced landing outside the high board fence around the polo grounds. I helped knock down a section of that fence to get the downed airplane onto the infield where it could take off.

The interesting part to me was that I was dressed in mechanic clothes, had a pair of big pliers with me, so I kind of looked like a mechanic and got a chance to help push that plane. When they got this fence down and the crew took hold of the plane, I noticed how they did it. I took hold of it, too, determinedly hung on, and got clear around into the infield before somebody kicked me out. I learned a lot about the plane in a couple hundred feet of hanging onto it. It was my first good look at an airplane. Later that same year, in 1910, I got a short hop in one. I was twenty years old.

Q: Some say the World War I German aircraft were inferior or overrated. Do you disagree with that?

A: I found nothing like that. I had to admire most of the engines. The BMW was the first overdimensioned and overcompressed engine. Remember, we hadn't gotten far with the superchargers that started with us and we were very much interested in getting better performance at altitude. Now this BMW engine was designed to be flown on throttle up to 7,000 feet, then you could open it up and get back to sea-level horsepower. *Overcompressed* meant that you didn't dare open it up until you got to the 7,000 feet because it would detonate, crack a piston, or whatever. It was a darned good deal. It made a sweet flying job at high altitude.

Q: When you left McCook years later, you didn't even have another job lined up. Why did you leave?

A: At that time, there was a rule that an officer could not stay on a job, a specialized job, for more than four years. So, my four years were coming up. It looked to me that if I went out an engineering officer, I would have to go to wherever they might send me. To the Philippines or the Canal Zone or somewhere. I had a family. I didn't want to take them around to those places. So, I decided to get out. I left the service. I received $2,400 cash and had no pension at all. That's the way it worked for both Reuben Fleet and me.

Author's note: The rule Hallett refers to was dubbed by several interviewed officers as "the Manchu Law." Until the late 1930s, the US Army required each officer to be posted overseas every four years. The officer's expertise did not matter. Overseas duty usually meant Asia, the Philippines—hence the Manchu allusion—though some were posted to the Panama Canal Zone. The rule not only was unpopular with officers' families, which led to officers resigning, it sometimes stopped valuable experimentation, both in the air and in the lab. Another issue affecting corps morale and causing early retirement was stagnant military rank and pay. After World War I, a junior grade officer such as a lieutenant could stay at that rank (and pay) for up to fifteen years. James Doolittle, for example, retired as a lieutenant after twelve years at that rank.

CHAPTER 2
ALBERT FRANCIS HEGENBERGER

INTERVIEWED FEBRUARY 1977

While at McCook, Albert Hegenberger was chief of the instrument branch and, later, chief of the equipment branch. He was the navigator on the first nonstop mainland US-to-Hawaii flight in 1927. In 1934, he was awarded the Collier Trophy for his development of a successful blind landing system. He retired as a brigadier general, was inducted into the National Aviation Hall of Fame in 1976, and died in 1983.

Q: First of all, my records indicate you were chief of the instrument division at McCook Field, correct?

A: Instrument and, later, navigation.

Q: My records also show you listed as making the Hawaiian flight with Col. Lester Maitland. Was that a McCook Field project? (*Note*: Lester James Maitland became a pilot during World War I, afterward being assigned to McCook as a test pilot. In the 1920s, he set many speed records and teamed up with Albert Hegenberger on a flight from Oakland to the Hawaiian Islands. He held several high commands during World War II. In the late 1950s, he became an ordained minister in the Episcopal Church, rising to the head of that denomination in Northern California. He died in 1990 at the age of ninety-one.)

A: Yes, that was a McCook project. The airplane—an Atlantic-Fokker C-2, named "*the Bird of Paradise*"—was delivered to McCook Field and run through performance tests, weight carrying and so forth, and then we tore some of it apart for bigger gas tanks and observation windows to take celestial shots.

Q: Where did the idea for the transpacific flight come from? Did it originate at McCook?

A: There had been approximately forty applications by pilots over a period of years—requests for approval to fly to Hawaii. And, of course, none of those were acted on for a long time because they were premature. No airplane capable of that range existed when the first request was made.

Q: In respect to Colonel Maitland, my research indicates he retired from the US Air Force in February 1944, when he was forty-five years old. It seems he retired prematurely. There's something there that I'm missing. Do you know of any reason why he would have left early?

A: I asked a general I know who retired here in Winter Park, "What happened?" He said that Gen. Henry Arnold was on a visit, an inspection trip, over in the United Kingdom. He toured from one base to another, and if there were any decorations to be awarded, Arnold would award them while he was at the base. Well, he got to Maitland's base, where he had a good, very efficient group. Among those on the list for decorations was Maitland, but they couldn't find him. It turned out he was drunk somewhere.

Q: Oh, is that right . . .

A: So, the rest of the story came from a fellow I know. He was a civilian employee in the US Air Force munitions office in Washington. I was ordered into the Pentagon on another project, and while I was there, I inherited this man as one of my subordinates. He told me that they got a telegram from Arnold, who OK'd getting rid of Maitland right away. They wanted to kick him out, instead of letting him retire. So, this man is said to have kept stalling on the thing and trying to find some way to let the matter die or to kill it or something, but he never could get anything through. He initiated paper for Maitland's retirement, but someone stopped it because Arnold had said "get rid of him." Finally, a telegram came that said Arnold was on his way back to Washington and this man had to do something, so he again put the papers through for normal retirement and that time they slipped through.

Q: Do you think that Arnold's suspicions were correct, that Maitland liked to tip the bottle a bit?

A: [Nodding] Yes, he did.

Q: What year did you first go to McCook?

A: I went there in February 1919. I was there until the summer of 1923. I was one of a group of officers that had been sent to MIT at the end of the war to take this postgraduate course in aeronautical engineering. I don't know exactly, but I think there were maybe sixty of us in that group. We all had some basic engineering, and they had decided they were going to develop an engineering division of the Air Corps, which then was the Air Service. It started out as the Aviation Signal Corps and was changed to the Air Service.

Q: So, you were the inventor of the earth induction compass, correct?

A: Well, the earth inductor principle was used as an engineering instrument for measuring the earth. It gave the direction of the magnetic lines of force. We had a spinning armature. Using it as a scientific instrument, you twisted this armature and tilted it till you got your maximum indication and it showed you the direction, using magnetic lines of force. Nobody was using that as a means of keeping a plane on course. They would just make a note that the earth's magnetic lines of force had a destination of so many degrees from true north.

Q: That's all they used it for until you used it as a compass?

A: Yes. I took it over, and we went to work in a little instrument shop. The lighter-than-air section at that time had a hundred thousand dollars that they wound up with toward the end of the year. They had the money, and the Air Service needed money badly for research and development. They couldn't see letting this money revert to the US Treasury when we had been asking for money for years and not getting it. So, they took it away from the lighter-than-air people and gave it to me. I had about a week to draw up all these projects to spend that money and get approval for it.

I placed that money with the Bureau of Standards. They had an instrument section that was doing some basic experimentation on new developments, which we supervised, that tested what the bureau built for us. And that's the story on the earth inductor compass. If it hadn't been for us, there wouldn't have been an earth inductor compass.

Q: That was before your Pacific flight, right?

A: Yes, because we gave Charles Lindbergh one to put on his airplane.

Q: Was the compass put together at McCook, the one that Lindbergh used?

A: No. It was built up in Pittsburgh. The Bureau of Standards built us one.

Q: You were at McCook when Colonel Thurman Bane was the administrator. What did you think of him?

A: He was a very forceful individual. He had vision. I don't know what engineering experience he might have gotten in the few years before World War I, but he was a forceful individual and I thought he was very keen. He was a very understanding individual. One time I gave flying training—illegally—to a nonflying officer there and checked him out solo. He cracked up the airplane. It was repairable, though. Bane could have skinned me alive for that, but he didn't. Another time I gave flying training to a Sergeant Cramer whose time was about up. He was getting out of the service to go home and said he wanted to solo. Well, I wouldn't solo him. I was cured of that.

He went up at noontime anyway and soloed himself, and did some stunting right over the field. We were in the cafeteria having lunch, and this guy is diving into the buildings, so we rushed out to see what the hell was going on. As soon as this sergeant landed, the officer in charge showed up, grabbed him, and threw him into the guardhouse. Bane finally let him go. Most commanding officers that I had experience with would have been so incensed about a thing of that kind that the guy would never have gotten out. So, Bane was all right. And he had a lot to do with the idea of building an engineering division in the Air Service.

Q: When Bane resigned, he was succeeded by Curry. Do you have an opinion about him? (*Note*: John Francis Curry flew combat missions in World War I, and after his service at McCook, he held various military commands and rose to the rank of major general. In 1941, he became the first national commander of the Civil Air Patrol.)

A: Curry was a good guy. He would play it safe, never doing anything very startling. He was slow and methodical, cautious.

Albert Francis Hegenberger

> *It started out as a turn indicator, not a turn-and-bank device. Development of it started when I ran across two instruments in a box of junk at McCook Field that had been brought over from Wilbur Wright Field, as Patterson was then known. When the war was over, they just gathered up everything, dumped it in boxes, and put it on a truck.*

Q: Now, what was your role in the development of the turn-and-bank indicator?

A: It started out as a turn indicator, not a turn-and-bank device. Development of it started when I ran across two instruments in a box of junk at McCook Field that had been brought over from Wilbur Wright Field, as Patterson was then known. When the war was over, they just gathered up everything, dumped it in boxes, and put it on a truck. This was in 1919. They unloaded that stuff in a bunch of sheds down in the northwest corner of the field. It was used for salvage junk, but a lot of it I could repair.

I got to rummaging through it and found those two what we now know as turn indicators. There was an instrument-maker still on duty at Wright, and I asked him what they were. He had a fair idea of what they were supposed to do, but he didn't understand it thoroughly. He said they kept files about the instrument somewhere, one signed by Shorty Schroeder, who flight-tested the equipment a few days before or after the Armistice. I ran down those reports. Schroeder's was very good, very exact, precise.

The instrument really gave you good information when the airplane was turning so that you could prevent it from getting out of control. Otherwise, you couldn't sense what was taking place while you were flying on instrument in the clouds. Well, I wrote the Sperry Company, and they sent Lawrence Sperry out. Lawrence and I did a little flying, first with our heads in the cockpit, later with a hood, to block out our vision. We started the ball rolling to standardize the instrument based on tests that we did.

About that time, we got in a shipment of German instruments that included a turn indicator, electric driven. They had used it on the Gotha bomber. It had the steel ball in the tube, liquid tube, so we appreciated that. We added it to ours and ordered some magnet turn indicators from the Sperry Company.

Q: I would never think of flying through clouds without all the proper equipment in the cockpit Before, people just went into the clouds. The mortality rate was high.

A: It sure was.

Q: I've read some stories where doctors in World War I believed that it took a certain person to fly through clouds. In other words, it wasn't the instrument; it was all in your mind.

A: When I started to fly, one of the tests they gave you was this whirling chair, the Jones Barany Chair. If you tucked your head down, when they stopped whirling the chair and told you to sit up erect, you were supposed to come up and lean over as a result of the turbulence created in the inner ear. If you didn't pass that test, you were thrown out.

Q: Are there any other instruments you worked on at McCook?

A: We had a rate-of-climb indicator, which is a good instrument. I don't know why they don't use it.

Q: The airplane I fly has a rate-of-climb indicator. Every plane I have ever flown has the indicator.

Q: Well, it's come back. It was out of the picture. The indicator, the only one built in this country at the time, was built at McCook, built by a Second Lieutenant Haines. It also was something we developed from that box of junk from Wright Field.

CHAPTER 3
THOMAS HARRIMAN

INTERVIEWED APRIL 1977

Thomas Harriman was a young McCook Field mechanic and the son of a McCook Field mechanic. He was a rolled-up-sleeves participant in the McCook story and observed history being made, on the ground and in the air.

Q: In February 1922, a lighter-than-air dirigible named "*Roma*" that the US had purchased from Italy burst into flames at Norfolk, Virginia. It was at that time the greatest aeronautics disaster in US history. One of the thirty-four people killed in the explosion and fire was your father, also named Thomas Harriman, a McCook Field mechanic. He was on the flight to maintain the engines?

A: He went to Langley Field, where the "*Roma*" was based, to install the engines—he and several other men. Quite a few went. During the first flight after the engine was changed, it hit high tension wires. He was riding down behind one of the engines and, of course, he was burned up in the crash. He was an ignition and electrical mechanic.

Q: At the time, you also were working at McCook? How old were you?

A: I was eighteen. I worked on the flight line. I did a little over forty-two years working on a flight line, till I retired. I never worked anywhere else on the field other than the flight line.

Q: Can you recall any of the projects done at McCook, the innovations they came up with?

A: I remember when they were working on the high-altitude record and some of the speed records across the country and things like that. There were about four civilian pilots, and the rest were military pilots. We were civilian mechanics. We didn't have any military mechanics, not in aircraft.

Q: Where did you receive your training as a mechanic?

A: When I started as a helper, I went to school at Scott Field and San Antonio and places like that. The men that I worked with were already mechanics, and when they returned from the war, they'd come right back into the hangars. That is where I got most of my experience, from them—plus all the schools I had to go to.

Q: I understand mechanics sometimes flew along on test flights as an observer. Who were some of the people you flew with?

A: I went as a mechanic most of the time. I flew quite a bit with pilots St. Clair Streett, Eubank, Harold Harris, and Pearson. (*Note:* [1] St. Clair "Bill" Streett flew in France in World War I, and in 1920, he led a squadron of DH-4Bs from New York City to Nome, Alaska, to show that air power could defend that distant territory. He was a test pilot and the commander of the Thirteenth Air Force during World War II. He was the first commander of the Strategic Air Command. [2] Eugene Lowry Eubank was a test pilot and later held several high commands, reaching the rank of major general. He lived to be 104. [3] Alexander Pearson Jr. was a test pilot at McCook and set a world speed record in 1923, as well as a transcontinental speed record. He was killed near McCook in 1924 while practicing for an air race. Pearson Field in Vancouver, Washington, is named for him.)

> *Well, some of the flights were interesting. The planes lost an engine once in a while, things like that. Nothing out of the ordinary.*

Q: Anything interesting happening during any of your flights?

A: Well, some of the flights were interesting. The planes lost an engine once in a while, things like that. Nothing out of the ordinary. Some of the test observers had to bail out, but I never did.

Q: Do you remember some of the airplanes then? Do you recall George de Bothezat and his helicopter?

A: I remember the helicopter. It's the one we used to get out on the end and hold it a little bit and then give it a push and step back. It had three or four props on it, if I remember correctly, and chain blades. It would get off the ground, but we'd just give it a little push as we walked away. It would hold in the air just a little while. Before it came outside for tests, we didn't see much of it till they pulled it out. There was a huge tent around it. It would just stay up in the air a little while, though, maybe 7 or 8 feet high. That was as high as it would go. It was awfully noisy, too.

Q: Do you remember other flying incidents at McCook?

A: One of our pilots was in Cleveland and he needed a blood transfusion, so we picked up about eight of the officers there at McCook and started up to Cleveland. We had just cleared the field when one of the gas tanks dropped out of the wing, hitting a cross-feed valve, so we shut off one engine completely and the other partially. We had one engine running and the other just catching and running a little bit. We turned around and went back to McCook, and they wired the tank back up and we went on again. That was in 1925, I believe.

Q: After McCook closed, do you remember what they did with the land?

A: For a long time, nothing happened there at all. It was just a big field with nothing but baseball diamonds and things on it. I don't think anything was done for a long time.

Q: Do you remember when the sign was put up on the hangar?

A: It was after one aircraft crashed there just as it was pulling out of the field, getting over the ridge and into some bad winds. It got a wing down and went down into the river with eight or nine people aboard. After that, there was a big sign at the end of the field, "This Field Is Small, Use It All." The plane wasn't from McCook. It came in from either Mitchel Field or Bolling Field.

Q: You must have done your share of flying in bad weather, as an observer. How was that?

A: You followed railroad tracks and sometimes you had to set down and wait. I landed twice with one airplane. I was traveling to San Antonio, and I changed an engine in it. They sent me another one and that one blew up. It was a PT8, a new airplane.

Q: Did you work at all with Jean Roche, the airplane designer and builder?

A: Very little, but he used to come down and help us out with problems, especially if we had trouble with high altitude or something. We didn't have much to do with him other than he would survey one of the jobs and give us an idea of what to do to correct a problem. One time we had an airplane that was having trouble at high altitude. You could hardly move the stick. But you'd get it on the ground and it would work fine. We couldn't help wondering what the problem was. So, Roche came along and took one of those CO_2 bottles and went all over those hinges on the stick. He produced exactly the trouble it was having upstairs. We cleaned all the oil and grease from the parts. He was the chief engineer, you know.

We had some interesting people here, aircraft manufacturers. Seversky and Vought would be on the flight line, especially when their planes were in the air. They were very interested in their planes. We especially liked Seversky. He was a nice man, a very good man. He understood a man's problems pretty well and this went over well with the mechanics.

Q: I was looking at a pay schedule for the 1920s. Did you as a mechanic feel that you were doing OK in terms of pay?

A: At that time, no. The pay was not very much for a mechanic at that time. It seemed all the young fellows wanted to work on airplanes. And there were a lot of men who just got out of the army, that's the kind of men we had in there. The pay wasn't much going in, especially as a helper. It was a time when you'd only get five dollars a day per diem and it was soon gone. You could always sleep in an airplane if the night wasn't too cold.

Q: Several people have mentioned the physical condition of Albert Stevens, the photographer at McCook. How far he used to run . . .

A: In the mornings, he would run all the way around the field. When it was time for him to come to work, he would be coming in from the last lap around the field. He also would go way out in the field with just his shorts on and sunbathe.

Q: Did he do all the running out of habit, or was he a fitness nut, or what?

A: Well, we have a lot more people doing fitness running today than we had doing it then. He was the only one I saw doing it in those days. He was kind of a loner that way. He only worried about photography and his exercises.

CHAPTER 4
HARRY ANTON JOHNSON

INTERVIEWED JANUARY 1978

Harry A. Johnson enlisted in the Aviation section of the Signal Corps in 1917. He was appointed a second lieutenant in 1918 and became a flying instructor. After little more than a year at McCook, he began a long career as a decorated US Air Force officer, finishing as a major general. He died three months after this interview.

Q: Can you give me any information about budget cuts or anything like that?

A: I was chief of the flight test section in 1926–27. I know we were cut practically every year, but I can't remember how much it was. I know I got to the place where we had two civilian test pilots, and we had to let them go because we didn't have the money. As it turns out, one fellow got a job at an aircraft company in Detroit, where he was killed, and the other got to be head of licensing and registration at the Civil Aeronautics Administration.

> *You know when Calvin Coolidge was president, he didn't see how we needed more than one airplane for all of us—the navy would use the airplane one week and the air force would use it the next.*

Q: During the 1920s, you did not have a president or a Congress that was in favor of aviation, isn't that correct?

A: Oh, Christ, for sure! You know when Calvin Coolidge was president, he didn't see how we needed more than one airplane for all of us—the navy would use the airplane one week and the air force would use it the next.

Q: I've heard a great many stories about Albert Stevens and those photographic missions he was on. Do you remember anything particular about Stevens?

A: He was a man who didn't have any regard for time. He worked down in the control equipment section, cameras and things. He'd get on a project and work. When he'd get to a certain stage at night, about ten o'clock or so, he'd lie down right on the counter, go to sleep for three or four hours, and then go back to work. Time to him meant nothing. He had a funny, funny gait, kind of like when people are chasing their dog team up in Alaska. The only thing he was interested in was photography. He and George Goddard worked side by side on the same developments.

Q: What was your position at McCook?

A: When I first went there, I was put in charge of maintenance, in addition to my other duties. We had about ninety men, all civilians. We gradually dropped on down to seventy-five. But you see, we handled not only the test work and so forth; we handled all the flying for all the personnel on the base. Once every three months, you see a major come out and he'd hit the ground thirty times—thirty bad landings—and you wouldn't see him again for three months. Usually they were flying a trainer. You couldn't get them in anything else.

Q: I understand there were different flight pay rates.

A: Yeah, you're going back to the original ratings of the Air Service in 1917. A pilot drew 25 percent of his base pay. A senior pilot drew 50 percent. A command pilot drew 75 percent. There were a dozen majors on the base, and all of them just flew enough to qualify for their flight pay. Thirty landings every three months. Hit the ground and bounce.

CHAPTER 5
LEIGH WADE

INTERVIEWED SEPTEMBER 1977

In 1919, after service during World War I as a flight instructor and aerobatics trainer, Leigh Wade came back to the United States and was assigned to McCook Field. During World War II, he held several top staff positions with the US Air Force in South America. He retired as an air force major general. He was inducted into the National Aviation Hall of Fame in 1974 and died in 1991 at the age of ninety-five.

Q: When did you first get into the service?

A: In 1916, I got into the North Dakota National Guard and into the Air Service the next year. After high school, I was going to become a doctor. I went to North Dakota on a dare, into the wheat fields. I was ready to go to the University of Michigan or Notre Dame, but I didn't come back to go. I was in Edgely, North Dakota, when Dr. Mosley came down from Mandan. We met and he invited me to come into the Mandan Drug Company, the idea being to get some experience in pharmacy that would help me in medicine. Flying was the furthest thing from my mind. The nearest I ever was to an airplane was at a county fair in Michigan, where they had a pilot who gave a demonstration. It flew around and landed, and they quickly put it in a tent and charged ten cents to take a look.

Q: What aviator was this?

A: I don't remember, but that was around 1914. I had no thought of flying at all. But when I joined the National Guard, we were mobilized and sent to a fort in Bismarck. There an airplane was leaving but the pilot had a forced landing on our military base. He taxied up and several of us went out to see and helped push it over near our tents. The pilot said he would appreciate any of us kind of watching over it, so some of us volunteered. We asked if we could sit in the seat and have our picture taken and we did. That was my first time ever in an airplane. It was a Wright pusher.

Q: Then you were sent to the Mexican border?

A: Yes. The reason I really got into aviation was the fact that there was no appeal for me to being in the trenches in France, even as an officer. It was a pretty rugged, dirty life. One day they called for volunteers for aviation. A fellow with the last name of Lee and me, with a first name of Leigh, were the two out of the company who stepped forward. That was a Saturday morning. The next Wednesday we were sent over to the hospital for part of our aviation physical.

Q: This was after the United States had entered the war in Europe?

A: Yes, this was along in the summer of 1917, in June. They started weeding out the volunteers who they thought would not make officer material. They called our names and I thought, "Oh, boy, the old skipper is really going to give us hell." Loyalty was one thing that was drilled into you, and I thought about what a fool I was. I remember thinking, *I'll probably never make it, and I'll get kicked out and have to go back to the draft*. Later, everyone else was dismissed and the skipper called the two of us in and told us to stand at ease.

We thought we were going to get a bawling out. Instead, he smiled and said, "I am going to lose you. They have approved you for aviation." He said we could go home to visit our families but be at New York Central Station that Sunday evening to leave on secret orders to Toronto, Ontario. And that's how I really got into aviation.

Q: Were you sent overseas after your pilot training?

A: We were the last class in Canada that year. Then we went to Fort Worth, Texas, at the end of October, assigned to the 17th Aerial Squadron. At Mitchel Field, I came down with the German measles. They didn't know what I had. On New Year's morning, 1918, they put me in quarantine.

Q: There was an epidemic in the country at that time, wasn't there?

A: Oh, yes. They took a barracks, and inside, they put some pipe up and around and dropped sheets on it to make a room. On one side of me was a case of black diphtheria, and on the other side was a case of scarlet fever. After several days there, they decided I had measles, and they moved me into the ward at the end of the barracks. They told me, "You get over in that corner. I don't care how cold it is—you stay away from us." And the squadron left, and I was left behind.

Q: So, you never did get over to Europe?

A: No, I did. I was assigned to go overseas because I was a rated pilot. Arriving in England, we got off at Liverpool and I was sent on to France. I became an instructor first, then a check pilot. I started the aerobatic training there. I flew Nieuports, and then for the aerobatics, we flew an English plane, the Avro. Anyway, in August 1919, I left France as a courier of special records. Then I was ordered to Dayton, to McCook. It was quite an experience because when I got there, the other test pilots hadn't been overseas, and they would say, "Here's one of those hotshots coming here to tell us how to fly an airplane." You could sense the attitude a little bit from the fellows, that I considered myself a hotshot, but I didn't.

Q: Was Shorty Schroeder one of the pilots at that time?

A: Yes, and Shorty was really a fine fellow. You couldn't find a better one. Shorty was the chief test pilot. I was under him. Then he left and John Macready, who was a captain, had charge of us. When he went to the engineering school, I was put in as chief test pilot. They were cutting down, so they made me chief of the flying section as well.

Q: I have a question about Schroeder leaving. I've heard the story many times about him going up 37,000 feet, losing his oxygen, his eyeballs freezing over, and then coming down safely. Was he disabled at all from that flight?

A: His eyes were bothering him somewhat. There was an effect from the high-altitude incident. It took him some time to get over it, because when he landed, he could barely see. He was very fortunate to be able to land safely. I believe they lifted him out of the fuselage. He went unconscious, and they took him to the hospital. When he came to, he didn't have much vision. Later, he had a chance to go to Chicago, where he was from. I really think his eyes bothered him, and that's the reason he left the service.

Q: Did you take part in the 1921 or 1923 bombings, the Mitchell bombing runs off Cape Hatteras?

A: Not too actively. However, I was ferrying supplies. There was a shortage of supplies, and they used the old Martin transport to supply. It had seats in it, and we took out some of the seats. It had little quarter-inch plywood doors that slid back and forth behind the cockpit. When you took off from Dayton, you had to make Washington for refueling because it was risky to land at Moundsville. I did once. When I took off, I started up this valley south of Moundsville and couldn't find the break. We were flying right down the valley, with rocks on both sides.

Although we didn't have full equipment for blind flying, I did fly blind and went up high enough that I felt confident that I would be over the mountains. And then flying through there, I could see a river, but I didn't know whether it was the Big Shenandoah or the Little Shenandoah. I knew we'd get through pretty soon, and we finally got out of that and into broken clouds. I didn't have enough gasoline and I had drifted to the south, so I had to make a landing. I landed in a grass field out there in Virginia. We went into town to call Bolling Field to get some gas sent out. And, mind you, of all the goddamn things in the world, they didn't have any gasoline to send me.

So, we bought common automobile gas and put it in. I still had enough aviation gas in the two gravity tanks in each wing to take off on and climb a little bit, and then I turned on this automobile gas. You should have seen the black smoke roll out when I turned it on. We made Bolling, anyway. We had them wheel out some barrels, and we drained this automobile gas out of the tanks into the drums. I told operations, "For God's sake, keep this. If you ever have anybody else that needs gasoline, you have this to send out. Just don't give it to that quartermaster." Then we went on to Langley, where they were happy to get the supplies and propellers and I don't know what else that was aboard.

Q: There were three McCook pilots on the round-the-world flight. How were you selected?

A: It's kind of interesting. When I was ordered from McCook Field to Bolling Field in October 1923, there was a morale factor. In air races and everything, Bolling always seemed to get chosen. So, I knew nothing about the world flight being planned until we got some mimeographed sheets with our name, serial number, and so on, and asked if we wished to be considered for the round-the-world flight. I didn't think that I or anybody at Bolling had much of a chance, especially me since I was the last arrival there. So, I just put down "Yes." In the remarks section about why I was qualified, I put down "Past experience."

I was living at the end of the officer quarters club with Bobby Walsh, who was the deputy commander. I had been out the night before at the British bachelors' big annual party that they had in those days. So, when I got up for inspection the next morning, I was pretty sleepy. I went to the operations room to try to get a little bet that no one from Bolling would be selected. I wanted odds. First, I asked five to one. No takers. Four to one, three to one. Still no takers. So, I didn't make a bet.

Mind you, I had four sets of orders in addition to being assigned to Bolling. One was to go to the Curtiss factory at Garden City and pick up an airplane and fly it to the West Coast. So, I tried to get Bobby Walsh to get these orders canceled. I got a phone call from Bobby and I asked him, "Which set of orders did you get canceled?" He said he didn't get any canceled. Well, as you may have noticed, I'm really fluent in profanity at times. Then he said, "But I've got Gen. Patrick's permission to be the first one to tell you that you've been selected for the world flight." I didn't know whether to believe it or not.

Then Bill Streett called and said that he had the permission of General Patrick to be the first to tell me. (*Note*: Gen. Mason Patrick was chief of the US Army Air Service during and after World War I.) We were all close friends, so I immediately said to myself, those two son-of-a-guns have gotten their heads together and are just calling to spoil my sleep.

So, I got in my old Chandler car and went over to the munitions building. Then I went on up to the Army-Navy club, where I normally played bridge on Saturday afternoons. I couldn't relax enough to play, so I didn't get into a game. When people saw me, they all started congratulating me. I just played along with them until Mike Kilner came in. (*Note*: Later a brigadier general, Walter Glenn "Mike" Kilner, was stationed at McCook in 1922. In 1939, he was appointed by Pres. Franklin D. Roosevelt to NACA.) I finally believed *him*. So that was when I first knew about it.

Q: You were command pilot of the "*Boston*" in the round-the-world flight, is that correct?

A: That's correct. Henry Ogden was in the second seat. He never was at McCook. I contacted many bases by telegram to select a civilian mechanic who was good on Liberty motors. I got five of them there to select from. Ogden impressed me the most, not only as a mechanic but as a man that could rough it a little. We might have had to rough it pretty hard. Anyway, the flight took me away from McCook Field. The next time I visited McCook was at the end of the flight. That was like an old home to Erik Nelson (pilot of the plane dubbed the "*New Orleans*"), Jack Harding (mechanic on the "*New Orleans*"), and me.

All of us pilots were single, except for Major Martin. For the other three airplanes, they selected bachelors because at that time they really considered it too much of a risk to leave a widow behind. They laugh about it now when astronauts go out and they're practically all married.

Q: I'm interested in the preparations for the world flight that took place at McCook. What took place there?

A: There was a committee formed, a secret committee. Billy Streett was one member of it. Erik Nelson had the engineering part of it and he chose the airplane. McCook was very important because of its development of instruments and instrument flying. We had the turn-and-bank indicator, an airspeed indicator, an altimeter, and the earth inductor compass. The latter was in experimental development at the time, and we decided to put it on and it worked beautifully. It worked beautifully all the way up to Alaska, down to Japan, until we got into the tropics and then, one after the other, the compasses went out.

The committee selected a navy torpedo plane as the basic airplane, and it was remodeled. The plane already had folding wings. Our wings would swing back, too, if you had to. We never had to. In Seattle, we put on pontoons. We went all the way to Calcutta, India, on pontoons. Then we put on wheels to England. The shipping facilities were so good that the pontoons we took off in Calcutta were the ones we put on in England. Shipping was as fast as flying in those days.

Q: It took something like four or five months to complete the flight?

A: One hundred and seventy-five days. We could have completed it in, say, two weeks, but the thing was that you had to change engines so many times. You couldn't have done it on one engine. The old Liberty engines wouldn't stand up that well. We did our own maintenance.

Q: And you finished the flight in a "*Boston II*?"

A: When I lost the original Boston in the Atlantic, I was picked up by the US Navy. I thought I was completely out of the flight. Then I received word from General Patrick that the prototype on which the four planes on the flight were modeled was being commissioned as the "*Boston II*" and was being flown to Pictou, Nova Scotia. I picked it up there and flew on.

Q: None of the people on the flights were injured during the trip?

A: No, because Harding and Martin were able to walk out of the mountains of Alaska after their crackup.

Q: Do you recall the Lepere airplane?

A: Oh, yes. That was the one that made all the high-altitude records. Schroeder flew it first.

Q: Did you have occasion to meet George de Bothezat?

A: Yes. To be perfectly frank with you, I think that de Bothezat placed too high a value on himself as an engineer. He tended to make some pretty big promises about what he could produce. That was his trouble.

Q: Another McCook Field character was Walter Barling, designer of the six-engine Barling Bomber. Any opinions about him?

A: He was a very dedicated and opinionated man. I never flew the Barling bomber. Harold Harris flew it. Some of us looked at him as kind of a joke.

Q: You mentioned, in passing, about an altitude record...

A: I wasn't out to set a record, but it happened with a Martin bomber with a Moss turbo-supercharger. That's the airplane from which Stevens parachuted on one flight. Anyway, Ray Langham and I were taking up the bomber to see how high we could get it. It was an open cockpit and it got pretty cold, but we made it. We came down, and I thought nothing of it being a record. They checked, but because it was not observed by aviation officials, you couldn't credit it as an official record. It was about 27,500 feet.

Q: There were trophies given out at McCook—the Flying Ass, the Bonehead, trophies for making notable mistakes in flight. Did you ever hear of them?

A: The Dumbbell, yes. We had some others, too. I don't think you'll find my name on any of them.

Q: How about Albert Stevens—did you fly with him?

A: I did in Dayton. He was down on the flight line one day in his coveralls, no insignia whatsoever. He said to me, "I want you to go on a photographic mission with me to New England." It sort of startled me. I knew him but not very well. I told him I had never flown any photographic missions, and he said he knew I could fly and that he had chosen me. He was pretty determined in a lot of ways. A very fine gentleman who sometimes would work in his lab until he was completely exhausted.

> *Stevens went for an altitude record that day. He had a little oxygen canister with a tube on it. It was strapped to his leg. When he jumped, the damned canister kept on going down. The jolt of the parachute tore it loose.... He landed over near Xenia someplace.*

Q: There is a story about him jumping out of an airplane without telling the pilot...

A: I think, as a matter of fact, it was his jump out of the Martin bomber I was piloting. The jump set a parachute record. Officially we couldn't get permission to do the jump, so that day when I came in and landed, I looked back and there was no Steve. I knew he had jumped. I did what you might call a little coverup. They said, "Where's Captain Stevens?," and I said, "Well, he must have jumped, I guess. He had a parachute with him."

Stevens went for an altitude record that day. He had a little oxygen canister with a tube on it. It was strapped to his leg. When he jumped, the damned canister kept on going down. The jolt of the parachute tore it loose. We expected to get to a high-enough altitude to require oxygen. So, he went from using the main oxygen tank in the airplane to using the canister of oxygen. But the canister tore off. He landed over near Xenia someplace.

Actually, I worked an awful lot of flights for parachute work. We'd take the old DH-4, which was pretty much used just for parachute work. We had a little platform on the side of the airplane. You'd step off from that. I flew an awful lot of those. It was fun. Looking down, you'd say, "Go ahead," and see the jumper go down and the chute open up. I never parachuted. Twice I needed a chute, but I didn't have one. Fortunately, I got out of those incidents all right.

Q: Did you say that you worked with variable-pitch props? What can you tell me about the Fairchild incident? (*Note*: Muir S. Fairchild was a pilot at McCook. After World War II, he became vice chief of staff of the US Air Force with the rank of four-star general. Fairchild Air Force Base in Spokane, Washington, is named for him.)

A: I recall when Fairchild reversed the prop and came down. I don't think he did it intentionally. In the old days, when you were gliding, every now and then you would sort of gun your engine a little bit to clear it. With that variable-pitch prop, once you started to glide, it went into the reverse pitch, so you couldn't gun your engine. What you did in a shallow guide is you kept some power on so the prop stayed positive instead of reversing. So that's what happened, I think, with Fairchild. Approaching the northeast corner of the field, there was a little pond. We called it Fairchild Lake after he gunned his engine and crashed into the pond.

CHAPTER 6
J. PARKER VAN ZANDT

INTERVIEWED JULY 1977

J. Parker Van Zandt earned a PhD in physics prior to serving in World War I. In 1927, he created Scenic Airways (still in business today) for sightseeing tours of the Grand Canyon. This led to his founding of Sky Harbor Airport, which serves Phoenix, Arizona. He became a sales representative for Ford Aircraft, demonstrating the Ford Tri-Motor throughout Europe, and managed airport terminals in Hawaii and the Philippines for Pan American Airlines. During World War II, he was a member of the Civil Aeronautics Board. He died in 1990 at the age of ninety-six.

Q: You say that in 1918 you tried very hard to go to McCook?

A: It was 1919. In 1918, the war was still on. I came back from France in the spring of 1919 to March Field and then wanted to transfer to engineering. Even then I was interested in the idea of air transportation. I assumed that the first thing would be to establish how to fly a reliable schedule over a given course, and for that, we had to do navigation and airway operation. I asked to go to McCook in order to help establish civil aviation in the United States.

Engineering school staff headed by Edwin Aldrin Sr. (in uniform). *Photo courtesy of the US Air Force Museum*

Q: The engineering school was started to give more training to Air Corps officers?

A: Yes, that's right. The young majors came back from World War I, and they had not had complete engineering training before being hurried into the war. The purpose was to bring them up to date and make them qualified to act as commanding officers in fields throughout the country. Lt. Ed Aldrin Sr. (father of astronaut Edwin "Buzz" Aldrin) and I were the two directors of the engineering school. Eddie was the senior director, as I recall, and I was the associate director. He and I instructed most of the courses. I taught the majors fundamental principles of gyroscopic operations and other basic aircraft principles.

A classroom in the first years of the Air Service Engineering School. *Photo courtesy of the US Air Force Museum*

Q: Can you tell me about the Dayton-to-Washington flight plans?

A: Our purpose in setting up the navigation branch was to develop a means of flying in any weather over a route that could be used for air transportation purposes, such as carrying mail, passengers, and cargo. So, we developed a model airway between McCook Field and Washington, DC, by way of Moundsville, West Virginia. We established fields along the route and beacons and developed a turn-and-bank indicator. Also, we developed what we called a Cloud Flying Instrument Board to convince the pilots that there wasn't static electricity inside the clouds. What really was happening was they failed to fly straight and level, and that made their compasses spin. It wasn't from any electrical thing.

Q: What was your opinion of Aldrin?

A: I thought Lieutenant Aldrin was a wonderful fellow to work with. He was very dynamic and forceful and had a positive character. Also, he was very ambitious. Our relationship was congenial. As far as I recall, we never had any disagreements or problems. I thought he was an intelligent and able partner.

Q: You were in the instrument branch?

A: I was in the division. I've forgotten what the name of the division was. There were several sections in it. I was chief of the navigation branch or section. Hegenberger was chief of the instrument section, I think. Then there was a parachute section and so on. A major was the director of all these different sections and branches.

Q: Who was your commanding officer?

A: Thurman H. Bane was the commanding officer. He was the one that I worked with particularly, but I don't remember the name of the major who was head of our branch. I thought Bane was a remarkably dynamic and forward-looking commander. He was a chap who was always willing to take a chance and try something new. He always was ready to praise people who did something unusual and well. He was equally ready to attach blame if they didn't. I thought he was a remarkably able leader in this kind of work.

Q: You left McCook in what year?

A: I left McCook in 1922 to go to Washington to help develop civil aviation under General Patrick. I left the service in 1925 to go with Ford Motor Company to develop a passenger plane.

Q: What were some of the projects that you worked on at McCook?

A: We developed the earth inductor compass, which Lindbergh used later on his transatlantic flight, in conjunction with the Bureau of Standards. By flying every week to Washington, I could use the facilities of the Bureau of Standards laboratories to develop the necessary navigation instruments. We also tried to work on the gyroscopic principle for direction-finding purposes. All the projects there were related to navigation.

Q: Did Lindbergh get his compass directly from McCook?

A: I think probably we supplied him. I couldn't say for sure. He might have gotten it directly from McCook Field because it was developed for McCook. The instrument that we developed through the bureau was the property of McCook Field, I'm quite sure.

Q: In developing your instruments, were you ever thinking about blind landings?

A: Of course, we were very interested in the question of blind landings. We also used it, for example, with the photographic section at McCook. They wanted to test out their cameras for mapping purposes. They had a Bagley camera, a three-lens camera that gave you perspective and depth on the ground. (*Note*: US Army Major James W. Bagley invented a state-of-the-art panoramic camera prior to World War I.) We took it down to the Moundsville area, where it was very hilly. I could fly it better, a straight course, with my head in the hood, looking at my turn-and-bank indicator, than they could fly by looking over the side and trying to line up things.

Q: How big were the engineering classes?

A: I remember that we only had eight or ten at the start. Aldrin and I were teaching them. They were largely majors in the class, all of whom had been early graduates from West Point and back from the war. We primarily taught them elementary or basic problems. The principles of lift. The principles of stress. Actually, all we really knew at that point were the basic principles.

> *It was a very good, congenial group of people at McCook because they were all interested in doing original things. It wasn't a stand-pat organization at all. We did have some practical jokers, such as Jimmy Doolittle and Oakley Kelly and others.*

Q: The working atmosphere at McCook was good, was it?

A: It was a very good, congenial group of people at McCook because they were all interested in doing original things. It wasn't a stand-pat organization at all. We did have some practical jokers, such as Doolittle and Oakley Kelly and others. One thing I enjoyed about McCook Field, which has nothing to do with practical joking, was that we had all kinds of aircraft there from the war. We had the British, German, and French planes and others, and we all had a chance to fly them.

I remember having great fun flying a Monosoupape. It fired on only one cylinder. You had to spin the rotating engine, and when it started off, the engine had a terrific gyroscopic effect and you had to immediately kick full rudder to keep it from going around in a circle. The only way to come down was to cut it. The engine ran at only one speed, so as you came down you glided until you finally landed. It was really quite something to fly. The Nieuport Monosoupape. I remember the first time I tried to fly that thing was quite an exciting time.

Then we flew the British SE-5s, a lovely little flying ship. It had a big dihedral so you just rocked in it, a very comfortable flying ship. So, flying all those planes was an interesting angle about being at McCook Field. Lieutenant Harold Harris was our test pilot and he was the one who usually did it first. If he survived, well, then the rest of us would have a try at it.

Q: How about social life at McCook?

A: I think it was very normal. Col. Bane had a very charming wife who was socially inclined, and as I recall, we often had social evenings. I remember going out with Colonel and Mrs. Bane. I was a bachelor then. Bachelors were more in demand to fill out a party. As I recall, Dayton was a very friendly town. The social life was very normal and very pleasant.

CHAPTER 7
JAMES H. DOOLITTLE

INTERVIEWED MARCH 1977

James Doolittle's accomplishments pre- and postdated McCook. In September 1922, before coming to McCook, he set a record by flying twenty-two hours from coast to coast, with one stop. As a civilian in 1929, he made the first totally blind takeoff and landing, relying on newly developed instruments. He rejoined the Air Corps in 1940 and led the famous "Doolittle Raid" on Tokyo in 1942. He commanded the 8th Air Force, retiring as a lieutenant general. President Ronald Reagan later officially awarded him a four-star "General of the Air Force" rank. The general was inducted into the National Aviation Hall of Fame in 1967 and died in 1993 at the age of ninety-six.

Q: You first went to McCook Field in 1923?

A: Yes, I had been stationed in San Antonio and had a change of duty station to McCook to go to the Air Service engineering school. My last duty at San Antonio was to go through the mechanics school and parachute school. I was very eager when the opportunity came to go through the engineering school. This had been on my mind for some time. The request had been made and the paperwork done during the time that I had been working on the trans-America flight. I originally was a mining engineering student before World War I, and I did not go back for my senior year but was very interested in engineering. After I got into aviation, my interest changed to aeronautical engineering.

Q: Did Billy Mitchell go around trying to recruit the best people that he could, including you?

A: I did know Billy Mitchell. I worked with him in 1921 during the bombing maneuvers off the Cape. As a matter of fact, I was his aide for one day. I knew him and admired him very much, so it is quite possible that we talked about this sort of thing.

Q: You were the chief test pilot, correct?

A: At McCook Field, I first went to school there. But I also did a lot of flying while I was in school, part of it in connection with two theses that I wrote, one for a master's degree and one for a doctorate after I went to MIT. I still had an umbilical cord with McCook, even when I was at MIT, and as a result of that, I did a lot of flying at McCook. When I came back to McCook for the second time from MIT, I was in charge of flight test research. I then was chief test pilot and in the engineering section.

Q: I read that you were removed as chief test pilot for low flying. Correct?

A: Not quite. What happened was that I was very interested in instrument flying, and I practiced it constantly. I got so that I could fly certain routes, for instance, from Dayton to Columbus and from Dayton to Moundsville, when other people couldn't. It wasn't because I was a better pilot. It was because I made a project of it and remembered every telephone pole, every windmill, every fallen tree along the route, so I could fly it when other people couldn't. This upset the commanding officer, a chap named John Curry, who then was a major or light colonel and later a brigadier general and a major general in World War II. He took a dim view of me flying when other people didn't fly. He said, "I'm going to take you off the job of chief test pilot and put you in the design section—you haven't enough sense to be a pilot." That was his precise statement.

Q: Was he a pilot?

A: He was a pilot of sorts. I was too proud to tell him that I had been practicing and because of that practice was able to fly when other people couldn't. It wasn't because I was a better flier. It was because I had trained myself to that particular phase of flying.

Q: I heard from another officer that administrators Curry and Bane were the types of pilots who always went flying with someone else.

A: I believe they each had their ratings, but they did very little flying.

A young James Doolittle and a Curtiss P-1 at McCook Field. *Army Air Service photo from the American Aviation Historical Society archives*

Q: The outside loop—was that at McCook Field? And did you just decide, "I'm going to try and do this," or did somebody tell you that he wanted you to try an outside loop?

A: Yes, it was at McCook. There were three of us that did a lot of acrobatic flying in competition. One was Al Williams, who was a very famous navy pilot. Another was a chap named Sanderson from the Marine Corps. At air meets, we frequently flew in competition. I was always thinking in the back of my mind, *Now what am I going to be able to do that is unique and will give me a leg up on my competitors?* The thought of doing an outside loop kept working around in there and, as far as I knew, had not been done. So, one day I took up an airplane and, as you say, went a little further, a little further, and finally went all the way around.

I immediately came in and landed. I got another test pilot named James Troy Hutchinson, a lieutenant, to come out and watch. I told him I was going to do something and then come down, and I wanted him to tell me what it was I had done. So, I went up and performed another outside loop. We were both very excited about it and were going to keep it very, very quiet so I would have it as a stunt to do the next time I was in competition with Williams and Sanderson. But somehow it leaked out and, very shortly, an order was promulgated by Maj. Gen. Mason Patrick, chief of the Air Service. He ordered that there will be no more outside loops. So, I never had a chance to use my trick in competition.

Q: There is a story out there that you had to spend some time in a hospital afterward because your eyes were bulging.

A: There was no discomfort whatsoever. It was anticipated that the negative g-force might cause some trouble, particularly in the circulatory system, and that you might have some small major arteries break in your eyes and they would be bloodshot.

Q: Test pilots today go through formal schooling. How about back in the 1920s?

A: Well, we had the engineering school. That was classroom only, but there was a certain amount of flying in connection with it. There was not a regular course in test flying, but there were courses in flying. That led to more knowledge as we recorded the results of aircraft activities.

Q: Your education was quite outstanding. Did you find that you did more engineering work than other pilots because of that? I don't believe the others had your education.

A: When I first went to McCook, all I had was three years of mining engineering but a great deal of mechanical engineering, both classroom and practical work in aircraft maintenance engineering. When I was on the Mexican border, for instance, I was an engineering officer for my flight. I wanted to know more than the mechanics that worked for me, and I always had a wrench or a pair of pliers in my hands. Sometimes when the commanding officer would come down, he thought I was a little oilier and greasier than an officer should be. I've always been interested in mechanics.

Q: Did you do any work at the drawing board?

A: Yes, I had mechanical drawing at the University of California when I was studying mining and had my drawing instruments. I quite frequently figured out things that I wanted to do and did the drawings of them before building them. My dad was a carpenter, and I was very handy with tools from the time I was a little boy. For our flight at the border, we had a closed truck that had lathes in it, a drill press, and all sorts of woodworking and metal-working tools. I had access to that and used it a great deal.

Q: There's been quite a bit written that industry wanted to bust up McCook because it was hoarding all the talent and competing with private industry. Is this accurate?

A: Most of the engineering work for the then Air Service was done at McCook Field. There was a lot of practical engineering work done in the repair depots, but most of the forward-looking engineering work was done at McCook. As a result, McCook certainly made an effort to get people who had some competence in engineering, particularly people who were creative. There is a tendency when new work is being done—new and interesting and exciting work that may be useful—the tendency is for people of talent, people of imagination, to migrate toward that.

So, there are two dynamics: There is the individual attempting to get where he can use his talents, and there are people running the show who are interested in getting these talented people to help them do a job. There are two forces working toward concentrating good people where interesting things are being done.

Q: Was industry coming to McCook trying to pull away some of these people?

A: I had two leaves of absence from the military to demonstrate aircraft in South America for the Curtiss company. But there was not really a concentrated effort on the part of industry to hire people out of McCook or out of Wright Field. It occasionally did happen that industry had a job that needed a particular chap, and if the chap was interested, he went with the industry. But I left the service for an entirely different reason. My wife's mother and my mother were both ill. I was a first lieutenant, and I got $166.66 a month. On that salary, we were unable to take care of our parents.

I had not yet been promoted to captain. I had been a lieutenant for more than twelve years. It was a financial obligation that we couldn't take care of on military pay. So, I went with the Shell Company and was paid exactly three times as much. I would not have left the service, had it not been for that financial obligation.

Q: The 1924 acceleration test you did—was that the first time an aircraft had been wired like that?

A: There had been an accelerator used before, but it was the first time that a comprehensive set of tests was made that took an airplane up to its failure point. It was a wood-covered wing, and after the last pullout of the dive, which I think was 7.8 Gs, I brought the plane in and found the wing had failed. The plywood had cracked. It had failed and given but not come off. Had I taken it up for an additional dive, there is no question that the wings could have come off.

The unique thing about the test was that it was orderly. It measured accelerations in various maneuvers, and it took the wing up almost to its designed stress point. In those days, wings were designed to withstand eight Gs, and I took it up to 7.8 Gs, where it started to fail. For the first time, we had an accurate measurement of whether or not the design formula was correct.

Q: The trim-tab test where the trim tab caused the rudder to fall off—do you recall that?

A: It was a moveable trim tab. There was a little control stick, we called it a pencil control, no more than 6 inches long. The rudder bar you worked with your feet. The first time I used the pencil control, it worked fine. Then I tried increasingly steep dives to see whether it would function properly at high speeds. In a very gentle dive, it started to vibrate. And as it vibrated, it broke the rudder cables. I was in a climb rate so strong that I couldn't hold the rudder. I asked the chap with me to put his feet on the rudder also. At that point, the rudder cable broke and it fluttered at will. I immediately pulled it up into a stall, and as soon as it stalled, the rudder quit vibrating and I just brought it down in a stall. I landed with no trouble.

> *The DH-4 wasn't too bad an airplane for its day. It was the only American-built airplane to get into World War I—it was British-designed but had the Liberty motor. So, an American-built airplane with an American-built motor flew in World War I.*

Q: There have been things written about the DH-4 airplane and that damaging one was not particularly frowned upon, just so they could be rid of it. Any truth in that?

A: The DH-4 wasn't too bad an airplane for its day. It was the only American-built airplane to get into World War I—it was British-designed but had the Liberty motor. So, an American-built airplane with an American-built motor flew in World War I. The DH-4 was a plane of average capabilities. The Liberty engine was for those days an engine of fair reliability. We would consider it completely unacceptable now. In actual combat, the gasoline tank was not self-sealing. As a result, many of them caught fire in the air, and it got the name of "the Flying Coffin."

When the war was over and some of us were interested in seeing better airplanes built, we found that there would be no better airplanes built for a while because of the great number of DH-4s and Liberty engines available. I must say that we did not fly them with the same care that we would have exercised if they were good, new, modern aircraft. I never heard of a chap being severely criticized for cracking one up.

Q: So, what happened if you did crash one? Was there a board to review the incident?

A: Normally, no. James T. Hutchison cracked up one in Canada. He had flown over to Canada to bring back some liquor, which was fairly illegal. When he started to take off, he cracked up. So, he just put a match to it and the thing burned. When it was investigated, however, the engine was intact and there were a lot of melted liquor bottles there. It was pretty obvious what he had done. Hutchinson had to pay for that airplane. I think it cost him $10,000. They took so much out of his pay each month for quite a few years in order to pay it. I don't remember anyone else who paid for an airplane that was wrecked. He paid for it because he caused so much embarrassment for the service.

Q: McCook Field itself—did you feel that it was unsafe?

A: The field when we first started was smaller than you would have liked. There were more obstructions around it than you like to have. But as airplanes increased in speed and performance, they also increased in landing speed and in takeoff speed. It's true there was a big sign, something like "This Field Is Small, Use All of It." But the sign was put up primarily to make sure you took off in more or less a north–south direction rather than in a westerly direction. The reason for the sign was to keep people from taking off the short way. The field was bounded by a levee and trees on the west side, along with a river.

So, it's true, the field gradually was outgrown. But at the time, in the early 1920s, we didn't think of it as being small, because the airplanes didn't require much room. Even then, if they were testing a new, larger airplane, takeoff ordinarily would occur at Wright, which later became Patterson Field. At McCook, there were no runways as such. What you had, hopefully, was a sod field. If you didn't, you had a dirt field that you would have a little difficulty flying from if it was too muddy.

Q: I've read stories that officers felt using a parachute took away the incentive for a pilot to bring an airplane back down. How did you feel about parachutes?

A: There were two things. One thing was the closed cockpit. We had all learned to fly in an open cockpit. When it came to flying in a closed cockpit, which was more comfortable and much more practical, there was a little feeling like in the navy when they went from wooden ships to iron ships. The old wooden ship people couldn't see how they were going to get along with an iron ship. We who had learned to fly in an open cockpit, with helmet and goggles, disliked giving up the insignia of our trade, which were our helmet and goggles. By the same token, we felt that we had gotten along for a long while without parachutes.

Before I went to McCook, I had gone to the parachute school and had jumped in a parachute. One of the things you did after you packed the chute, as part of your course, was to jump with the parachute you packed. Even so, we thought of a parachute as being probably unnecessary. However, we hadn't been there too long when Harold Harris was flying a new Loening high-wing monoplane fighter aircraft, and he had aileron flutter flying right over the field about 1,000 feet. The wings disintegrated, and it became necessary for him to jump. As far as I know, he was the first man in this country to jump and save his life with a parachute. He would surely have been killed without the chute.

Some of us witnessed it. Quite a few of us. It was at the noon hour or just before the noon hour, and quite a few of us were out on the line, watching his takeoff. As a matter of fact, Thurman Bane, another chap, and I were shooting traps just off the flight line, and we saw the thing from its inception. I distinctly remember Colonel Bane wringing his hands and saying as the plane disintegrated, "Oh, my God. Oh, my God. Oh, my God." How happy we all were when we saw the parachute blossom and Harris come down safely. From then on, I don't think any of us hesitated to use the parachute. We had the object lesson that we needed to take us away from our pride and toward using good judgment.

Q: When did it become mandatory?

A: I don't remember, but all of us who were doing test work used parachutes from then on by choice. The chute was a little uncomfortable. It was not as comfortable to sit on a parachute as it was to sit on a cushion. Because of the heat of the backpack and seat pack, you were a little encumbered, and it took a little while for pilots who hadn't seen Harris to accept that slight discomfort in the interest of getting some very good insurance.

Q: In 1924, you were supposed to make a flight with Macready, a transpacific flight. Was this a McCook project?

A: It was our personal project. It never came to fruition because there were so many problems and largely because it would have taken quite a bit of money, which in those days was very difficult to acquire. We did work out a plan but were never able to get it approved.

Q: You were the type of man who got enjoyment in doing something for the first time, like the outside loop. Why is it you never tried for the Orteig or Dole prize or tried the Atlantic flight like Lindbergh? (*Note*: The Orteig Prize of $25,000—offered by New York restaurant owner Raymond Orteig—was for the first aviator or aviators to fly nonstop from New York to Paris or vice versa. The Dole Prize of twenty-five thousand dollars was offered by James D. Dole of the Dole pineapple empire for the first fixed-wing flight from Oakland, California, to Honolulu, Hawaii. Though Maitland and Hegenberger were the first to successfully complete this Pacific flight, military pilots were not eligible for the prize. Several pilots were killed competing for these awards.)

A: I never tried for the prizes because I was in the service. I did want very badly to go on the world flight and was not chosen for that in 1924. No particular reason I wasn't chosen, except that they had some boys who were going to do a real good job of it. I would have liked to go on the South American flight. But I wasn't interested in anything outside the service, and Lindbergh's flight and the Dole flight were outside the service.

Q: Do you know the story about Fairchild and reversing the pitch of the prop on approach?

A: The first controllable-pitch prop was not really a controllable-pitch prop. It was a reversible-pitch prop. The idea was to shorten the landing by reversing your propeller pitch upon landing. Sandy Fairchild was the test pilot on that project, and he took off and had just gotten airborne when the prop reversed of its own volition. This put him in a stall, and he landed in the river right next to McCook Field. I think that little accident put the controllable-pitch prop back about twenty years.

Q: The various trophies for notable mistakes—the Bonehead and all that—was that at McCook Field only?

A: I think that was largely McCook Field because most of the testing was done at McCook. I never knew it being at any other field.

Q: There is a picture hanging in a museum of you standing next to the Flying Jackass trophy. Do you care to say how you won it?

A: I did indeed win the Flying Jackass, much to my embarrassment. I won two awards, one later. Oddly enough, I've forgotten why I won it. I won it legitimately, I'm sure, by consternate stupidity, but I've forgotten just what exactly the stupidity was.

Q: Some of the planes had "P" numbers on the tail. What was the designation?

A: "P" in those days meant pursuit. They didn't use "fighter plane." They called it "pursuit." "O" meant observation. Then there was "GA" for ground attack—the GAX, GA1, and so on.

Q: Did you know the airplane designers Newell and Niles? (*Note*: Joseph S. Newell and Alfred S. Niles authored several books for engineering students. Niles was a professor of aeronautical engineering at Stanford University for thirty-two years.)

A: Yes, they were two very fine, absolutely top, civilian designers. At McCook, there were both civilians and military people. The civilian test pilots were Louis Meister and Ralph Lockwood. The rest of us were all military. At one time, we had another test pilot, Art Smith, who was a superb flier and test pilot, but he didn't stay for too long. The sections were usually but not invariably run by military officers. There would be both military officers of technical competence and outstanding civilian technicians in the different departments. This was true in the design section and the maintenance section. Most of the maintenance people were civilians.

That was one of the unique things about McCook Field at the time. It had a larger percentage of civilian workmen than at any other military field, as far as I know. Some of them were extremely competent. I would say *most* of them were extremely competent.

Q: A friend, I understand, gave you a Sperry turn indicator in 1927 for use on a flight?

A: The indicator was under test when I came through to get permission to make the one-stop transcontinental flight. I saw the indicator for the first time and borrowed one from a project engineer, whose name I have forgotten. It struck me as something that would be very valuable on the flight. I explained my need, and he very kindly loaned me one. It was that simple.

Q: Tell me about the time you and Albert Stevens couldn't make any headway against the wind?

A: One of the airplanes at McCook had a Liberty engine and a supercharger on it, and was designed for high-altitude flying. Stevens wanted to take a series of high-altitude pictures of readily measurable things on the ground and check the barometric altimeter against the scale that was then used to see if it was correct.

We started flying west, and the winds were so strong at high altitudes that although at low altitudes we progressed as far as Richmond, Indiana, by the time that we had gotten to altitude, we had been blown back almost to Columbus, Ohio, clean back over Dayton to Columbus. So, we just kept heading west and landed back at Dayton. We always had headed west. Our flight was blown back almost 100 miles.

On that same flight, we also were testing out a liquid oxygen system. Apparently, it didn't vaporize especially fast, and we both passed out for a period of time and the airplane flew itself for a while.

Q: There is a story about a pressurized cockpit that developed a problem. Was it Macready or Harris involved in that?

A: Harold Harris. They put in a pressurized tank, and on top of the airplane fuselage, they had a pump. The pump was driven by a little propeller, which compressed the air in the tank in which the pilot sat. Harris took it up on the first flight. A relief valve was supposed to open if the pressure got greater than normal atmospheric. The valve stuck and Harris found himself in a very bad position, with the pressure getting greater and greater. He had trouble remaining conscious.

He couldn't dive down in order to get to the ground, because that made the propeller go faster and pump some more. He finally managed to get down and was barely conscious when he did. They reengineered it and put a regular pipe valve in there in addition to the automatic relief valve, so if the thing happened again, the pilot could turn on the regular valve and equalize the air pressure. They ran a series of tests and introduced the idea of having a "manual override" for when stuff didn't work right.

Q: I've heard stories about yourself and three dummy parachutists at a picnic . . .

A: Oh, yes. Parachutes were tested by throwing them out with dummies attached, and we had three of those dummies we called Hart, Schaffner, and Marx. They each were made of very heavy rope bound in such a way to look pretty much like a person, so they would react pretty much as a person would when attached to an opening parachute. So, we were having an air show, and we arranged for one of the parachutes to not open.

I was on the reviewing stand. I was tasked with telling Thurman Bane's successor, a man named McIntosh, when the parachutes opened that the nonopening one was on a dummy. I stood next to him to tell him of the joke, to tell him not to get upset. It was a very unpleasant job because he didn't think it was very funny. There was no official reprimand. He just indicated his dissatisfaction with that sort of stuff.

Q: The parade for you after you won the Schneider Cup—was it through downtown Dayton? (*Note*: Correctly called the Schneider Trophy, it was a prize awarded for a race involving seaplanes and flying boats. Land-based pilots, such as Doolittle, normally did not participate. The annual event spanned 1913–31.)

A: They put a white rowboat on a flat-bottomed truck and put me in the boat dressed up in an old-fashioned admiral's outfit, with a fore-and-aft hat, lots of gold braids. They told me either I could ride through town dressed that way untied or they would tie me up and, tied-up, I would ride through town dressed that way. I went along with them and rode through town dressed as Admiral Doolittle. This was just a gag by my brother test pilots. Like the various trophies, it was just a way to break up the monotony.

> *During the 1920s, we didn't feel we had any enemies. Hitler hadn't started to act up. We felt that we had fought a war to end all wars. We did want to remain strong as a nation, but we thought the likelihood of another war was quite remote. By the early and middle 1930s, we began to realize that the world situation wasn't calm.*

Q: In a place like McCook Field, where the latest developments were produced, was there any problems with security against spies?

A: No. During the 1920s, we didn't feel we had any enemies. Hitler hadn't started to act up. We felt that we had fought a war to end all wars. We did want to remain strong as a nation, but we thought the likelihood of another war was quite remote. By the early and middle 1930s, we began to realize that the world situation wasn't calm. Of course, at the tail end of the twenties, you had the Great Depression, and people were more worried about that than anything else. It wasn't till the Depression ended and Hitler began to make noise that we really had a feeling of insecurity.

Q: How about the life of officers and families at McCook?

A: We lived off the post in Dayton. I guess there wasn't much of anything different for the wives. I suppose they felt a little more apprehensive about their husbands being test pilots because the attrition rate was very high among test pilots.

Q: Was depression experienced among pilots and families when a pilot was lost?

A: You were very distressed when you lost a close companion, but no depression. Distress rather than depression.

Q: You made a parachute jump across the river from St. Louis. What were you doing there?

A: Walter Beech made a very fine little airplane called the Beech Mystery Ship. It was a low-wing externally braced monoplane, with wheels and pants, and it had a Wright Whirlwind engine. It had very good performance for its day. The Shell Company bought one with a large set of wings for aerobatics and cross-country flying, and also bought a small set of wings, interchangeable with the large wings, for racing. It was quite a bit faster with the small wings.

Jimmy Haizlip, who was working for Shell at the time, had an accident and cracked it up. We still had the wings, so I bought the debris and had the airplane redesigned. It was my personal airplane—I paid for it myself. It had the old landing gear, but the gear was fared in better than it was fared in before in order to pick up a little speed. To do all that, torque tubes in the ailerons were bent. I did the design, and that was stupid because the torque tubes then permitted just the tiniest bit of give.

So, I was running a speed course on the first flight, right on the deck, with this rebuilt racing plane, and the ailerons started to flutter—fluttered right off with a good-sized piece of the right wing. The plane just automatically turned on its back, and I fell out at about 400 feet. This was due entirely to a stupid piece of redesign. That was in 1931. I remember because right after that airplane crashed, Matty Laird asked if I wanted to fly the "Laird Super Solution," and I did and won the Bendix with it in '31.

CHAPTER 8
HAROLD R. HARRIS

INTERVIEWED DECEMBER 1977

During World War I, Harold Harris became the first American to fly over the Alps, from Italy to France. After his McCook Field service, he did much test flying of crop-dusting aircraft. Later, he became a vice president of Pan Am Airways, living in Peru for three years. At Pan Am, he introduced several industry firsts, including toilets in airliners. During World War II, he reenlisted and set up the Planning Section of the Army Air Transport Command. General Harris died in 1988 at the age of ninety-two.

Q: The de Bothezat helicopter—were you the first to fly it?

A: Col. Thurman Bane was the first one to fly it—the reason being that he was the commanding officer of the post. He never did any testing. I don't know how good of a pilot he was. He felt that the de Bothezat was a baby of his because he ramrodded the appropriations for it. So, he was going to prove the thing was right and made the first flight, if you want to call it that. The highest the thing could ever get was 6 or 8 inches off the ground. I don't think Bane ever got it more than a couple of inches. That was true of all the helicopters before Sikorsky's time.

Q: With ground effect in mind, are you of the opinion this helicopter flew?

A: No. No helicopter could fly until Sikorsky got his rotational twisting of the blades. All the helicopters that I had anything to do with, starting in 1920, all of them were just within ground effect.

Q: Were there any other attempts at helicopters at McCook?

A: Not that I know of. I'm pretty sure that I'd know about it if there had been any. After Bane, Art Smith was selected to fly it because he was quite small. Bane probably thought the total weight would be all right with Smith flying. Art couldn't do it. So, even though I was a good deal larger, I got the job.

Q: What did you think of de Bothezat himself?

A: He was a very interesting gentleman, very interesting. He had a high squeaky voice, almost a falsetto. It was startling to see this burly frame and then this funny little voice would emerge. But he was a very able engineer. Very able. He made a very successful living after the helicopter debacle, if you want to call it that, designing and constructing ventilation fans for buildings.

Q: About the P-80 flight with the pressurized cockpit, is there anything you can add about that flight?

A: I was thinking about it the other day. Ross McFarland became very well known in the aviation field by his basic book on how a human being fits into an airplane and how an airplane and a human being fit together in the air. He was for many years at Harvard the Guggenheim Professor of Aerospace Health and Safety. What I'm trying to say is that he was an authority on things of that sort and wrote much of the basic material on human behavior in the air—fatigue, the effect of hypoxia, and all that. A few years ago, he gave a lecture. In it, he said that he made an exhaustive survey of aviation history and came to the conclusion that I was the one that made the first pressurized flight anywhere.

Q: And you're not concerned about John Macready's claim to have been the one making that flight?

A: I'm not concerned about Macready's story. I'm just sorry for Macready because nobody ought to get caught in lies. They ought not to make them up in the first place, but to put it in print is very bad. I was in South America on a flight, left in December 1926, and his story came out about that time. I never corresponded with Macready about it. The only thing that I did, the only letter I ever wrote Macready, outside of a cable I sent him complaining about him stealing my experience—I sent him a congratulatory letter on his eightieth birthday. Otherwise, I never had any real correspondence with him.

Engineering Division's USD-9A—the first aircraft with a pressurized cockpit. *Army Air Service photo from the American Aviation Historical Society archives*

Q: After that test flight, did the testing continue or was it dropped?

A: It was dropped. It's a pity, too, because it had very important possibilities for the future, as time has proved. For what reason it was dropped, I don't know. The plane was rebuilt. Safety devices were installed, including a ball-peen hammer, which could be used to knock out one of those bull's-eyes if you had to. Up till the time I left the field, in February 1925, it never flew again. What happened after that, I can't tell you, but I don't think it ever flew again. E. L. Hoffman was a hell of a fine, important person to get things started and get 'em done. Hoffman never got any recognition from anybody, as far as I know. (*Note*: Maj. Edward L. Hoffman was in charge of the Equipment Branch at McCook. In 1926, he was awarded the Collier Trophy for developing a practical parachute.)

Q: There are a lot of people like that, doing little bits of progress that advanced aviation. Doc Burka was another one . . .

A: Well, Doc was a different kind of fellow. He was a nice, able citizen in his own field, but Hoffman was over all of it. He had all the night-lighting and parachutes. All of the equipment was under Hoffman. How he managed to keep everything moving smoothly ahead without any trouble, I don't know. He had some pretty specialized guys that were working for him.

Q: The emergency parachute jump that you made at McCook in 1922—what type of airplane was it?

A: A Loening experimental fighter. Let's see. (*Note:* Harris looked in a logbook for that period. The columns in the book were labeled *Date*, *Type of Plane*, *Type of Engine*, *Type of Work Done*, *Detail of Work Done*, *Duration*, and *Maximum Altitude*.) Let's see what we have here. Yep, a Loening, PW2A.

The remains in a Dayton backyard of "P-233," a Loening PW-2A aircraft. Harold Harris survived this crash by utilizing his backpack parachute. *Army Air Service photo from George Goddard collection*

Q: You had no ill effects from parachuting that day, no trauma?

A: I was in the hospital with my leg. As a matter of fact, General Mitchell happened to be on the field at that time, and he came in to see me.

Q: You dropped one 500-pound bomb in the offshore ship bombings in the early twenties. Did you do anything more?

A: No. I was just one of the pilots in the bombings. Actually, I was a little more than that because I was doing the liaison flying between Dayton and Langley Field for General Mitchell. As a matter of fact, I cracked up that plane in trying to get back to the field. Have you run into E. P. Warner? No? He was a very, very able aeronautical engineer out of NASA, but it wasn't called NASA then.

Q: It was NACA.

A: Right. E. P. Warner happened to be at McCook and asked if he could ride back to Washington with me. I said, "Sure." He was a very nice guy and very able citizen. We took off quite late in the afternoon and overnighted in Moundsville, West Virginia. You young people don't realize that airplanes didn't fly very far in those days. They flew a short way and landed and refueled. Anyway, we overnighted there, and I told E. P. that we had to get out of there quick in the morning because the fog came in from the river there. We needed to get out of there just about daybreak.

So, we got going at the crack of dawn and climbed up through the fog. We got up over the clouds on a compass heading. Remember there were no radio beams and anything like that in those days, no maps either except road maps. I guess we flew for about an hour and forty-five minutes, by compass, and I thought, *Well, maybe I've got a tailwind. I'd better find out where I am pretty quick or I'm liable to find myself out over the ocean.* So, I found a hole and we went down. We didn't recognize anything—just farmland.

We found a likely looking field, shot it a couple of times, and went in and landed. This was a DH-4, not a DH-4A. It was going to be broken up anyway, though I didn't want to be the one to break it. It just about came to the end of its landing roll when the right wheel caught in a hole, probably a groundhog hole of some kind, and it sheared the gear off. It landed in a heap. We were in Falls Church, just outside Washington. So, we called up and informed them that we were all right, but the plane was a total wreck. We took an automobile and drove on into Washington. I borrowed a plane from Bolling Field and got down to Langley in time to report to General Mitchell. He hadn't the foggiest idea why I was reporting to him.

Q: Was Eddie Warner at McCook?

A: He wasn't stationed there, but he was there a great deal because of his work. Anyway, I said to him, "Eddie, damn it, here I've been worrying myself to death up here, sitting up front"—of course, there was no intercom in those days—"I hope you weren't as worried as I was." And he said, "No, I wasn't worried. I was reading the minutes of the Peace Conference."

Q: About the bombings, I don't suppose the Ostfriesland was one of them you attempted to bomb? (*Note:* This German battleship was sunk by aerial bombing in July 1921, as part of a demonstration to show the military potential of aircraft.)

A: That was bombed later. The ship I bombed was a cruiser. I don't even remember its name. There were no real preparations at McCook for the bombing. We were an experimental place. We didn't enter into the operational phases of the work, except by accident. But it was a big deal with the Air Service. General Mitchell got pilots from everywhere. That's how I happened to be there. I didn't kill myself with glory on that one, having trained as a bomber pilot in World War I. The plane I flew was a B-1 Martin bomber.

Q: The Barling bomber was huge.

A: Yes, the tail surface was probably as big as the lifting surfaces on the de Havilland. Walter Barling was a very nice little Britisher, a very nice little guy. He was competent. I think his big weakness was the fact that he was so meticulous in every detail that the company that built the airplane went broke. He just insisted on doing things just this way, every nook and cranny. And, you know, it was like God himself. I was no help to him, I'll say that. The last design that he made in Great Britain cracked up on takeoff and killed the crew.

I told grounds crew people, "Look, I don't know who designed the tail surface on this bomber, but let's make sure that if this thing goes up on its nose, like the job did in Great Britain, that we have something up front to take the shock. We ought to have a set of wheels up front." So, at my insistence, another set of wheels was built for the airplane. They were later removed because it was found they were quite unnecessary.

Q: I've heard stories about the bomber, mainly adverse, such as it couldn't get to Washington because it could never make it over the mountains.

A: That wasn't so. We had conversations about taking it to Washington so General Patrick could show it off to the congressmen who held the money. He personally talked to me about it. I said, "Well, General, if you'd like to have this in Washington, I'll sure try to get it there. But I do want to point out that if one of the engines lets go en route, it might mean getting banged up in the hills." The plane didn't have any extra power. He thought he better let it be.

Q: Do you recall offhand what the bomber's maximum altitude was?

A: Yes, 16,000 or 18,000 feet.

Q: What about stability. Did it feel stable?

A: Very good. It was a very good airplane. It wasn't a fighter. It wasn't supposed to be very maneuverable. It never flew in or out of McCook. I wouldn't have tried it.

Q: General Patrick seems to have been an interesting man. He did not begin to fly until he was sixty years old. How would you rate him as a pilot?

A: A very, very fine man. The only occasion I had to see his piloting was when I acted as an aide one time and we flew to Chanute. It was a dual-control de Haviland, a very fine airplane. He flew it part of the way back. In those days, you had to follow a map and check off checkpoints. You automatically start crossing section lines at a particular angle, and you knew that was going to bring you to where you wanted to be. But the general didn't seem to get that idea at all. He couldn't fly very straight.

When we got back to McCook, I looked down and the big flag was up on the flagpole. That meant there was a general officer on the post. In other words, General Mitchell had come in. I saw that and pointed down. We couldn't talk. I pointed down to the big flag, but he didn't know what I meant. He wanted to land the plane, so we came in and he landed downwind. There wasn't much wind, but there was enough that the flag was flying out. A few years later, I attended a reception for General Patrick, and the hostess asked if he knew a Lieutenant Harris. "Yes, I know Harris," he said. "He's the fellow that let me land downwind in front of General Mitchell." He was a fine fellow.

Q: I ran across a story where *Aviation Magazine* reported a Washington rumor that had General Mitchell taking over McCook Field. Ever hear that?

A: Well, he would have been a wonderful fellow to take it over. But nobody could fill Thurman Bane's shoes. Even Billy Mitchell couldn't, I don't believe. Billy Mitchell would have done a much-better job at public relations. Bane didn't care about those things, but he got things done. He got things started and made it happen.

Q: You were the chief of the flight test section, correct?

A: Yes and Florence Fairchild was my secretary. She was a lovely, lovely lady. She finally married Muir Fairchild, whose wife had died. I was the best man at their wedding.

Q: Fairchild ended up with four stars, didn't he?

A: Darned right—and he deserved them, too. I take a lot of credit for that. Fairchild and I were together in Italy. After the war, I stayed in uniform, and Fairchild went back to Spokane to go into business. We were pretty close in those days. When they finally decided they wanted to get some of those pilots back into uniform—they didn't have enough pilots—I sent the information out to Muir Fairchild and urged him to come back. This was in 1920. I urged him to apply, which he did. Thank God.

Q: The "honeymoon special." What exactly was it?

A: What happened was they took the gunner's compartment out of the rear area of a DH-4 and built two seats facing, one toward the tail and one toward the nose. They added a canopy over the top. It was useful because you could pull the top down and look out. It had these Plexiglas windows all through it, so you could look out and not be disturbed by the wind. The pilot was out in the air, but the two passengers were enclosed.

Q: Back to Fairchild, I read somewhere that he was scheduled to go with Kelly on the coast-to-coast flight. The article says nothing about why he was taken off the flight....

A: I'll tell you why. We were running some experiments on reversible-pitch propellers, and we had one on a Jenny. Fairchild was the test pilot. This was the one where he reversed it and ended up in a pond. He broke his arm and couldn't go on the flight. Bane's brother-in-law, Lt. Ernest Dichman, a pilot and engineer, did a lot of the engineering for the flight. Dichman, Fairchild, and Kelly did all the flying in the thing. Macready was a Johnny-come-lately and had nothing to do with the flight except to go for the ride.

Q: The self-sealing tanks—were they at McCook?

A: Yes, just coming in. They did quite a bit of experimental testing on the firing range with various self-sealing devices. Some of them worked; others didn't.

Q: The runway surface at McCook—was it cinders, dirt, or grass?

A: Grass. There was a little concrete, but it wasn't long enough to land anything on it. It was badly sited. If you ran off it, you ended up in some buildings. You just took off in any direction.

Q: What about the sign painted in 10-foot-high letters atop a hangar? The sign read, "This Field Is Small, Use It All."

A: The reason that sign was put there was because some cocky guy with a Martin bomber full of people, instead of using the whole field, he took off from the middle of the field and didn't quite make it. He piled up down there at the bridge. Everybody was dead, and that's the reason they put up that sign.

Q: Did you ever win the Flying Ass Trophy?

A: I don't know what that is, but I am sure that I deserved it, even if I didn't win it. The first one I ever heard of was the "Cup of Good Beginnings and Bad Endings." It was invented by Rudolph Schroeder. I should have won whatever dumb trophies were being handed out because I sure cost the government a lot of money in cracked-up airplanes.

Q: About the time you left—in 1925–26—there was a great exodus of people, real good talent, from McCook. Officers, engineers, mechanics going out to industry. This was good for industry, but it was bad for the Air Corps. Were you approached by Huff and Daland? (*Note*: Thomas Huff and Elliot Daland designed the first crop-dusting aircraft.)

A: Yes, I was, I guess, probably the first.

Q: I read that the aviation industry complained about McCook Field right from the start—that it was hoarding talent. Is this true?

A: The people at McCook did do some design work and actually built one airplane. Also, they built an engine. It was an eighteen-cylinder, water-cooled engine, put into a well wing. I guess it was supposed to be a long-range observation plane. I had the job of flying the thing, its first flight. I was smart enough—lucky, really, I wasn't smart—to get quite a bit of altitude before I started to make a turn with it. Well, this was a low-wing monoplane, internally braced, and the bracing was not sufficiently sturdy. When you put the aileron over a little bit, it would twist the wing. Brother, if you think that wasn't a trick to get that thing back on the ground. . . . The engine was designed at McCook and was a total wash.

Q: The airway that you had between Dayton and Washington with a stop-off in Moundsville,

West Virginia—were there any electrical devices on the ground at Moundsville?

A: No. It was an airway because we designated it an airway. The only thing there was a refueling setup. There were no bonfires in between at night. We did a great deal of flying that route. What happened was the federal government was then running the airmail, and they wanted to operate at night and had nothing at all to operate with. They asked us to develop aids on the ground and in the airplane. Hoffman assigned an electrical engineer, Lt. Donald Bruner, to the electrical side of it. I handled the flying side. Bruner and I did an awful lot of night flying. I had been a night instructor in Italy during the war, so I didn't have any particular problem with night operations.

Q: What type of devices were on the ground?

A: To show you how stupid people are, instead of us going to the lighthouse people to find out what they had learned over the centuries, we learned it the hard way. The first tests that we held were with big searchlights standing vertically. That was fine if you were right over it, but unless it was reflected from a cloud, you could never see it. Eventually, we used rotating beacons that, as far I know, are still in use.

Q: Does the name Eddie Allen ring a bell? (*Note*: Edmund T. Allen was a test pilot at McCook Field in the final days of World War I. Later, he became the first test pilot for NACA.)

A: Allen was an extremely fine aeronautical engineer and pilot. I always had great regard for him because he was so confident and so quiet about it. He never threw his weight around at all. He was a little guy who had done a lot of flying in the early 1920s, in gliders in Germany. As a matter of fact, he got his face all smashed up in a glider. Allen finally ended up as the head of test work for Boeing. He burned to death in 1943 in a terrible accident in the first B-29.

Q: Was McCook the only place that you know of that worked on brakes for aircraft?

A: As I told you, we carried up dummies to test parachutes. The DH-4 wasn't very good for this because you could only carry one dummy along with someone to dump it, so we borrowed a Douglas torpedo plan from the US Navy. Then you could drop two or three at a time. Anyway, when these planes landed, you had to have two men out on the field to hold the wingtips. I got to thinking, *Well, this is silly having two mechanics out there just to help the pilot turn it around.* I believed that if we could get a kind of lever to clamp down or pull up on the inside wheel, the pilot could turn the plane around himself.

I was about to leave, so I turned over to the hangar superintendent the request to rig up a device of that sort. He got to talking with Mac Laddon, who was a civilian engineer, and Mac thought, *Well, this is just ridiculous. Why don't we do it right and make brakes?* So, he did, and that's how brakes for planes got started at McCook.

Q: What was the US Navy's role at McCook?

A: They tried to learn all they could. The navy was so deficient in its landplane operations that they had me do their test flying in the early days. I did the test for the first torpedo plane up at the Martin factory. The navy didn't have anything to do with the test. I loaded a torpedo on the airplane and flew it down to McCook, where we ran a performance test on it. Then the navy brass wanted the airplane in Washington, so I flew the plane there with a torpedo on it.

Q: You were McCook's chief of the flying section at a time when there wasn't much funding. Any interesting stories during that time?

A: We did what we were instructed to do with what was available. In 1923, our speed course was a 2-mile stretch in a meadow at the old Wright Field. It was marked with pylons, and you timed yourself with a stopwatch. It always amused me to think, *Here we put out all these ponderous reports on the performance of airplanes based on some of the sketchiest darned material you can possibly imagine.* These pylons were nothing but lathe with a little fabric on them. Whenever a farmer would come down there to mow that field and take away the hay, he would move the pylons. So, what started out an absolutely perfect 2-mile course probably ended up being two and a sixteenth or something.

Anyway, on that course, you were flying right on the deck. There was a little backroad used only by farmers that worked in the area. The road had plenty of signs on it that read "Beware of Low-Flying Aircraft." But there were no guards or anything of that sort because there wasn't enough traffic on the ground.

> *Hoy came in after he and his observer ran the speed course. The mechanics were cleaning up the thing and asked him, "Where did you get all this blood on your spreader bar?" He said, "What?" It seems he had taken the head off a driver of a little truck on that road. He didn't know it, but I guess the driver of the truck knew it.*

Hoy Barksdale, for whom Barksdale Field is named, was flying the speed course with a modified DH. It had a spreader bar on the fixed landing gear between the wheels. Hoy came in after he and his observer ran the speed course. The mechanics were cleaning up the thing and asked him, "Where did you get all this blood on your spreader bar?" He said, "What?" They investigated and found he had taken the head off a driver of a little truck on that road. He didn't know it, though I guess the driver of the truck knew it.

It wasn't Hoy's fault. The poor guy killed himself. You could write a lot of books about Hoy Barksdale. He had the fastest reaction time of anyone I ever saw, and it saved his life. He was flying a speed run on that same course in an experimental DH with a steel fuselage. The tail broke off. Well, you can imagine, running along at 130 miles per hour, which was top speed in that particular plane, flying 6 to 8 feet off the ground and your tail breaks off.

It just throws you right over, inverted, yet he got out of that airplane and pulled his rip cord. He came out of it alive. He had so much forward velocity that even though the chute was probably only partially open, it would break his fall enough. Another man, Bob Anderson, who was in the plane, was killed. Then again, this rapid reaction is what killed Barksdale. He later got a plane into an uncontrollable spin and bailed out, but he pulled his chute too soon and hooked it on the tail.

Another thing that happened at McCook was the testing of a Verville Racer for competition purposes. It was a monocoque. It was enormous and had a big Packard engine up front. It was the same airplane in which C. C. Moseley won the Pulitzer Race in Long Island the following year. (*Note*: Maj. Corliss C. Moseley, McCook Field test and racing pilot, left the military in 1925 and founded Western Air Express. He eventually established civilian flight schools to support the war effort, teaching twenty-five thousand pilots and five thousand mechanics.)

This must have been in 1921, and Schroeder was the pilot. The plane was so blind forward that you couldn't see anything. I don't think he even had a periscope, like Lindbergh had on his plane. Anyway, Schroeder wanted to get some movies of this thing landing. We had the movie guy out on the field, and Schroeder came in and landed right into the camera, seriously injuring the cameraman.

Q: You used to have public shows at McCook, once a year. In the 1923 air show, you demonstrated the Barling bomber.

A: I flew the Barling all the way from Carlton, hopped out, and flew the helicopter, the de Bothezat. As a matter of fact, we had a stopwatch, and that was the best flight the de Bothezat ever made. It must have been well over a minute.

Q: I remember reading that you said the de Bothezat had the best altimeter that you could have—a rope with markings a foot apart. Do you have any other stories of those times?

A: One had to do with the world *flight*. At the time, I thought it was pretty hectic—amusing, too. Remember, three planes got as far as takeoff from Scotland for Iceland, and all of them got to Iceland except one. Leigh Wade had to go down in the drink with the *Boston*, and the plane was lost. Well, in order to have three airplanes in the proceedings, regardless of the fact that actually only two made the whole flight, we had a spare, which was all just standard. In all respects, it was the same as the others, except it didn't have the world flight insignia on it.

The insignia was quite a complicated thing. So, we got a message from Washington to get this thing painted up so that Wade could take it from somewhere up in Nova Scotia, down to Boston, and west from there. Well, this was a weekend, and we had to find a sign painter first. We found him. I went out later in the afternoon to see how he was getting along, and there was no sign of the guy. The sign was about half done. We weeded around in the hangar there and finally found him drunk underneath a bench. These were Prohibition days. What had happened was that the airplanes all had a tank built in, carrying a gallon of alcohol. It was in reserve in case the plane went down.

Q: Was it grain alcohol?

A: It was to drink. And he had found this tank. Damn it, now, we were really in trouble. I got a couple of fellows from the hospital to help me. After a lot of coffee and cold showers and whatnot, we finally got him back on the job and got it done in time enough so that it could go. But it was touch and go for the whole time.

Q: Was this alcohol tank standard for the time?

A: No, it was just for the world flight. It was to drink in an emergency. It was all sealed up. Nobody knew it was there except the crew.

Q: I ran across a letter written in 1924, which would have been right after you left McCook. Billy Mitchell writes, "McCook is pitiful, practically nothing going on." This was a year before his court-martial. Do you agree with that description?

A: You've got to remember about Mitchell: Either things were going the way Mitchell wanted them to go or else they were terrible. You see, after Bane left, there wasn't any leadership that amounted to anything. I mean these commanding officers came in by way of their seniority, not by way of their ability. I don't mean that in a bad way because they were all nice guys. Curry, who I presume was in command when Mitchell wrote that, was a cut above the others. But there wasn't any real dynamic drive at the top.

Q: Bane was a hard act to follow.

A: That's exactly right. They were doing the best they could with what they had. I can't entirely endorse what General Mitchell said.

Q: You were married at the time you were at McCook?

A: Yes, and everybody lived off post. Nobody lived on the post except Bane. He had quite a nice place. Reuben Fleet lived with him there for a while.

Q: Did you spend much time with Ed Aldrin?

A: Oh, yes, very much. I'm very fond of Eddie Aldrin. He was not particularly well liked by a lot of people, but I thought he was a damn able guy.

Q: Was he a pilot?

A: Yes. He had his wings, but didn't do much flying, except enough to get his flying pay. That was the thing that used to tee me off. We had a Martin transport, one of the first passenger planes that Martin built. It had, I think, ten seats in it. I was a first lieutenant drawing 25 percent flying pay, and all the military aviators on the post had to get their flying time in. So, they would all come out at the same time, and I would fly eight or ten of them for their flying time. They got 75 percent of their base pay against my 25 percent of piddly base pay. The 75 percent went with the rating of military aviator. These were all West Point fellows.

Q: What were you rated?

A: Pilot. Military aviator was a rank. It was just like saying PhD. You had to pass a series of tests. You had a flying test. I couldn't get it because they stopped giving it out. That used to tee me off to no end. I was such a rascal then. I'd do a lot of wild maneuvers with the airplane to make the boys earn their money.

You were talking about McCook stories. I had an interesting experience with Isaac M. Laddon. He had been an automobile designer in Cadillac before World War I. Cadillac had taken a contract to build airplanes from a French design, the LePere. The LePere was a fine airplane, as I remember. Too bad it didn't happen earlier, because we would have really had a first-class airplane if we would have had the LePere instead of the DH-4.

Anyway, among the airplanes Laddon designed was the LePere. He did the spadework of laying out the spars and stresses, along with tending to all the other problems that were inherent in the design and building of an airplane. He went to McCook and was employed there as a civilian engineer, so I knew that he had something to do with the work that had gone into building this airplane. It wasn't ready for testing until after the war ended, and I was doing the testing.

I would make climbs to the ceiling, and I asked Laddon if he would like to go for a trip. The plane either had to carry his weight or the weight of a gunner or some ballast. And Mac said, "Sure, I'd like to go." Well, it was a very cold day. In those days, it took about seventy minutes to climb to the absolute ceiling. He was bundled up as much as he could. There were no heaters, of course.

When we got back on the ground, I said, "Mac, how did you like your ride?" He said, "Oh, I got awful cold and then I began to think about the design of those spars and how I really fudged them." He said, "You know, I learned a good lesson from that."

Q: Would you mind mentioning about your ear?

A: Well, yes, I had an infected ear when I was three and they took out my eardrum. I haven't had an eardrum since I was three years old. There's no secret about it. When the FAA finally came into existence, or CAA, or whatever it was, they wanted to rule that I couldn't fly an airplane with passengers aboard. It was all right with me. I didn't want to fly anymore, anyway.

CHAPTER 9
HOWARD CALHOUN DAVIDSON

INTERVIEWED SEPTEMBER 1977

After departing McCook Field activity, Maj. Gen. Calhoun Davidson held several high commands. On December 7, 1941, he was commanding general of the Hawaiian Interceptor Command at Wheeler Field in Hawaii, after which he became commanding general of the 7th Air Force. He died in 1984 at the age of ninety-four.

Q: You graduated from West Point?

A: Well, a friend of mine from our hometown of Horton, Texas, went to Texas A&M after high school. This was in 1907. He came back and said you should go back to A&M with me. Well, I had one more year of high school. He said, "C'mon, they'll give you an examination and you can get in probably." So, I went back with him. By the way, the whole cost of school—board, lodging, tuition, and everything—was $250 a year!

Anyway, when we got there, the dean of admission asked for my high school certificate. Forty of us said we didn't have one, so we had to take an exam. It was in algebra on quadratic equations. None of us had taken it. I looked at the questions and saw that I couldn't answer any of them. I quietly folded up the paper, put it in my pocket, and slipped out of the exam, thinking that was that. The next day, they published the results. Thirty-nine of them were admitted on condition, and I had been admitted scot-free! They thought that I had lost my paper and didn't want to make any fuss about it.

So, I was at A&M about a year and a half when I got an appointment to West Point in 1909. The first two years at A&M helped me get through West Point. I had a terrible time. I could never make good grades and finally graduated eighty-fifth in a class of ninety-three. I had an especially difficult time in French, taking an exam and just barely passing it. But all the others had failed in mathematics, which I hadn't failed in. I graduated in 1913, but my record at West Point still is below sea level in French.

Q: When did you get into aviation?

A: In 1916, after serving six months in the Philippines. I reported to North Island, where I took aviation training in about October of that year.

Q: When did you first go to McCook?

A: I came back from France in 1919 and was sent right to Dayton. I was assigned first to the engine testing section. In my time, we were testing the BMW and the Mercedes that the Germans had developed. They were six-cylinder motors and had been very successful in World War I. The motors of the allies in that war were more experimental. The Liberty was a completely experimental thing. At Dayton, we learned that it took ten years to get the bugs out of a new motor. We fooled around and designed and built the Liberty motor, sending it into war without having done all of that testing that it should have had. Afterward, we did a lot of that testing at Dayton to improve it. The engine that impressed people the most at Dayton was the BMW. We never could find out what made it so efficient.

Q: Do you have an opinion about the Liberty engine?

A: When they finally got the bugs out of it, it was a pretty good 400-horsepower engine. But in World War I, they didn't have the bugs out and it wasn't very reliable. Quite a few of the engines made it overseas. Most of them didn't. In my experience as an air officer of the Seventh Corps, the engines in our airplanes were Samson and the airplanes themselves were French. The fighters were Spads or British Sopwith Camels or French Nieuports.

Q: How long did you stay at that position at McCook?

A: About six months working on engines. Then I fell into supply for about a year. One of the jobs was to get rid of all the useless "air equipment" we had. We had dozens of wings for airplanes that didn't exist and everything like that. I think when I took over, we had about four million articles on the supply list. We surveyed those things and got rid of them as fast as we could.

Q: You mentioned the engineering school...

A: The engineering school was like production engineering. We went through the shops just practically like mechanics. We had to learn, for instance, metal spinning and making things on lathes. We had to glue boards together for a propeller, make our own templates and mark it out, and then actually whittle out a propeller, which would be used in service. Things like that. We did have about a month or so of academic stuff, especially mathematics. When we'd start, we were given a book with about a hundred problems in it. We'd have to work out those problems.

Q: I thought the year at the engineering school was all in a classroom environment.

A: Not much classroom. It was almost production engineering work. Besides making the propeller, I had to make a chest and finish it, and then put fifteen coats of varnish on it—give it a piano finish. Made it out of cherry wood. We had millions of feet of wood at Fairfield Depot to make wooden propellers. We could buy it at reasonably good rates because they had no use for it. They had mostly gone to steel propellers. We would get it and make furniture out of it. One of my assignments was to build this chest and finish it just like a piano.

Q: Was the runway at McCook grass or cinder?

A: Grass. I never saw a paved runway until years later. It just had a big tee that would point to the wind. There weren't any landing instructions or no controls at all like we have now.

Q: You mentioned the field was formerly swamp . . .

A: We were sitting on a crust of about 12 to 15 inches of dried soil. Underneath that was just mud. Bolling Field in Washington was exactly the same way. We had a Vought, a Bristol, or something or other, a dive bomber. I tested it. The wings came off, and it hit Bolling Field. It took seven days to just locate the airplane fuselage that had gone down through this crust into the mud.

Q: You were close friends with Thurman Bane. He passed away in 1932. Do you have any idea what caused his death?

A: I think it was some kind of brain tumor or something like that. He was interesting and was a very good type to have in charge of a place like McCook Field. Because when he graduated from West Point in 1908, there was a system for selecting officers for the Ordnance Corps. You couldn't just graduate from West Point and choose the Corps. You had to pass an examination, and then they'd choose you. The chief of ordnance came down and visited the school and he said, "Bane, how are you doing?" And Bane said, "Oh, all right, I guess, but they work us too hard here." And the chief said, "Well, if you want to get ahead, you have to work harder than the other fellow or assume that God gave you more brains." Bane used that a lot to make other people get busy and work their brains to try and improve themselves.

Maj. Rudolph "Shorty" Schroeder preparing for a high-altitude flight with an oxygen tube in his mouth. *Photo courtesy of the US Air Force Museum*

Q: Dr. George de Bothezat did his work at McCook. There's a story going around that he talked Bane into dropping the variable-pitch propeller project.

A: I think that is absolutely true. de Bothezat had everything in his helicopter except some kind of balance. Now this Spaniard built the autogyro and that automatically balanced it. But de Bothezat never did have a successful machine. Bane thought the world and all of him. He was a Russian and came over after World War I to get a job. Bane asked him, "What can you do?" He said he could do anything. So, Bane asked him to design a bomb sight that would keep the hairs on the target all the time. He did, but it was about as big as this overstuffed chair. The principle was there, but he couldn't sell it in the United States. He went over to England and tried to sell it to the British, and they rejected it, too, because it was too big. But later it was taken up, and some of it was in the Norton bombsight, which was good.

Q: You remember Shorty Schroeder...

A: He was a test pilot and his specialty was high-altitude flying. We had an old airplane called the LePere, a French airplane. It was the only one in existence over here. They rigged it up with the supercharger. He took it up—it was an open cockpit airplane—took it up to about 35,000 feet. In those days, we had to buy our own goggles. His goggles got clouded up with snow inside at 35,000 feet, probably about 50 below zero. He had oxygen, but it came through a little tube, no bigger than an ordinary wooden match. He reached up to clean the snow off, and just at that time he pushed up his goggles to clean them and that tube froze and shut off the oxygen to him.

He passed out, and the airplane went into a nosedive, full power, and came down from 35,000 feet to about 2,000 feet. That change in pressure was almost like hitting him in the head with a hammer, and it woke him up. He was close to McCook Field, so he shut off the motor and successfully landed and then passed out again. They rushed out and got him. The doctor said his heart was about double the size it should have been. It enlarged trying to get the blood to him, you see. His eyeballs were frozen—everything was wrong with him. The doctors had a field day examining him, never having had a specimen like that before. In two weeks, his eyes got all right, and he was back flying.

A funny sequel to that is that by that time I was supply officer and Bane said, "Get us a supply of oxygen that's dry." So, I put in an order to the oxygen people, and they got this dry oxygen and were filling a tank for us and it exploded. I thought, "Oh, my God, we got somebody who will sue the government for millions." I rushed over to the oxygen plant to see the man and he said, "The only thing it did to me was it blew the shoes off my feet." I asked, "What can I do for you?" He said, "Give me another pair of shoes and I'll be all right." I rushed him to a shoe shop and bought the shoes myself so he wouldn't have too much claim against the government.

We destroyed, I guess, about four million dollars' worth of useless equipment—wings for airplanes that didn't exist, fuselages with no wings. All sorts of things like that.

My job, mostly, was cleaning up the supply of materials. We destroyed, I guess, about four million dollars worth of useless equipment—wings for airplanes that didn't exist, fuselages with no wings. All sorts of things like that. We were spending money to keep them listed in good shape. We finally rigged up a scheme where we could survey them and just get rid of them—sell them or whatever.

Q: So "surveyed" meant destroyed?

A: No, it meant that you put it before a surveying officer, and he'd say whether or not it was serviceable or unserviceable. If it was unserviceable, you would either sell it, if you could, or destroy it. Get rid of it so we could get it out of our records. For example, we had a Barling Bomber and it had a good idea in it—a propeller on each side, both run by a crankshaft off the same motor. By making them turn opposite, you got rid of all the torque. But it wouldn't fly, and it sat on the field until all the fabric rotted off the wings and everything. I don't know who concocted the idea, but General Mitchell came through. They had a test of incinerator bullets, and they shot some of those into the bomber and it burned up. Before they did that, they removed all this complicated mechanism so if it was any good it would be available.

Q: This is interesting. The Barling bomber did fly, it just didn't fly that well, I think—not as well as they expected.

A: It may have flown once, but it never flew while I was at McCook Field. It sat staked out. They didn't even put it inside a hangar. Just staked it out until it was almost a complete wreck. Then they got mechanics to take out all the interesting parts. They're probably in the museum in Dayton today. So, that's the way you surveyed. You had to say it was worn out from wear and tear, even though you couldn't say the bomber was worn out through wear and tear because it couldn't fly.

Alfred H. Hobley ran the section testing all the supplies that came in. Everything that came in, I had to buy it and it had to pass specifications that we put down. Gasoline, for instance. We didn't buy it by octane. Why not? It all relates back to Schroeder making an altitude flight. When he got up to about 30,000 feet, he noticed that the glass tube on the pipes feeding the gasoline from the tank to the carburetor had bubbles going through there. That was because the gasoline we bought was what they called "casing head gasoline." They'd compressed the gas coming out of the well, turned it back into a liquid, and when it got up to 30,000 feet, the atmosphere was so thin that it turned back into gas. It was feeding gas through his pipe and not gasoline. So, we put in a distillation test so that if it had gas in it, it couldn't pass.

Q: I asked you about an "almond borrow engine"—does that ring a bell?

A: I think we called it a "wobble plate" engine. It had a shaft and a plate on it, and that plate would wiggle back and forth as the shaft turned and that made the pistons work. They've got something similar to that today. The shaft that turns the plate is on, say, a 45-degree angle, and the pistons work on this plate so that you can see when the shaft turns it pushes those pistons around. They had it at McCook, but it was almost too radical for them to deal with. I think the civilian people developed it since.

CHAPTER 10
HESTER CHRISTIANSEN

INTERVIEWED APRIL 1978

Hester Christiansen was there at the beginning of the McCook saga. Assigned to the facility as a telephone operator, she began work at the field before the administration building even was fully constructed. Her memories were of the human, rather than the technical, side of McCook Field operations.

Q: Your husband was a mechanic during World War I?

A: He came over in 1917 to go to school at Yale, where he had a cousin attending. The war broke out and he was crazy about flying, so he enlisted in the Signal Corps, was sent to Texas, and then was overseas all during the war. He was with the 12th Squadron. At one time, he was with General Mitchell in his squadron. But he wasn't a flier; he was a mechanic. It was through that that he came back to the United States after the war, gave up his Danish citizenship, and became an American citizen. General Mitchell was responsible for sending him to McCook Field to get a job.

Q: When you came to McCook, there really wasn't a McCook. You were actually the first person there, working as a telephone operator even before they completed the buildings.

A: That's right. The field was under construction, but the administration building was practically complete. I was sent from downtown out to McCook Field as a telephone operator, with a small PBX exchange in a great big room. They told me that eventually they would have a large telephone exchange put in the room. It was October 1917.

Q: When you first got to McCook, what do you remember? Any airplanes?

A: I don't remember airplanes because I was in that office that was on the opposite side of the field from the hangars. We were very busy. We had a line that went to Indianapolis too, I think, the Sixth Corps area. I forget what they called it then. I never took a Civil Service examination to continue on in telephone operating because I wanted to go on into something else.

Q: I am interested in any good human-interest stories . . .

A: Bob Mayer is one. I think he was one of the most interesting people at McCook. They had a main entrance to the field through which all employees had to come, and Bob Mayer was in charge of that, of security. Harry Carpenter was his assistant. They handed out passes to the employees as they came in, and Bob could remember everybody's name and each person's number. He was with them all those years and then went on to Wright-Patterson Field. He was strict without making anyone mad. He was very well loved by all the McCook Field people.

Anyway, he memorized everybody's name. He knew people who had come back, who had been working at a field out of town and then came back to McCook. The minute they'd come in, Bob would say, "Hello, Mr. So and So." He always knew their names. He would write them a special pass. All the employees had a badge with their name and number on it, and these badges sat on a rack behind Bob. He would reach up and get each person's badge the minute they came through the door. It was ready for the person. The main entrance was on Keowee Street.

You know, everybody at McCook was very friendly. It was a very friendly atmosphere. We had regular dances, and I played piano for them. Actually, several of the boys from the squadron played instruments. It was down at the post exchange, which was just a place that the boys could go to get candy and crackers and things like that, like a snack bar. The exchange was located on down toward the hospital, down beyond the home of the commanding officer. There was a cafeteria on the field where a great many friendships were made and many have continued to this day.

> *I loved working at McCook. I thought it was wonderful. You were all the time rubbing shoulders with people who had been places and done things. Having had only a sixth-grade education, I always have felt my years spent at McCook Field, where I was able to associate with all these wonderful people who were making history—well, that was an education in itself.*

I loved working at McCook. I thought it was wonderful. You were all the time rubbing shoulders with people who had been places and done things. Having had only a sixth-grade education, I always have felt my years spent at McCook Field, where I was able to associate with all these wonderful people who were making history—well, that was an education in itself.

For instance, General Mitchell came to the field several times and was very friendly. Orville Wright came to the flying section many times. He was a shy but cordial man. Major Napier was in charge of the hospital there. He was a handsome man. Others I met included de Seversky, and Sikorsky, and de Bothezat. I got to know many manufacturers, including Glenn Martin, Anthony Fokker, Grover Loening, Chance Vought, Larry Bell, and Lawrence Sperry. General Pershing made a tour of the field one time, which was exciting.

The pilots had fun with each other. After a test flight that ended in the mud or some such result, during the meeting upstairs, they had "trophies" laid out on the table. As a result of the discussion, a pilot who ended up in the mud or something was presented a trophy—Alibi, Bonehead, Donkey—and it would be on his desk until the next episode.

As a joke, they also had what was known as a lung tester. It was a small can with an opening on top and a stem that you put in your mouth. When you blew into it, black powder would spray over your face. The person blowing in it didn't know it, but everyone else did. That was used mainly when someone from another field came in and did a little too much bragging.

There was an awful lot of cooperation between the heads of departments and the personnel. They were very kind, I thought. I never could find anything wrong with any of them. The men I worked for, people like Muir Fairchild and Harry Johnson, they just turned things over to you and let you go ahead and handle it, you know? There were no powerplays going on all the time, like I noticed after I went to work somewhere else.

CHAPTER 11
ALAN MORSE

INTERVIEWED NOVEMBER 1976
During World War I, Alan Morse was a balloon pilot in the US Navy and served overseas. With a degree from MIT in engineering, he worked at McCook for four years, beginning in 1921. Later, he was employed in test labs for the Civil Aeronautics Administration.

Q: When were you at McCook Field, and what did you do there?

A: I was there from 1921 to 1925. I started out in the static test area and then moved to the wind tunnel.

Q: Please share some of your memories of McCook.

A: Well, I remember being present at the first flight of the Barling bomber. The plane was constructed at Teterboro, New Jersey, taken apart, and shipped by train to Wright Field, where it was reconstructed. On the day of the flight, Harold Harris and Muir Fairchild were the pilots. A mechanic—I don't recall his name—and Mr. Barling were on the flight. Mr. Barling's position was in the forward gunner's hole. I had the highest regard for the flight and for Mr. Barling.

In those days, the distance from the control wheel to the control surfaces was of great concern because of the human strength required to push and pull the controls. The primary concern was getting the tail off the ground as soon as possible to reach flying speed as soon as possible. This, of course, meant that if the crew pushed too far, it would cause the nose to hit the ground. That's why wheels were mounted on the front to prevent this. As far as the control surfaces, the plane was perfectly aerodynamically balanced.

The throttles were interesting. The Barling had six engines with different types of throttles. The pilot's throttle was exactly like a joystick, and power could be reduced or given to the right three engines or left three engines by simply pushing the throttle to the left or right. This throttle could be overridden by the engineer, who sat in back of the pilot and had six separate throttles. His function was to exercise the power of the six engines, among other duties.

I remember the "Cycleplane." Its inventor, Gerhardt, used to run up and down stairs in buildings at McCook to build up stamina. Somehow, by using a stopwatch, he was able to get a reading of his "horsepower." I was present for the first flight of the Cycleplane. The craft was pulled and managed to get airborne before the wings folded and it crashed. Gerhardt was laughing so hard when the rescue people arrived to rescue him from the wreckage. I believe that was the only attempt to fly this type of airplane.

> *I remember the Cycleplane. Its inventor, Gerhardt, used to run up and down stairs in buildings at McCook to build up stamina. Somehow, by using a stopwatch, he was able to get a reading of his "horsepower."*

When I was working in the wind tunnel, a model of the MB-3 was put in the tunnel for a test. It was shown to be very unstable with much yaw. I felt that this was because of the very short length of the MB-3. The model was split at the tail, and the equivalent of 4 feet was added to lengthen the aircraft. This had good results in the tunnel, so it was added to the actual aircraft and flew well. I think this was the last time such a short aircraft was designed.

There was a time in the early 1920s when I was an observer on a high-altitude flight at McCook. The pilot was Harold Harris, and the airplane was a DH-4. I remember that we reached 29,000-plus feet and it was time to go home. I think Harris was hungry for lunch, and to hurry up the descent, he started slipping to the left and then to the right and by this method was able to come down very fast—so fast, in fact, the gas tank collapsed from the pressure.

There was a test pilot named Brookley who I looked up to as a sort of hero. I always admired him as a skilled pilot. (*Note*: Wendell Holsworth Brookley died while test flying in 1934. Brookley Air Force Base in Mobile, Alabama, now closed, was named in his honor.) One day, Brookley asked me for a ride into town in my Ford Model T. I was more than happy to give my hero a ride and, on the way, decided to exhibit my skill as a car driver—by driving into the traffic head-on to pass slower traffic! I doubt I impressed Brookley, but I did scare him a bit.

I remember it was Muir Fairchild who reversed the prop on the JN-4 while it was still in the air. He managed to land the plane in a pond near McCook. The pond was ever after known as Lake Fairchild. Some other pilots were cowboys. Every post had its cowboys, which is what I call a pilot that would just about try anything and expect to get away with it. They usually did. The commanding officers never stepped in.

CHAPTER 12
DARLENE E. GERHARDT

INTERVIEWED DECEMBER 1977

Darlene Crist met Dr. William Fred Gerhardt, developer of the "Cycleplane," while working together at McCook Field. They were married in 1924 in Boston while visiting close friends James and Josephine Doolittle. During World War II, she worked at Wright-Patterson Air Force Base. After World War II, she was secretary to various high-ranking US Air Force officers, including Gen. Albert Boyd, sometimes referred to as "the Father of Modern Flight Testing." During this era, she also was a secretary in the intelligence office at Wright-Patterson that oversaw "Operation Paperclip." That top-secret operation gathered knowledge from former German aeronautical engineers and rocket scientists. She retired from government service in 1968.

Q: When did you come to Dayton?

A: My father was a railroad dispatcher and we moved to Dayton in 1910 because the railroad offices were being moved from Lima. He took me and my older brother out to Simms Station, outside Dayton, to see the Wright brothers and their colleagues fly. That was the first time that we had seen an airplane. We lived, at that time, within a few blocks of the Wright bicycle shop and the Wright home. We occasionally passed by those places and were very much conscious, as much as anyone was in those days, of the importance of it. We felt like we knew what was going on. We became very fascinated with aviation at the time, such as it was.

After I graduated from high school in 1919, I went to business college for a year, at Miami-Jacobs Business College in Dayton. I had known a number of people who were a little older and were at Ohio State. One time while I was visiting a friend, she suggested that I see if I could get part-time work at the university. I was offered the job of working for the dean and secretary of the College of Commerce and Journalism. It was very nice, and I had a very interesting period there. I also took courses in journalism and enjoyed that very much.

Anyway, I came back at the end of the school year, and a friend who knew the personnel man at McCook Field suggested I try to get a job there and stay in Dayton. I only had a passing interest in aviation at that point. But staying sounded like a good idea. I thought that perhaps I could work for the summer and then go back to Columbus in the fall. I interviewed and was accepted. This was in 1921, when I was twenty years old. My first job was working for Lieutenant Monteith, who was working on his book *Simple Aerodynamics and the Airplane*.

I was very awed by him because he was a dignified, reserved man who seemed to be highly respected by everyone. A very attractive man. I always think that office arrangement has a lot to do with your work. I sat in the same office with him and with three of his assistants, so I was present and had an opportunity to watch and see the people who worked under him in the airplane section, who were in design groups.

Q: Who were some of the people under him?

A: The three design groups were headed by I. M. Laddon, A. V. Verville, and J. A. Roche. And there were many fine engineers under them, such as Ray Whitman, LV. Kerber, Max Short, and others. They were an interesting group, designing experimental airplanes. At that time, the heads of the aircraft organizations, such as Glenn Martin and Donald Douglas and numerous others, came into the office and held conferences there. So, I had a chance to listen. I always was very interested in what was going on.

A great many of the men at McCook were World War I pilots, practically all of them. These men were not college-boy ages. Most of them, the officers especially and the civilian designers, had been involved one way or another in World War I. They were men in their twenties and thirties. The war seemed very close because they were still talking about episodes and things that had happened.

May I go back a little? Because I was going to work at McCook and I had never been up in an airplane, one of my friends suggested that I should go out to Jack Stinson's. You couldn't call it an airport. It was a field where he kept his plane. It was somewhere south of Dayton. This was in 1921, and I was very happy to take a flight. My first time in the air.

So, it was all very interesting. One of my duties in working for the chief of the airplane division was to be the secretary of the accident board. People were kind to me. Claude Buchanan, the assistant to Lieutenant Monteith, took me down to the shops where they were building airplanes and repairing airplanes. He gave me a thorough education in airplane structure, as far as you could learn of it that way. People took the trouble to explain things to me and take me to the wind tunnel to see how that worked. I had a great opportunity to learn.

I also was secretary to the inventions board. That was one of the more amusing things because we got a lot of crackpot ideas in there. I used to see these drawings come in on all kinds of paper . . .

Q: Do you remember any of those ideas?

A: I remember two because, in later years, one turned out to be not so ridiculous after all. It was for the airplane fuselage to be covered in isinglass, the forerunner of plastic. It was what they used for film on windows and things like that. Somebody said that that way they could see the structure through the isinglass and see what was going on. That was good for a very big laugh, the idea of covering it with a transparent material. Now it's being used in a different form. In another instance, someone suggested that instead of landing gear, they should have little feet that ran along the track. I don't know how to describe it but instead of landing on a wheel, the little feet would land the plane.

Eventually, I thought it would be more fun, from what some of my friends said, to work in the flying section. So I transferred and was seated next to Lieutenant Brookley for about a year. He was a lot of fun, a cutup, and we had sort of a mock feud going on about different things that we disagreed on. We would argue playfully. But he was a very fine pilot and was open to innovations.

He was the first one to develop skywriting. I don't remember whether he was the one who devised the method of smoke coming out, but he went up and practiced it. He used to sit and work out the letters upside down or backwards, you know, and then go out and practice with skywriting. That was here at McCook. It was perfected in various ways. Then he and some of the other pilots liked to do stunts. He and James Doolittle and Pearson devised all sorts of little stunts. One of them was tying the tails of their planes together with ribbon, the planes standing not too far apart, and then going up and doing stunts and returning with the ribbons still tied to each aircraft, which really took a lot of skill.

They practiced flying in formation, the three of them. In September 1923, they had the biggest air show that had ever been held out here at McCook. One of the stunts they had worked out was flying a plane with a cockpit somewhat covered so that you couldn't see the head of the pilot, and they had a dangling head underneath the fuselage. When the plane came in, it looked like the plane was upside down, quite close to the ground, and the pilot's head was dangerously close to the ground. Of course, everybody screamed!

Darlene Gerhardt, with hands in pocket, surrounded by McCook Field pilots and staff posing in front of mistake "trophies." Over her left shoulder is Harold R. Harris and over her right shoulder is civilian test pilot Louis Meister. Wendell Brookley is attempting to engage her in conversation. *Photo courtesy of Darlene Gerhardt*

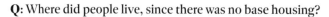

Q: Where did people live, since there was no base housing?

A: There was no base housing, except for the base commander and possibly someone at the base hospital. Young officers would take an apartment or a house together. Some of them lived at the YMCA. I suppose a few of them had their own apartments. Some lived in people's homes. Transportation was poor. We didn't realize it then because everybody was used to using trolley cars. But transportation to the field, although it was really close in, was a problem for anybody who lived any distance. It was the custom for people to pick up others, either by arrangement or haphazardly. People would just walk down the street from McCook after work, and others would come along and pick them up. It was just part of the way of life there.

Because people didn't get around as easily as they do now, home entertainment was more the thing to do. People got together in their homes. In general, most of them lived in the same area, the Dayton View area, within a mile or two of McCook. I think this changes the way people live. There were hotels and some places of that sort where you could go to dance and have dinner. So it was all in a very small geographical area where this took place. And, living next door, people became quite intimate and acquainted. People often reminisce about their neighbors—"I lived close to Doolittle" and "The Aldrins lived down the street from me"—that sort of thing.

Q: What were some of the social events here at McCook?

A: The officers had periodic dances, which they held in the building that had the big room. I'm not sure if it was a gymnasium or a dining room or what. Anyway, it might have been monthly, dances. Of course, it was very important to be invited to these dances—at least it seemed that way to the people that went around with the officers. We would have felt hurt. I can remember one incident when I wasn't going and I was upset about it. We also had picnics each year, and we looked forward to them and planned them. It was just a get-together for everybody with all kinds of old-fashioned stunts and balloons. It was held near the river so there were river sports.

Q: What are your thoughts on General Mitchell?

A: I would have no objection to telling about the thrill I got from hearing his story about the Mitchell-Langley bombings, which he told to the officers at McCook shortly after the bombing test. I was the backup stenographer. Fortunately, I was not the first stenographer, because it was so interesting that I think I missed taking down a good bit of the information that he gave. He was so enthusiastic, and it was all so different and so shocking to see those pictures of invulnerable vessels going down under the bombs.

Q: You talked earlier about Mitchell's manner, his flamboyancy...

A: He was an attractive man. His walk and his whole demeanor were something you would expect a movie star to have. He carried a swagger stick. His clothing was not strictly the regulation uniform. He was a debonair sort of man, a lot of personality, very friendly and open. That is, he was friendly with people under the circumstances when I saw him. I understand he could be very dictatorial at times. It was always a special event, I think, when Mitchell visited the field and went around and talked to people.

Q: He enjoyed influence at McCook?

A: Well, he only made visits to McCook. He was, at that time, assistant chief of the Air Service and was not the one that made the top decisions. But I think he had more to do with the things that happened at McCook in the subsequent years than any other person. He was very much a driving force, I believe. He fought for things. He was interested. He appreciated the steps that were being taken. Since my opinion is also based on what I knew he did afterward, maybe I'm reading something into it. But I feel that he was the impetus for many of the advancements that took place at McCook.

Q: OK. Now the "Cycleplane" of your husband, William Frederick Gerhardt. Was anybody else working on anything like that?

A: I don't believe so. Fred had the type of mind to want to do something new and different. He did experiments with helicopter-type things. He did a lot of flight testing. I don't think the idea of the Cycleplane or a foot-powered plane had even been thought of in any plans or schedules that were ever made at McCook Field. I think it simply was a brainchild of Fred's, with the help of Mr. Pratt and others. Fred was the inventor. He had the patent. He was the one who really designed it. Mr. Pratt had worked on a number of the drawings and fittings; he had a great deal to do with it and helped build it. It was built first in a barn. I don't know its location, somewhere in Riverdale. I did not know Fred well at that time. I know his parents helped. They all glued wings and wood.

Q: There was no government money involved?

A: No government money. There was no grant. It was not programmed in anything at McCook Field at all. He was given permission to test it at McCook Field because after it was assembled, it was too big to be anywhere except a big hangar. This was not a stunt. He firmly believed that flight by manpower was possible and that this would revolutionize a lot of theories that people had about the lift of surfaces and that sort of thing.

Q: Did he take a lot of heat from people as far as joking?

A: Yes, he did. Once it was built and put together—and this was quite a project, under difficult circumstances with limited funds—people found out what was going on, and they thought it was just a big joke. Most of the people I would think who saw it thought that it was a weird-looking object.

Engineers who worked on it were very enthusiastic about it. I think Harold Harris encouraged him to do this and was interested. There were probably others. I know there were one or two who disparaged the whole project with some venom. It was built. It was tested. There was a motion picture made of it actually in the air. Of course, they had to tow it at first in order to get it started.

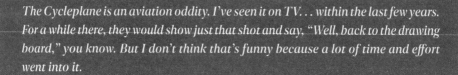

> *The Cycleplane is an aviation oddity. I've seen it on TV... within the last few years. For a while there, they would show just that shot and say, "Well, back to the drawing board," you know. But I don't think that's funny because a lot of time and effort went into it.*

Q: How high did he get off the ground?

A: A few feet off the ground, maybe 10 feet, something like that. I am familiar with the term "ground effect." I doubt he ever got beyond that. I think it was maybe as high up as a man, 6 to 10 feet. The film actually shows it, without being towed, in the air, propelled strictly by foot power. I believe they made more than one test.

But one film they made ended with the Cycleplane cracking up. It crashed together in the middle with all those wings, and it made for a very foolish-looking object. The Cycleplane is an aviation oddity. I've seen it on TV here in Detroit within the last few years. For a while there, they would show just that shot and say, "Well, back to the drawing board," you know. But I don't think that's funny because a lot of time and effort went into it.

Q: And your husband was the pilot in that film?

A: Yes, he was. I don't believe anyone else ever piloted it. Harris was there during testing. It attracted a lot of attention—worldwide, really. There were articles, though I don't have any of them, but there were articles in foreign papers about it. It aroused quite a bit of interest outside McCook Field. I would have to say that Fred was a scientific genius. He was asked to give talks at the International Mathematics Conference and submitted scientific papers. He worked mathematically, not mechanically. This wasn't something tried out one way and put together another. It was all worked out in a mathematical fashion.

After the crash in the film, he redesigned it with four wings instead of seven and using Japanese silk instead of a sort of Japanese paper, like on the first one. He had the interest of a number of important people. Bill Stout was very much interested in it and always had a great deal of faith in Fred's ideas. He put a little money into it. They formed a little corporation for the Cycleplane, I think, with Mr. Deeds here and Kettering, and a few other people in Detroit.

At the time, Fred was doing consulting work and really had no funds. His parents had put their money into the first one and were older and unable to help. So, he had to get money to actually construct it. It was done in the most inexpensive fashion possible. He had the help of a young graduate of the University of Michigan who was more intrigued, I think, by Fred's abilities than anything about the project itself. He wanted to help Fred.

He came down to Detroit and stayed with us for a year or so, just putting his time and effort into helping Fred build the second plane, because he was sure Fred knew what he was doing. Others seemed to have faith in him. Woodworking was done by the Requarth

Lumber Company there. They did a lot of the construction, gluing the wings, parts, spars, and everything together in our apartment basement. They finally got it together and constructed, and had high hopes for proving his theory.

Q: Where was the second Cycleplane kept?

A: At McCook. There were only one or two buildings left there. The whole field was being dismantled but he was given permission to move it out there. Shortly, he was told that the building would have to be demolished. The weather had been bad, and he hadn't been able to get it out and make the actual test. So, he had to move it away from there. It took a box as big as a boxcar to put it in. It was shipped to Detroit and stored in the balloon hangar up there in Grosse Ile, Michigan. Later when he was at the university, the wings were removed and were taken to the laboratory. They were to be reglued and checked preparatory to making a test up there. During the work, one of the students flipped a cigarette into the wings and the entire structure was destroyed. That was his last attempt.

Q: Looking at this as far as aviation history, what would you say about McCook's place in it?

A: I'd quote some of the other people who have said it was the hub. It was the nucleus, but I truly believe it almost was magical, that in one place there came together all of these talented, ingenious people who had the place, the enthusiasm, and the background to do some miraculous things, though money sources were limited. It was fun there.

Author's note: Darlene and I stayed in touch for several years prior to her passing in 1995. The Cycleplane concept was ever on her mind. She was very aware that people around the world were working on accomplishing the first human-powered flight. On August 23, 1977, success finally came at Shafter-Minter Field, a few miles north of Bakersfield, California. The Gossamer Condor, designed by Dr. Paul B. MacCready and powered by pilot Bryan Allen, a championship bicyclist, flew the first figure-eight course, thus demonstrating true man-powered flight. Darlene was elated at Dr. MacCready's success. On June 12, 1979, the Gossamer Albatross, another MacCready design also powered by Bryan Allen, flew across the English Channel.

CHAPTER 13
LOUIS HAGEMEYER

INTERVIEWED JULY 1966

Louis Hagemeyer had a forty-year career in government. Most of those years involved research in aerial photography and related projects at McCook Field and, later, Wright-Patterson Air Force Base. Because of his professional focus on photography, he spent years working alongside George W. Goddard.

INTERVIEW CONDUCTED BY GEORGE W. GODDARD

Q: When the Armistice was signed, you already had orders to go overseas, correct?

A: Yes. In a month or so, I was transferred to McCook Field—I think it was around January or February. I was assigned to the equipment section. I don't remember the original commanding officer, but E. L. Hoffman became the commanding officer. Since I had done some photographic work prior to that with Pathe News, I suggested to the commanding officer, Thurman Bane, that there was an opportunity to enhance the research effort with motion pictures. As a result, he authorized the organization of the first motion picture group in the Air Service that was composed of three people.

Q: I remember flying you when we made those films of the Guardian Angel tests.

A: Yes, I remember that. The US government had agreed to buy the rights to that patent provided they made three successful jumps. It was the type of parachute where the chute was contained in a package under the fuselage and a rope came around and fastened to a harness and a jumper. When the aviator jumped, the weight of the body pulled the chute out of the pack on the bottom of the fuselage. They completed the three jumps, so they successfully concluded the contract as far as the payment was concerned when this Englishman decided he wanted to make another jump. It was about 4:30 when everybody was leaving McCook. He made the fourth jump, and the rope hooked on to the rocker arm that controlled the tail surfaces on the outside of the fuselage. The rope snapped and the parachute, of course, stayed with the airplane and he fell. I believe it was 1,500 feet.

Of course, parachutes were one of our major motion picture subjects for coverage because, at that time, they were in the early development stage when nobody was certain exactly what would happen. I recall in one case they were uncertain how far the parachute would clear the tail surface. I sat on a 14-inch platform out on a wing holding a camera, tied to a strut, so I could see the parachute going by the tail surface. I had many thrilling experiences of that nature in connection with parachutes.

Q: How many years do you think it took Hoffman to develop the chutes before they issued the order that everybody had to wear one?

A: I would say about five years. I know we did wear parachutes when I was on my way with some equipment for Billy Mitchell's bombing tests in 1921. I recall wearing my first parachute then. On that particular flight, of course, flying from Dayton to Langley Field, you always had to land at Wheeling to take on gas, then at Washington to take on more gas, and then on down to Langley Field. If I remember correctly, on that particular flight, Leigh Wade was flying, and Jack Harding was with me. We were in a twin-engine transport and, after taking off from Wheeling, we got involved in a storm over Uniontown.

It was so rough that, with our engines wide open and our nose pretty well down, we were reaching 1,500-feet altitude, and we decided we'd better use these parachutes. However, they decided that Hagemeyer would be the first one to go, and when Hagemeyer turned chicken and wouldn't go, nobody would go. We finally made a forced landing at Manassas, Virginia. I don't recall the exact date of that, but it probably was in the late spring or early summer of 1921. By the way, do you recall "Roaring Al" Hobley . . . ?

> *The lawmaker said that nobody was going to tell him what to do and that he was staying right there. About that time, Hobley says, "Fire!" All this Vaseline and BB shot came out the back of the gun, all over the congressman. That Palm Beach suit looked like it had smallpox.*

Q: Very well. He was a colonel.

A: At this time, I think he was a major. Anyway, they were to test a gun at McCook that was developed as a nonrecoil gun—a 3-inch, nonrecoil gun—on the gun range. Around the time when they were ready for their test, a congressional committee came over from Washington and the congressmen wanted to witness the test. This gun had a barrel about 15 feet long that split in the middle, and you put in two shells. One shell carried the explosive charge, and the other half of the barrel carried another shell that was loaded with Vaseline and small BB shots, so they counteracted the forces and you had a nonrecoil gun.

Everybody in this congressional committee, incidentally, was dressed in Palm Beach suits. This one congressman, who wanted to be sure he didn't miss anything, got in back of this gun. Hobley tried to get him to move out, telling him it wasn't safe, but he insisted. Finally, they got into an argument and yelled and screamed. When he yelled at the congressman, the lawmaker said that nobody was going to tell him what to do and that he was staying right there. About that time, Hobley says, "Fire!" All this Vaseline and BB shot came out the back of the gun, all over the congressman. That Palm Beach suit looked like it had smallpox.

Q: Weren't you engaged in some work with Colonels Deeds and Kettering—some kind of drone? (*Note*: Edward Andrew Deeds was president of the National Cash Register company headquartered in Dayton. Deeds partnered with the Wright brothers in an early airplane manufacturing venture and led the military aircraft [mainly DH-4] production effort in World War I. In 1917, the newly commissioned officer was largely responsible for choosing the McCook Field site. Charles F. Kettering was a prolific inventor and holder of 186 patents. In 1918, he designed and tested the "aerial torpedo," nicknamed by many "the Kettering Bug." It was considered to be the first aerial missile. He went on to head research at General Motors for twenty-seven years.)

A: You're probably thinking of the craft they actually tested down in Florida, which Kettering had designed. Stutzman was actually the mechanic working on the thing. They were quite successful and flew it, if I remember correctly, something like 39 miles under radio control. I think it probably should be considered the first flying missile with wings that was radio-controlled. Kettering was responsible, I guess, for the development of the engine and other mechanical features, though the aeronautical design was done at McCook.

Q: Other McCook recollections?

A: Well, there was Schroder's high-altitude flight when he froze his eyeballs. He was at about 20,000 feet, and his goggles fogged up. He pushed them up on his forehead in order to see better to come in for his landing. He made a good landing, but he had a quarter of an inch of ice over both of his eyes. The doctors at that time said they didn't know how he could even see the field to come in, but he did.

Also, any time a new airplane was to be flown, General Mitchell would come out and, usually, make the first or second flight in it. If it was a two-place job, he accompanied the pilot on the initial flight. If it was a single-seater, after the initial flight, he invariably flew it himself on the second flight.

Q: I remember when I was at McCook Field, General Mitchell came out and said he was going to make me his photographic officer on the bombing exercises. I think you were sent down to install the cameras. What kind of cameras did you use?

A: Mostly Akeley cameras, the camera the great explorer Carl Akeley had developed for hunting big game. These were all hand-cranked cameras, so we modified them to make them a little more suitable for aerial work. It wasn't until later that we developed a motor for the camera. The advantage of the Akeley was that with one hand you could rotate the camera vertically or horizontally, leaving your other hand free to turn the crank. When I photographed bombing tests, I used a DH-4 as the camera ship.

Q: You or Hoffman had a concrete wall to test plane fires, correct?

A: Yes, the concrete wall with the ramp going down the side of the hill. They'd take the wings off the planes, since they would contribute nothing to learning about fires. The fuselages with the motors running wide open would run down and hit the concrete wall, usually resulting in fire. We had to put up some protection with railroad ties on each side of this thing, and we used high-speed cameras to photograph the origin of the fire. We were able to pinpoint the start of the fires, which in most cases was at the smokestack. The stack would be quite hot and the gasoline from the ruptured tank would hit the red-hot valves at the exhaust and start the fire. As a result of these tests, they were able to eliminate quite a bit of the fire hazard in aircraft.

Q: After a series of bombing tests on the coast, you went back to McCook?

A; Yes, and it's rather amusing how we got back, because after the bombing nobody had any gas. The pilot and I spent most of the night going around with any kind of can we could get, draining the gallon or half gallon out of the bottom of the tanks of all the other planes without anybody's knowledge and pouring the gas into our airplane's tank. At daybreak, we were able to get away and had just enough gas to get back to Washington. Everyone else was stuck there for about a week, because the barge that was coming down the canal to bring the gasoline had developed some trouble and didn't get through.

Q: At McCook, they developed the armor-plated airplane. You did a lot of photography with that, didn't you?

A: To keep the engine cool, you had to keep it at full power all the time, because of the weight of all the protective armor. The pilot couldn't throttle down the engines and stay in the air. I went on a lot of maneuvers with different planes. I remember the air races in Detroit in 1922, when for the first time, a plane reached the speed of 200 miles per hour—I think it was about 205 miles per hour. I recall at that time that someone stated we had reached the maximum speed of aircraft because the human body would not stand any faster speed. The pilot had partially blacked out in turns on the pylons in that race.

I don't recall the name of one airplane for sure, I think it was a Lawson. Anyway, it was a ten- or twelve-passenger plane and they brought it to McCook to set a new official altitude record. Since they wanted to publicize it, they got some chorus girls from the local theaters to ride the airplane. They got up to around 12,000 or 15,000 feet, and as you know, when an airplane hits its maximum ceiling it wobbles quite a bit. All the newsreel cameramen were around McCook Field to get this landing. After it finished its roll and had turned around, we could see things flying out of the airplane. These girls had been all dolled up with these picture hats, and when they got down, we found out that what we'd seen were these hats flying out of the windows. That was around 1925–26.

Q: What were some developments at McCook of which you felt particularly proud?

A: On one of the parachute tests, Art Smith was flying me in a Curtiss Jenny. I was using the Akeley camera for the first time, standing up in the rear cockpit looking through a little rubber eyepiece. I told Art to circle this parachute as it was coming down. He did, but he got so intently interested in the parachute and maintaining his circle around it as it approached the ground that he failed to notice his altitude.

As I was looking through this eyepiece, I suddenly noticed a building getting pretty large. I looked up and saw we were about to stick a wing in the ground, so I took my left foot to hit the stick to pull the other wing up, and around that time, we hit the ground and washed off the landing gear. That convinced me that we needed the type of viewfinder you could see through without actually putting your eye to the camera. We added to the Akeley a viewfinder that gave us a 2-by-5 or 3-by-5 image on the top, which gave you a much-larger image and also permitted you to see what was happening on the outside.

Q: You took a lot of pictures of the de Bothezat helicopter at McCook, didn't you?

A: I probably spent as much footage on that as on any single project we had. Almost every morning, we had to go out there about five o'clock. de Bothezat had this thing set up in a hangar-like building, and we'd have to go out and get all set up and then pull this thing out of the building—literally pull it out—because de Bothezat wouldn't allow enough people around there to see this thing. He kept it highly secret. We had to fly this thing, or do whatever testing we were going to do, and get it back in the hangar by seven o'clock, because he didn't want the people who started coming to work at 7:30 to see it. He was very secretive about the project, and that went on for months and months.

Q: Do you have any stories about Albert Stevens?

A: He was an individual, as you know, who would work on a project until he was no longer able to stand. One morning, I came to work in what they called the museum building at Wright Field. As I was walking in the door, one of the fellows came running out. He said, "There's a dead man up there." I went upstairs and there was Steve, lying on the cement floor sound asleep. He'd been working for three or four days without sleep, and when he felt like sleeping, he'd lie down on a desk or the floor—wherever he happened to be. He passed out for twelve or more hours.

Q: You have talked about a flight to the West Coast that took you ten days. Why so long?

A: This was in a DH-4 airplane and, as you know, in a DH-4, you couldn't fly over 200 miles most of the time without gassing up. After a couple of days, we got to Wichita Falls. We took off and hit a sandstorm. Since we could only fly up to 12,000 feet or so, and the sandstorm was higher than that, we had to come down and landed at a place that was really nothing but desert. We'd go to bed at night, pull up the sheet over our heads, and when we'd wake up in the morning, there would be a quarter inch of sand on top of the sheet. That storm lasted three days, so when we finally did get away, we had consumed eleven days going from Washington to San Diego. That desert town, by the way, was Midland, Texas.

CHAPTER 14
FRANKLIN O. CARROLL

INTERVIEWED JULY 1966
After McCook Field, Franklin O. Carroll was head of several commands dealing with research and development. In 1945, he became commandant of the Army Air Force Engineering School at Wright Field, which later became the Air Force Institute of Technology. He retired a major general and died in 1988 at the age of ninety-five.

INTERVIEW CONDUCTED BY GEORGE W. GODDARD

Q: About the early days at McCook and the engineering school there . . .

A: I never attended that school, but I was an instructor in mathematics there. The man I've always credited with being the father of the engineering division was old Colonel Vincent, who was the chief engineer of the Packard Company. He told the story that in the early days of 1917, there were two missions—one French and one British—who came over to this country to see what we had in the way of aircraft engines for fighter planes. He found that each of them had an enormous number of models—I think the French had thirty or forty and the British had the same thing—so the supply situation was just getting out of control.

So, he went to Washington and proposed that they set up what was called a "mammoth engineering division or department." He worked with another officer who was in charge of handling aircraft production at the time. Vincent was thinking more about engines at the time, and the engines we had were being tested by the Bureau of Standards at that time. His idea was to get the two coordinated, to get one organization to handle both the airplanes and the engines, as well as all the other equipment that you needed to make an airplane. It was in May 1917 that he proposed the formation of this department.

He first proposed that it be set up in Washington, but they couldn't find a suitable place, so then he went out to the Indianapolis Speedway, but they couldn't set it up there either. Then he went to Dayton to see what could be done. Do you remember Moraine down south? They had a little field and a contract to build DH-4s, so Colonel Vincent proposed that they set up this outfit down there, but they didn't think they could spare the space. And so on. Finally, it was suggested that they use a location at the junction of the Mad River and the Miami River. That was agreed upon as a suitable place, and that's where they set up McCook Field.

At first, they decided to build an eight-cylinder engine, for which Colonel Vincent got approval. In thirty-three days, they had built one engine and delivered it to the Bureau of Standards. They didn't build many eight-cylinder engines but went to the twelve-cylinder that became known as the Liberty engine. In the meantime, he'd been talking to the people in Washington, proposing the establishment of this engineering department.

Q: When was McCook Field actually established? (*Note*: He responded partially by reading from a prepared text.)

A: I arrived in Dayton on Sunday, October 14, 1917, to take active charge of building, engineering, and developing facilities at North Field. That was the original name of this open area at the junction of the Mad and Miami Rivers. The field later was renamed McCook in honor of Gen. Anson McCook of Civil War fame. One of my first important jobs was to obtain a meeting of the minds as to what activities should be centered at McCook Field. I advocated the following: "The engineering organization at McCook shall prepare and distribute specifications covering all airplanes, airplane engines, and airplane accessories required by the Army Air Forces. The engineering division at McCook shall be responsible for checking and approving all proposals submitted to the government to cover the cost of constructing sample aircraft equipment, in accordance with government specifications."

You see, our country had done it differently than any of the other countries. The British, for example, had what they called the Ministry of Supply, headed up by a civilian organization that determined what their military services would get. We, on the other hand, had determined our own requirements, had written our own specifications, and were responsible for checking all proposals.

"Furthermore, we shall pass on all contractors' drawings of aircraft equipment, with a view of gradually bringing about standardization." That's another big thing: the US Air Force always has held the fundamental principle of trying to standardize as much equipment as possible. "Furthermore, McCook Field shall be responsible for testing and finally accepting or rejecting all equipment built for the Army Air Force. McCook Field is charged with the design and construction of all the experimental equipment, conduct acceptance tests and, finally, approve such equipment before it is released for production." That's the only portion that's been modified. These others have remained fundamental principles for the Air Force.

But industry began to protest, I think rightly, that the Air Service should get out of the construction phase, because the companies were struggling to get along and this was really taking business away from them and retarding their efforts to get started. So, after 1924, no more airplane engines were designed or built at McCook Field.

I've always been proud that Jean Roche and I designed and built the last plane to be manufactured at McCook Field—the Corps of Observation XCO-6. He was a Frenchman who came over early in the First World War and designed some of the early training planes. He was head of the Corps of Observation design unit. Boulton and Larry Kerber were heads of the bombardment section, and I. M. Laddon, as I remember, was primarily concerned with transport. Fred Verville had fighters.

Q: Do you recall any interesting events during the early designing of these airplanes?

A: The first plane didn't have brakes—you had to use your throttle and pull back on the stick to dig the tail in so it would slow you up. Laddon was given the job of developing brakes for the airplane, with the primary purpose literally being to stop a plane before it hit the fence at the other end of the field in case of a forced landing. But it didn't take long to find out that brakes were very handy just for moving planes around the field, taxiing them up to a hangar, and so forth. Laddon designed the first airplane brakes used in this country, I'm sure. None of the airplanes overseas had brakes either.

I was one time voted the pilot most unlikely to succeed. They had just repaired a bomber wing that had been damaged, in the shop at McCook. They rolled it out on the line and asked me to fly it. I got in and started the engine and I had to make a sharp turn, which you did, of course, with one engine, depending on the direction you were turning. However, I didn't turn sharp enough and hit a gas pump. I knocked off the wing opposite the one that had been repaired.

Q: As an aside, I went there in 1919 and there was a guy who'd been an ace overseas. He was spinning a Thomas-Morse, and he pulled out too late and crashed into the trees at Triangle Park. We all went over there and found him sitting in the top of a tree. He'd crawled out of his plane and was looking all around to find his goggles. The fire department came over and put a ladder up, and when he got down, he started looking for his goggles. He said, "I wouldn't lose those goggles. I had those over France." He wasn't concerned about escaping death. He was worried about those goggles. Anyway, were you there the time de Bothezat tested his autogyro?

A: I was the pilot. He got a contract to design and built the first helicopter the United States would own. We had project officers in those days who were responsible to the commanding officer, Thurman Bane. Our principal duty was to keep track of the correspondence and write out a brief almost daily, which would be sent over to his office to keep him up to date. Sometime in 1922, they assigned me as the project officer and the flight test officer for the helicopter. It flew all right as long as it was within the ground effect—the ground wash from the propeller blades. But when it began to get above that, the machine became unstable in all directions.

> *Harris had on a parachute and he jumped out, and the fool thing opened. I remember he landed on a grape arbor away from the field, practically unhurt. After that, people started thinking maybe they ought to wear those things....*

Q: Did he prove anything by that at all, did any of his ideas get into future use?

A: I don't think so because even the autogyros that came along before our present helicopters were constructed differently. I mentioned testing parachutes. You know, we didn't wear them for a long time, and people around McCook Field weren't particularly interested in wearing them anyway after watching so many of them land out there. The old dummy would come down in the field and the parachute wouldn't open—and everyone figured that would happen to them.

Harold Harris was head of the flight test section at the time. He went up in 1923 or 1924 to test a Loening monoplane, as I remember, and something happened. Harris had on a parachute and he jumped out, and the fool thing opened. I remember he landed on a grape arbor away from the field, practically unhurt. After that, people started thinking maybe they ought to wear those things, though it wasn't until 1925 that parachutes became mandatory. But his jump really sold the boys at McCook on wearing a chute.

Do you remember the Custer jumping balloon tested at McCook? If you jumped, it would take you off the ground, and if you had some wind, it would blow you on over fences and houses, and pretty soon you'd come down. Of course, if the wind happened to change and blow you back, that was fine. It seldom did, and you had to pick it up and bring it back in the truck.

Then there was Lt. Harry Sutton, the only man I ever heard of who jumped twice from the same airplane on the same flight. They were having trouble with one of the old Douglas aircraft that had poor spinning characteristics, and Harry was given the job of seeing what they could do to correct it. They built some containers that were put in the wings and filled with shot. We had some controls that enabled him to release them if he needed to. Anyway, he got into a spin and couldn't get out of it, so he jumped. When the wing came around again in the spin, he landed right on top of it and had to jump again. So, as far as I know, he's the only man who ever jumped twice from the same airplane on a single flight. That was in the middle 1920s.

Do you remember Pearson? He was flying one of those planes and put it in a spin, deliberately. Pretty soon we saw him falling and everybody waited for him to open the parachute, but he never did and was killed, out west of McCook. When we went out to examine the airplane, we found the entire parachute had been cut off his back and was still lodged in the flying wires. He got out all right, but when the wing came around—again, it was just at the wrong time—it sawed his parachute right off.

You remember the Barling bomber, of course. They wanted to fly it to Washington to show what a wonderful airplane it was, but when they began to figure the amount of fuel they'd have to put aboard to get it the 380 miles to Washington, they realized it would be unable to get over the Appalachian Mountains, which shows what a limited range we had.

CHAPTER 15
OAKLEY KELLY

INTERVIEWED MARCH 1966

Following Oakley Kelly's historic 1923 transcontinental flight, he piloted ninety-four-year-old Ezra Meeker in the same Fokker T-2 the next year. They flew along portions of the Oregon Trail that Meeker had traveled as a young man by ox cart while migrating from Iowa to the Pacific Ocean. The flight was to generate support for the preservation of this route. Later, Kelly was assigned as a squadron commander at Pearson Field, Vancouver, Washington, and retired as a colonel.

INTERVIEW CONDUCTED BY GEORGE W. GODDARD

Q: When did you first go to McCook Field?

A: About February 1919. It was in the early spring of 1922 when Capt. Muir Fairchild and I thought up a coast-to-coast flight and talked it over. In those days, the trouble was to find an airplane capable of making the flight. It so happened that the only thing we could think of that would do the job was a German Yonkers, the first all-metal airplane. We had one at Dayton with a BMW engine, 185 horsepower, with low fuel consumption that would have made it possible for us to carry the load and make the trip. But it was a foreign airplane, so there was no sense in going on with that idea because there was no chance of getting approval in Washington.

> *Colonel Bane went on into the dressing room to get his flying gear. I didn't know it at the time, but later events proved that we were on our way from that moment when he took a look at that long red line on the map.*

Then they bought this Fokker, and I was assigned as project engineer to do acceptance tests on the plane. I was rooming with Ernest W. Dichman who, incidentally, was the brother-in-law of Thurman Bane, the commanding officer. Dichman took an interest in the project and volunteered to run static tests on the wing to see how much load we could carry. I was then in charge of airplane maintenance and, in addition, was a test pilot in the flying section.

To promote the idea, I posted a large map of the United States on the wall of my office. It was located in such a way that pilots passing through on their way to the locker room just behind my office would walk right into the map. First thing, Thurman Bane came in there and looked at this long red line stretching from New York City to San Diego, and he reared back and said, "What's this?" I said, "Well, colonel, that's a little flight I'm planning to make one of these days." He snorted a bit and I said, "It's a nonstop flight from New York to San Diego." Colonel Bane went on into the dressing room to get his flying gear. I didn't know it at the time, but later events proved that we were on our way from that moment when he took a look at that long red line on the map.

Later, we prepared all the information we could get hold of to determine the performance of the airplane, to see how much we could carry. It was easy to figure the distance we could fly; then we had to apply that to the altitude of the country—the mountains in the West—to see if we could clear them. Our ability to clear the mountains depended on how much gasoline we'd burned by the time we reached them. To avoid the high altitudes and carrying the extra fuel, it was necessary to fly about 360 more miles from San Diego to New York compared to flying from New York to San Diego.

We tried it originally from the West Coast, setting up a route through the passes—that's where we added the 360 miles to the distance. On that eastbound flight, the engine failed when the water jackets cracked, and we lost our coolant and were forced to land at Indianapolis. But that established a record in 1922 and brought the Air Corps some very desirable publicity.

After that failure, we spent the winter around Dayton, then went to New York to pick up what is known as a Hudson Bay high—high barometric pressure up in Canada, producing east and northeast winds across Pennsylvania. Then you want low pressure down in Texas, giving you a counter-clockwise wind direction. So, if you put the two together, you've got a prevailing east–west wind. That occurs four or time times in the spring, as a rule. That atmospheric condition was forming on May 1, when we made our plans to start the next day. We were able to take off from New York at noon the next day.

Q: What field did you take off from?

A: We had the airplane at Mitchel Field and moved it over to Roosevelt Field. (*Note*: The Mitchel facility was named in honor of former New York City mayor John Purroy Mitchel, who was killed in flight training in 1918. Roosevelt Field was named in honor of President Theodore Roosevelt's son, Quentin, who was killed in combat in 1918.) We had 745 gallons of gasoline that had been shipped in steel drums in a boxcar from San Diego to Dayton. Some was used in Dayton, and the remainder was trucked to New York to fill the plane. The petroleum companies took the tip and went on to improve their gasoline. Anyway, we cleared the Alleghenies with 2,800 feet indicated altitude. Theoretically, the airplane was capable of taking off with a full load and climbing to possibly 4,000 feet—no more than that. We were never able to get it that high in the first hour after takeoff because of the weight of the fuel.

There was a little trouble with the voltage regulator, which cut out too soon after we crossed into New Jersey. It was necessary to remove the switch from the instrument panel and adjust the voltage regulator with the engine running at full power and a full load on there, or turn around and go back to New York. We were about 80 miles out of New York when that was indicated on the instrument panel. It took about thirty minutes to do that, but there was no effort ever made to put the switch back on its mounting post—it was left hanging on the ignition wires on the instrument board. As I've said before, that is not a form of maintenance that is recommended, because there is a danger of direct short in your ignition system by the metal mounting post.

Q: Was seating side by side?

A: No, in those days, we didn't have a copilot. The pilot rode in the nose beside the engine, and the alternate pilot would be in the rear of the airplane. There was no communication between us or between ourselves and the ground. The airplane didn't even have any lights on it. There was nothing dangerous about that, because we were probably the only ones in the air over the United States that night.

Q: Did you have any trouble maintaining your location?

A: The plan was to go to Dayton and, if everything was working all right, continue. Otherwise, we were going to land at Dayton with whatever was giving us the trouble. Anyway, the plane cleared ground at 11:36 Eastern Standard. We never changed the clocks in the plane from Dayton time when we went to New York, all time recorded was Central time. We passed Dayton about five in the evening. It was dark by the time we got to Indianapolis, and we'd asked the balloon service at St. Louis to turn on the searchlight for us and they did. We passed St. Louis about nine o'clock at night.

Q: What altitude were you flying?

A: We tried to save the engine some—throttle it back to 1,520 revs. I don't suppose it was capable of more than 1,540 with the fixed-pitch propeller. I'd say we were about 2,000 feet off the ground. We'd been under heavy clouds from Indianapolis and were starting to come into the effect of that Texas low. We expected to encounter some rain. Certainly, there was no moonlight. After we passed St. Louis, we had to keep dropping down and we got on the Missouri River. When we left Jefferson City, we had to strike out cross-country on a regular course. We were guiding the airplane by lights on the ground—farmers' homes—because there weren't very many towns in western Missouri.

Q: Did you have a turn-and-bank indicator?

A: We had a turn indicator. The bank feature was merely a ball on a bent tube, but that wasn't any good as a turn indicator because the centrifugal action on the steel ball would throw it clear over to one end, and it would stay there. However, the turn indicator was of value to us. We had a set of instruments in the back for the copilot and a set up front for the pilot. Instruments were very limited in those days. We didn't have a radio on that airplane—no contact with the ground whatsoever after we left New York.

About midnight, we got out of the overcast and came into bright moonlight, which was a help. I picked up a railroad track—all this time we'd been flying by dead-reckoning. We ran over the town of Spearman, Texas, at three thirty in the morning and I was able to definitely establish our position, so that worry was out of the way and we continued on in the daylight. We'd purposely delayed the start from New York for at least an hour so we would be past that point in daylight—we didn't want to run into the mountains in the Albuquerque vicinity at night. Our maximum altitude, by the way, was in central Arizona at 10,500 feet, but that was soon lost, and it settled down to 9,500.

The real trouble was on the first flight from San Diego east. There's a pass in the Oregon Mountains very close to White Sands. It's a V-shaped pass—short but very narrow. The plane went through there with probably a 200-foot clearance above the ground and at full power. I was afraid to go into the pass, thinking I'd encounter rough air, but it was the smoothest sailing I've ever had. There was no space to turn the plane around anyway. After you entered the pass, you had to keep going.

Orville Wright (*center*), a frequent visitor to McCook Field, flanked by Oakley Kelly and John Macready. *Photo courtesy of the US Air Force Museum*

Anyway, that same afternoon on our way to San Diego, traveling north of Alamogordo Valley at full power in good weather, for no reason at all the bottom fell out from under the airplane. I know now it was caused by a terrific and dangerous downdraft coming from high mountains just east of our course. That cold air was coming down at five o'clock in the evening to fill up that White Sands country. That was a dangerous spot. The airplane was mashed down to the ground until when I pulled back on the stick to avoid a crash and sagebrush went through under the wingtips—I was within 10 feet of the ground. But we continued on and arrived in San Diego at 12:26 Pacific Standard time—twenty-six hours and fifty minutes after we took off. Eventually, we flew the plane back. It's in the Smithsonian now.

To close out this about the flight, a lot of people have tried to write articles that injected a considerable element of thrills into the flight. But it was actually made by paying attention to details prior to takeoff. It's not something you can do after you're in the air. After you are up there, you have to hope for good luck with your equipment.

Q: You had a good team . . .

A: Macready came along late in the picture—after the plane had been flight-tested and the plans all made. He was actually a student in the engineering school and had been in charge of operations in the flight test before he entered the engineering school. Dichman was the man who probably did as much in planning the details and starting up the flight plan. He was an aeronautical engineer.

Q: Did you have any dealings with General Mitchell?

A: Oh, yes, my career would have been a lot different if General Mitchell had remained in the service. One other story with a McCook angle: Who built the first instrument-flying plane in the Air Corps? I did and was reprimanded for doing it. It was when I was in the Philippines, right after McCook. I took this airplane and converted it into an instrument flying with a hood over it so you could pull it back when you needed to see out. We wrote up the specs and sent them to Dayton, to McCook. The answer we got back referred us to circular number so-and-so. It said that "all experimental and research work will be conducted at Dayton, Ohio."

CHAPTER 16
GEORGE C. KENNEY

INTERVIEWED MID-1960S

George Churchill Kenney was a World War I fighter pilot and was first posted to McCook Field as a student in the Air Service Engineering School. He returned to McCook to develop techniques for mounting machine guns onto aircraft. During World War II, he held various commands, including overall commander of Far East Air Forces under Gen. Douglas MacArthur. In 1945, he became the first commander of the Strategic Air Command. He retired a four-star general and was inducted into the National Aviation Hall of Fame in 1971. He died in 1977 at the age of eighty-eight.

INTERVIEW CONDUCTED BY GEORGE W. GODDARD

Q: I'd like to get your opinion on Billy Mitchell and the tremendous work he did to build up aviation. He could get to congressmen and get things acted on, where an ordinary fellow in the army couldn't get in the front door.

A: Of course, eventually he'd have to run into the army people and they'd block him off because the army in those days—the navy, too—didn't understand what aviation was going to do. Years before World War II was ever thought about, Billy was thinking on it. Back in 1923, he had a conference out in Dayton attended by the section heads. He had told whoever was in charge—I think it was Thurman Bane—that he wasn't satisfied with the stuff out on the line. That day he flew an observation airplane with some experimental stuff on it. It had been built out at McCook Field, and it wasn't any good—no improvement on what they'd had five years before.

> *The general turned to Bane and said, "T. H., you seem to have run out of ideas here. Go on down to the conference room, bring the sections chiefs, and I'll give you a few to work on." He went down there and told them, among other things, how to build a jet engine.*

The general turned to Bane and said, "T. H., you seem to have run out of ideas here.

Go on down to the conference room, bring the sections chiefs, and I'll give you a few to work on." Of course, that insulted the whole gang there. They thought they knew all there was to know about aviation. He went down there and told them, among other things, how to build a jet engine. He said, "I've been down to the power-plant lab and I've seen that work you're doing on that new engine that they say is going to turn out 600 horsepower.

"You know what's going to happen to all the work that new engine does? It's going to turn crankshafts and push pistons up and down and wear out bearings and wear out the sides of the cylinders and expend a whole lot of engine internally doing no useful work. Then it'll push a lot of stuff out into the open through the exhaust pipes. What's left will turn a silly little fan out in front and what's that fan doing? All it's doing is putting a thrust to the rear and the reaction to the thrust is what makes the airplane go forward. Now the most important part of all that power that's being used there you're throwing away. It's going out into the air through the exhaust pipes."

We all looked at him, a few of us kids—you know, like Roy Harris, and me, who had sections. We worshiped old Billy and anything he said was gospel, but we didn't know what he was talking about. He looked all around and said, "You're a dumb bunch. I suppose I've got to tell you how to build that engine.

"Well, go get yourself a big piece of pipe about 10 feet long and 3 feet in diameter. Bore a hole in the top, pour gasoline in it, and touch a match to it. Then all this stuff will blast out through the rear and the reaction will shove this thing forward. Just tie it onto an airplane." We didn't know what he was talking about, but it was the jet engine. Billy always was way ahead of his time in envisioning what was going to take place.

I remember one time I said something to him about speed—that pretty soon speed would threaten to tear an airplane apart if it went much faster. He said there was no speed too great for man to travel. Of course, Billy didn't have much patience. He wanted to get things done. He didn't like hanging around until a whole lot of people made up their minds. I remember one day there was something about the army and navy and development and experimental stuff. He says, "Why, don't be silly. To entrust the development of aviation to either the army or navy is just as sensible as entrusting the development of the electric light to a candle factory."

Because of his impatience, and because he probably couldn't have spelled *tact* if you'd given him a dictionary to study from, he was bound to have a collision with the general staff. In fact, in those days, if you didn't follow the line, you could get into a clash with the general staff of the army without very much trouble.

Q: In the first war, what were the de Havilland DH-4s mostly used for?

A: They put them into the first-day bombardment group. We watched them get shot down and burned up just about as fast as we put them up, because that plane had a pressure-feed system on the gasoline and if you hit any of the system, you had a fire. Our stuff was gravity-fed from a little tank above the carburetor. It pumped from the main tank up to this little tank. You could shoot holes all through that thing and you wouldn't burn up—unless you got an incendiary bullet through a busted line. The DH with its pressure feed, as soon as you touched anything, about 10 pounds of pressure sprayed that gasoline all out into the air. I saw good strong kids that cried when they saw they would be flying that DH.

I remember one outfit that had been flying Breguets, which was a good, stable job that you could land on a tennis court. It carried a pretty good load. It was kind of clumsy, but it didn't burn up if it crashed. The French used them, and some of our squadron used them. When they took them away and gave those pilots DH-4s, that crowd was ready to go over the hill.

Q: When you came back from the occupational forces, where did you go?

A: All over. I went to McAllen field down on the Mexican border and I went up to Camp Knox to sell the military some ideas about working with them. After about six months, I went to the engineering school at McCook. Ours was the second class. Eddie Aldrin was the instructor. From there, I went to the Curtiss plant to be the government representative. Then to Wright Field about 1923 to run the factory section. I was at Wright Field for about two years, then to the tactical school at Langley, to the command staff school at Leavenworth, Kansas, and then they shipped me back to McCook Field again. I was only there about a year.

CHAPTER 17
REUBEN H. FLEET

INTERVIEWED MARCH 1966

One of Reuben Fleet's military assignments prior to McCook Field was to establish the first airmail service. This was in 1918, between New York City and Washington, DC. After leaving McCook, he earned a reputation as a determined businessman. His company, Consolidated Aircraft, sold aircraft to the military, including more than 18,000 B-24 Liberators and 3,300 PBY Catalinas. In 1973, the Fleet Science Center was established in Balboa Park in San Diego, California. Fleet was inducted into the National Aviation Hall of Fame in 1975 and died the same year.

INTERVIEW CONDUCTED BY GEORGE W. GODDARD

Q: When did you go to McCook?

A: I reported for duty at McCook Field on January 5, 1919. I served there until November 30, 1922, when I resigned from the service and got out completely, without any pension or anything. Colonel Bane retired as of that date, as did Maj. George Hallett, chief of the power-plant section.

Q: You were then in charge of what?

A: I was the contracting officer for the Air Corps. During my four years in that job, I allowed 28,000 contracts, most of them with assistants' names signed to them, like purchase orders. There were also about 6,000 contracts with the names of both parties signed at the end, with about 6,500 firms in America, embracing all kinds of endeavors. When I resigned, within twenty-four hours after it got out in the press, I was offered three jobs.

The first was vice president and general manager of the Boeing Aircraft Company in Seattle, the offer coming from Bill Boeing himself, who was a friend of mine since he was nineteen and I was fourteen. He coached me. I played ball with him, and we also flew together whenever we had a chance. I didn't solo until I came down here. I reported for duty in San Diego, March 22, 1917, at the Signal Corps Aviation School.

Q: You said you were offered three jobs when you got out.

A: Yes. The next one was from C. M. Keys—in 1922, he was head of the Curtiss Aeroplane Corporation in Ohio—as an advisor at a salary of fifteen thousand dollars. Oh, I forgot to say Boeing offered me ten thousand dollars a year as vice president and general manager.

Q: Boeing was a pretty small outfit then, wasn't it?

A: It was pretty small. He was in the timber business. My father had bought most of his timber from his father, Wilhelm Boeing, who was an immigrant from Germany. He had gone to Upper Michigan and bought a timber claim. He logged it off, and with the money he had made there, he bought another one. He kept going on like that in Upper Michigan. They then discovered iron ore on his property. When Bill's father died, Bill and his twin sister were nineteen. Bill then came out to our county and lived there five years before moving to Seattle.

Anyway, the third offer was from the Gallaudet Company, which offered to make me vice president and general manager. They were in the aircraft business and had built a factory in East Greenwich, Rhode Island. I decided to take that offer. They asked me, "How much do you want?" I said, "Ten thousand a year." They asked, "How long a contract?" I said, "I don't need a contract. If I'm not the right man, then you don't want to be saddled with me. If I am the right man, I won't need a contract to hold my job." So, I took over their management.

The Gallaudet Company had been run by Edson Gallaudet, a fine gentleman, a Yale graduate and very popular man. But he was a man who would take a contract with fifteen unsolved problems in it, the failure of any one of which would spoil the whole damn job. After observing several bad business decisions made by Edson Gallaudet, I did a survey to see what the company had done. To my surprise, I discovered that they owed three million dollars and they expected me to make that three million dollars back. They had nothing worthy of continuity or worthy of perpetuity.

> *The chairman said, "This is the first honest report we've had. We may just as well have taken our three million dollars, put it in the toilet, and pulled the chain." After that, I canceled several jobs and started making them money.*

So, I said in my report to the stockholders that I find the company owes three million dollars and it's worth one hundred thousand dollars, if they could get it. The chairman of the board asked if I could get it, and I said, "No." The chairman said, "This is the first honest report we've had. We may just as well have taken our three million dollars, put it in the toilet, and pulled the chain." After that, I canceled several jobs and started making them money.

I later purchased 51 percent of the Gallaudet Company. With $25,000, I formed a new company on May 29, 1923, without any debt of any kind, called Consolidated Aircraft Corporation. My sister and I owned it all. After about a year, I worked up to employing 450 people and I couldn't get any more, without importing them from New York, Boston, or

New Haven. So, I decided to move to Buffalo. I went to see about the Curtiss plant that the army had built for Curtiss during the First World War. It was 37 acres under one roof.

Q: When you moved in there, what contracts did you have from the Air Corps?

A: I had no contracts at all. I had to go down to nothing. We dropped down to seven people. I went to Texas taking Clark with me to Brooks Field. (*Note*: Virginius Evans Clark was a former McCook Field commanding officer and inventor of the "Clark Y Airfoil.") There, we took an aircraft with a side-by-side cockpit, where neither pilot could see the other side of the cockpit; rewelded it into a fore-and-aft job; and called it "the Camel," because it had a hump in it. The instructor sat in the front and the student behind. It made such a hit with the boys that we landed a contract.

This was a total civilian industry contract. The contract office that I previously ran at McCook was irate when it found out, but I talked Gen. Mason Patrick, head of the Air Service, into awarding me the contract. In the end, 221 of this Clark design were built as the Consolidated PT-3.

Now, you'll remember, George, when you learned to fly and I learned to fly, whenever there was a crash, the front seat man always was a goner. Sometimes the rear seat man was a goner, too, but we always knew the front man was a goner. I said to Patrick, "The airplanes that I'm building are going to be entirely different from that. There's not going to be any goners. There's not going to be any fires in crashes."

Author's note: A story often told reflects on Fleet's brashness as a businessman. The head of the Army Air Corps at the time, Henry "Hap" Arnold, received word that Fleet was in Washington and about to pay Arnold a visit. Arnold is said to have had all the chairs removed from his office in an effort to induce Fleet to shorten his visit. Fleet arrived. After a few minutes, he sat on the edge of Arnold's desk and remained perched there until a business contract was signed. On the day Fleet retired from the Air Service, he boasted he was going to "make a million dollars." He went on to make much more than that and died at the age of eighty-eight.

CHAPTER 18
JOHN A. MACREADY

INTERVIEWED FALL 1967
John Macready is the only pilot to date to have won the Mackay Trophy three times, 1921–23. Colonel Macready was inducted into the National Aviation Hall of Fame in 1968. He died in 1979 at the age of ninety-one. Merced (California) Regional Airport / Macready Field is named in his honor.

INTERVIEW CONDUCTED BY GEORGE W. GODDARD

Q: When did you first get into the service?

A: Well, I was in Searchlight, Nevada—thirteen saloons and two grocery stores. That was before World War I in 1917. A recruiting sergeant came into town. I'd never seen a soldier before then. I went over and enlisted in the cavalry and was sent to Reno. On the train, I saw something about this new thing "aviation" that looked like it might have some merit in military affairs. You had to be a college graduate. You had to be physically OK. I had graduated from Stanford with a degree in economics, and I was in the AAU boxing championships—a three-time lightweight champion—so I thought I would give it a try.

When I got to Reno, I asked to be transferred into aviation. I waited around for a couple of weeks at this hotel in Reno before I was transferred as a private first class in the Signal Corps and was sent to the University of California. There it was all close-order drill and internal combustion engines. Nobody knew anything about aviation. I remember the textbook we had there, a character was called "Grandfather Gravity." Anyway, I went to ground school there and then to San Diego for flight training. After a while, I was the officer in charge of flying at Brooks Field, Texas, a school for instructors. Finally, I was transferred after World War I up to McCook Field in Dayton as a test pilot. That was in the early part of 1919.

Q: Who was chief of the test pilot branch? Was that "Shorty" Schroeder?

A: No, it was Ralph DePalma, the automobile racer. At that time, McCook Field was what they called a "slackers paradise." All the rich men's sons went there to just put in time. Ralph DePalma was not a flyer, but he was in charge of flying. I remember the first week I got there, there was a Captain Jones that took a plane up that had been built there, I think. He stalled out, crashed, and was killed. In the flight test section was Lt. Harold Harris, who was chief of the section for a while. He was a very fine pilot. He's as well known today in Peru as George Washington in the United States because he started Pan American Airways through South America.

While I was a test pilot at McCook, in about 1920, Capt. Albert Stevens, who was in charge of the photographic department, wanted to make a photographic flight. I talked it over with the commanding officer, Thurman Bane, and he named me the pilot on that flight. This first flight was a scientific thing. We were to go to Ensenada, Mexico, and photograph the eclipse of the sun, which happened on a certain date. We also were to fly the airmail route and pick out emergency landing fields for the airmail pilots. So, we started out and picked out fields where the mail service might land because, in those days, the planes' Liberty engines were unreliable. We worked our way across the continent till we got to Ensenada.

On the date the eclipse was to happen, it was very foggy. We got through the fog, but there were clouds above. We started through those clouds at 16,000 feet, and the eclipse took place while we were in the clouds. We could just see that it got dark and the strange colors that emerged while the eclipse was taking place. It was kind of a ghostlike kind of a thing. Anyway, we came down and worked our way across the continent again, picking out fields as we went. The interesting part of that flight was that we got back without cracking up the plane. It was a successful flight, but we didn't get a chance to photograph the eclipse.

Then there was the time Oakley Kelly and I made our cross-continental nonstop flight, in May 1923. Then Captain Stevens agitated for another flight in 1923, probably around July. I remember going down to Washington with Captain Stevens about that. We went to see Stephen Mather, the first director of the National Park Service. The problem was there was no money to finance the photographic flight. Mather said that he would put up six dollars a day of his own money. So that was the basis of the flight.

I'll tell you about Stevens. He was a very unusual character. I have never seen anybody like him in my life. He was great big, powerful, broad-shouldered, a thin type of fellow. He had a wonderful mind. His intelligence truly was unusual. He had no inhibitions. He was a very athletic fellow and not at all interested in money or fame. The job, that was all he was interested in. He was the one, in my opinion, who developed cameras at that time. I would be down in his office, and he'd be working with tools on the cameras. He would work out all his changes and then take them down to Fairchild, and that company would then incorporate the changes into new cameras. In my opinion, Stevens was the one who really developed those first cameras.

As I said, he was a very strange fellow. On these trips we took, he would get his sleep in snatches. He could sleep any time, any place, two hours at a time. He would lie down on the floor, if he wanted to sleep, and go to sleep right then. He would sleep in the plane while we were flying. We were in open-cockpit planes, and if I saw something that we should photograph, I would have to reach around to the rear cockpit and tap him on the shoulder or shake him a bit to wake him up so he could take the picture.

I remember one time in Dayton there was a party at the home of Edward Andrew

Deeds, president of the National Cash Register Company and cofounder of DELCO. Stevens and I were invited. It was a very dignified affair, with many important people there. Stevens got sleepy and went to the middle of the floor and slept. Right in the living room, with the people there. If I had done that, I would have been shot. But he did it and only got written up.

Anyway, the second flight that Stephen Mather more or less financed was a flight to photograph national parks and anything of interest near the parks. We were given blanket authority. When we started out, we didn't even know where we were going. They wouldn't do things that way nowadays. We didn't even have to keep in touch with McCook Field. We didn't telegraph to let them know where we were or anything. We just started out and flew where we wanted to and took pictures. We also were told to pick out more emergency landing fields for the mail service.

We usually wouldn't know where we were going to land ourselves. We just picked out fields. If it was in flat country, it wasn't much of a problem, but when you got up in the mountainous country, it was different. Sometimes a friend would pick out a field next to a town. Most of the time, though, we'd have to fly around a town looking for a place to land.

At that time, a plane was like a flying saucer today. People weren't used to them. In many of the mountainous areas, they had never seen an airplane. So, we'd circle around several times looking for a place that had possibilities, and then we'd swoop down two or three times making several low passes, looking for rocks, bushes, ditches, or anything. You would be taking a big chance anyway.

We could see the people watching us, and after we landed, they would start to gather around. They came by automobile, horseback, wagons. Now there was a lot of work to do besides just flying and picture-taking. At that time, the gas came in 100-gallon drums and it was quite a job to put 133 gallons of gasoline in a plane through a shammy, lifting it up a pail at a time. That was the first thing we had to do after landing. Then we would have to tune up our engine to see that it was all right. We'd have to arrange to get the gasoline. Anyway, everywhere we went, the people were very helpful.

I would work on the engine. This was a DH-4 with the Liberty engine. As I was working, Stevens would be in the rear cockpit and he'd shout up to me, "Mac, can you finish this up by yourself? I'd like to get my running in." I'd say OK, and pretty soon he would come out in his BVD's, in his underwear. He had put a red stripe around the waist and a red stripe down the sides so that they'd look like running pants.

Stevens always claimed that if he got out of the cockpit and ran around in his BVDs, he could get arrested, but if he had those stripes down the sides, it was OK. People would be there interested in what we were doing, and he'd start out on his run. That's how he kept in shape. At dusk, I'd see him coming back in.

Then it was a question of staking down the plane for the night. The crowd was always very helpful. The leader of the Boy Scouts would take charge guarding the plane. We would then get into a car and drive to the little town. The people driving us were interested in a little conversation, but when Steve got in the car, he'd just get in the back seat and go to sleep. That's how he got his sleep, in snatches, all the time. After a night in the town hotel, we'd get out and do our job, taking pictures.

One place we landed was Pocatello, Idaho. I had a friend there, Harry McDougall—subsequently killed in 1928 during a Pocatello air show. He was an ace in World War I. He said he'd pick out a field for us and put down a big white sheet. When we got to Pocatello, we looked down and the field was too small, but we had to get in anyway because we were out of gas. I made two or three shots at it and finally stalled it in. We then couldn't get out. So, the Chamber of Commerce of Pocatello had a meeting and the mayor and chamber decided to build us a field.

> *During the chamber meeting, we were invited to a party. At the party, Steve was the center of attention of the girls. All of a sudden, all went silent. I looked around and there was Steve in the center of the room, sound asleep. You can imagine how the girls felt who had come out to see him.*

The next day, the mayor called for volunteers. About forty or fifty men came out, including the mayor, who put on a brand new set of overalls and put a shovel in his hand to have his picture taken. Anyway, they built a field so we could get out. During the chamber meeting, we were invited to a party. At the party, Steve was the center of attention of the girls. All of a sudden, all went silent. I looked around and there was Steve in the center of the room, sound asleep. You can imagine how the girls felt who had come out to see him.

Stephen Mather wanted Glacier National Park photographed particularly, so we spent a lot of time there. There was a field near there in Kalispell, Montana. We spent several days at Glacier Park. I was the pilot, and Steve did all the photographing. I did exactly what he told me to do. Sometimes I had to kick the plane up on a wing so he could take a picture straight down. Over some of those places like the Grand Canyon, you would get buffeted pretty badly by the wind, and he was in a dangerous position. I was strapped in with a safety belt, but Steve had to stand up in that back cockpit to take the pictures and was taking a pretty big chance. The air got very bumpy, and I had to maneuver quite a bit. Anyway, we continued our photo flights all throughout the west to San Francisco. We landed at Concord, because there was no airport in San Francisco at the time.

On the way back east, we stopped off in Las Vegas. At one time, I had been the Justice of the Peace in Searchlight, Nevada. We landed in the sagebrush near Holbrook, Arizona. Then there was no other place to land. Some of my old friends from Searchlight were to come out to meet us. They told us that they were going to put out a sheet in the middle of a field. As we got close, I knew we were about to run out of gas. I could see heavy rains out on the desert, just downpours. I knew we were going to crack up before we even landed. We couldn't help it. We were out of gas and had to get down. The field they picked was way too small, and sure enough, when I brought the plane down, it cracked up.

Q: Did it turn over on its back?

A: No. It went into a ditch and upended. We spent the night in a hotel. The next day, we were out there in our coveralls, taking the plane apart in order to do the repairs. We had to do all the repairs ourselves. It was a dirty job. The Schusters, who were big shots in Holbrook, invited us out to Sunday dinner. It got to be near noon, and I told Steve we had better get dressed up.

I took off my coveralls and put my uniform on to look proper. Steve said. "Oh, this is all right. I'll go the way I am." He still had his dirty coveralls on and grease all over his hands. So, we arrived at the Schuster mansion on the top of a hill. They came to the door with the ladies all in nice dresses, and there was Stevens in his old coveralls and dirty hands. The first thing he said was, "Hey, you have any place for me to wash up?"

Turns out the storms all over the desert had washed out their water system, and they didn't have any water. The ladies explained very quietly to Stevens that the pump had burst in their basement. Steve said, "Let me take a look at it." We went down into the basement, and the pump was underwater. He asked if they had a wrench, and they got him one. He went down in his coveralls under the water, his head fully submerged. You could hear him clanking on the pipes as he was working on that pump below the surface.

After a while, he got it going. The people were pleased. Mr. Schuster was a pretty big fellow, but he got out one of his suits and gave it to Steve, who took off his wet coveralls and hung them out to dry. He put on the oversized suit, and we had dinner. He did things like that, and people would take it as a matter of course. If another person did it, it seemed totally out of place. He'd get by with it.

We landed on a dry lake out in Arizona one time. A bunch of Native Americans came up bareback on horses. They didn't speak English. We got along very well with them. We had cracked up the airplane, though, so we shipped it back to Dayton and got on back. After we returned to McCook, we went down to Washington to meet with Gilbert Grosvenor, president of the National Geographic Society, and other government officials. I gave a talk, and Steve gave a talk. His talk was more impressive because it was more scientific.

Q: About your high-altitude flight. When did you make that flight?

A: Well, truthfully, I can say that from 1920 to 1926, I did all the high-altitude flying there at McCook. First, it was the LePere, and then they built another, the XCO-5.

Q: The LePere had the Liberty engine with the Moss supercharger. (*Note*: The inventor was Stanford Moss, General Electric Company.)

A: Yes. The Lepere and XCO-5 both had that supercharger. General Electric Company had developed it on the top of Pikes Peak in Colorado. Then it was shipped from Pikes Peak to McCook. Then Rudolph Schroeder, a test pilot at McCook before me, took the LePere up to 33,000 feet and lost consciousness. In those days, you took the oxygen out of a welder's flask. He had trouble with his oxygen tube and lost consciousness. His plane fell for 6 miles, and he just regained consciousness before he was about to hit the ground. He landed the plane, but the gear was smashed a bit. It was repairable. I think that was the last altitude flight that Schroeder took. He was in the hospital a while because he had frozen his eyeballs.

I was assigned to that job then, and I carried it right on through until I resigned from the Air Service in 1926. I would say there probably were fifty flights made to altitudes above 30,000 feet. Once in a while, you would try for a record. Orville Wright was always the official observer. I know that many times I got higher than the world's altitude record, but there would always be some sort of a technicality in the recording equipment or some little thing of temperature that would cause a problem. Orville Wright was so conscientious, super conscientious; the flight would just be thrown out. He would have to personally send everything back to the Federation Aeronautique in Paris. (*Note*: The FAI has sanctioned all aviation records, worldwide, since 1905.)

My highest record was 40,800 feet. That one was authenticated by Orville Wright. But, in the meantime, there had been a Frenchman, Jean Callizo, that had gone above that altitude. After that flight was sanctioned on paper, they found out that he had been tricking them. He was stripped of all his honors and senior rank and disgraced. That was a big story in those days. There was another French pilot, Joseph Sadi-Lecointe, who was trying for altitude records as I was. I would go up to 38,000 feet or so, and he would go up also.

Q: What was the reason for developing the second high-altitude airplane, the XCO-5?

A: The LePere was too heavy, and it wasn't a proper plane.

Q: Did Roche have any part in that?

A: Well, Roche did. There were a lot of them who did. I think Mac Laddon did. It was in the engineering division. It was a team effort, built by McCook Field for high altitude flying only. It was built out in the shops at McCook. Not an outside thing at all.

Q: It was much lighter? It had a much-higher-lift wing?

A: Yes, that's right, and an improved supercharger. That was the whole theory behind all of those high-altitude flights, the development of the supercharger. Here's how it went. General Electric Company did the work on Pikes Peak. And there was this Doctor Moss, who would come down about every six months. Now Doctor Moss hardly knew what was going on. The supercharger was developed by a fellow named A. L. Berger at McCook Field. He was an educated mechanic, a very good mechanic. You would never make a high-altitude flight when something didn't go wrong with the supercharger. Something always would happen.

I would come down, and Berger would be there. We would talk it over. I'd just tell him what happened. I'm not an expert engineer or anything like that. He would then ask questions and take the supercharger into the shop. Berger would work on it personally—his welding, his changing and making things a little different. There were excellent shops there at McCook. He's the one that developed that supercharger. And that's the supercharger that was in existence during World War II. After he would reinstall it in the plane, we would make another flight, going up a little higher, maybe to 38,000 feet. The highest that Orville Wright ever actually authenticated was 40,800 feet.

Q: This second airplane, the XCO-5, what was the performance of the airplane in landing?

A: Well, it was very slow. Getting into this high-altitude stuff a little more, when we first started out, there was a fellow named Roy Langham who flew as an observer. He was a tough little fellow. He would go up and write down the instrument readings. But after we would get up to a certain height, he wouldn't write anything anymore, and we couldn't figure out what the matter was. We learned the thing was his mind wasn't working because of the altitude.

Q: What about the de Bothezat helicopter?

A: I was the test pilot. They had it attached to the ground by ropes. It would rise up about 5 or 6 feet. That's as much as it ever got off the ground. I sat in the seat, but it wasn't a flight or anything, I was just doing what I was told. I didn't have any contact with it later.

Q: Just mention some of the people there. Wasn't Eubank there? (Eugene Lowry Eubank became a major general during World War II and died in 1997 at the age of 104.)

A: Yes, he was adjutant at McCook. Eubank was never in the flying section. After Kelly and I made our transcontinental, nonstop flight, I was in charge of the section, and we used to play little practical jokes. There was a fellow named William N. Amis there and Eugene Hoy Barksdale. There was Alexander Pearson (*Note*: He was killed at McCook in 1924, and Pearson Field, Vancouver, Washington is named for him.) and Frederick W. Niedermeyer (*Note*: He was killed at McCook in 1922). He was the first one. Ralph Lockwood, a civilian test pilot, was there. Louis G. Meister was another civilian test pilot. They were the two civilians.

Franklin Carroll was there. Arthur Roy Smith was a civilian test pilot who was killed in 1926. Of course, Doolittle was there. He didn't test-fly very much, but he was there a little bit. Eugene C. Batten was there. Harold Harris was there, of course, along with Leigh Wade.

Q: What were the early types of airplanes we had?

A: Well, this is the way the thing was. I went up there and the first thing they did was get all these German planes over and all the planes used in World War I. They were tested comparatively. You would read about Baron Manfred Von Richthofen going up to an altitude of around 20,000 feet. Well, we tested those planes, and they wouldn't get above 17,000 feet. That was the absolute ceiling. We found out all this stuff that had been broadcast around had been grossly exaggerated.

CHAPTER 19
JEAN ALFRED ROCHE

INTERVIEWED MID-1960S

Jean Roche went on to design several light single-wing aircraft. One of his more famous designs was the Aeronca C-2, first flown in 1928. This single-seat aircraft is commonly known as "the Flying Bathtub" and helped spawn the popularity of civilian aircraft. He died in 1981 at the age of eighty-six.

INTERVIEW CONDUCTED BY GEORGE W. GODDARD

Q: Well, my friend, you were in the US Air Force for how many years?

A: Forty-two years.

Q: When did you first report to McCook Field?

A: In 1917. I came from Washington, where we had been translating French and English drawings into American style, so that we could manufacture such airplanes as the Spad, the SE-5, and the Bristol fighter.

Q: Who were some of the people who came after you arrived? I know you were the first of the aeronautical engineers. Many others came after you. Just name a few.

A: Some of the others? Well, Isaac Laddon came from the automobile industry in Detroit. (*Note*: He was designer of the PBY Catalina, B-24 Liberator, and B-36 Peacemaker.) There was B. C. Boulton. (*Note*: He later was a design engineer on the Martin B-10 bomber.) L. V. Kerber came from MIT. (*Note*: He later became president of Spartan Aircraft and cowrote several engineering books.) And Alfred Verville was also there. (*Note*: He later designed flying boats, racing aircraft, and commercial cabin airliners.)

Q: How did they ever come to select McCook Field as the site for the program?

A: Well, there were some politics in the background. But it was a good selection because it was in the center of the automobile industry of the United States. Capitol and manpower were available there for designing airplane engines and airplanes themselves.

Q: Did Orville Wright have any interest there?

A: Orville Wright, of course, had started the first airplane-making in Dayton and done some of his initial flying there. That was after he came back from France and the Kitty Hawk site in North Carolina.

Q: He didn't do much development after 1917, did he?

A: No. After 1917, he gave his patents to the Wright Aeronautical Corporation, and he didn't have much to do in developing new types.

Q: Wasn't Wright having some trouble there with the Langley patents? Wasn't there some friction between Wright and Langley about certain parts of an airplane that had been patented?

A: Yes, there was a great deal of contention as to who was the author of the first flying machine. It is true that the Langley machine was capable of flight, but it lacked a suitable engine, and that was why the Wrights got ahead of Langley, producing a practical flying machine.

Q: Langley's was more theoretical than practical, wasn't it?

A: Well, Langley's machine was a tandem monoplane. It could have been practical, but the engine development was not sufficiently advanced. So, it could be said that the greatest contribution the Wrights made was the engine with which they powered their airplane.

Q: Charles F. Kettering was quite active at McCook at that time, wasn't he? (*Note*: Kettering was a businessman, a prolific inventor with 186 patents, cofounder of Dayton Electric Company [DELCO], and head of research at General Motors from 1920 to 1947.)

A: I saw very little of Kettering.

Q: He developed that flying missile there—the Kettering Bug? Some say it was the first smart bomb . . .

A: That was done in great secrecy in Kettering's private laboratory.

Q: Did Wright have anything to do with that?

A: I do not know that Wright had anything to do with that. I have a friend, Harold Morehouse, McCook Field's small engine designer, who worked on the engine, which was a two-cycle, high-speed engine.

Q: Who did the radio control of it?

A: I do not know who was in charge of the radio control development.

Q: But it was radio-controlled, wasn't it? The idea was to fly this over the German lines and drop dynamite down on their storage warehouses.

A: Yes, that's true, but the trouble with this flying bomb was that it could be interfered with and misdirected by the enemy. There was also some fear of its accidental misuse over friendly territory. That's why it was not continued.

Q: How many airplanes did you have when you first started the field there at McCook?

A: Oh, at McCook Field, we probably had a few dozen airplanes of various makes. We had some foreign airplanes brought over from Germany, France, England. Nearly all the war types of aircraft were represented in our inventory.

Q: You had some civilian pilots there too, in addition to some military pilots. Do you remember? Was the test pilot Ralph Lockwood one of those people there?

A: Yes, there was Lockwood and Art Smith and Louis P. Moriarity, who was killed at McCook in 1922.

Q: There was a lot of flying done at McCook Field, and the field had a pretty good safety record. I guess they had the cream of the crop of the pilots.

A: Yes, they were all the very best pilots of the Air Corps.

Q: What was the first design work you did, and when did that start at McCook Field? What were you trying to accomplish?

A: In 1917–19, Col. Virginius Evans Clark, who was the first commanding officer of McCook, had written a specification for a military combat airplane. The first job I got at McCook Field was to design that airplane.

Q: A fighter?

A: It was a two-place observation airplane, equipped for defending itself in case it was attacked. It was a biplane.

Q: You always advocated monoplanes over biplanes.

A: Yes, that's true. But in the early days, the fighting all had been done with biplanes that required great rigidity and ability to turn, which a monoplane could not have. That was why until 1928 all military aircraft were biplanes.

Q: A few of them were triplanes as well.

A: There were a few triplanes, but of course the more wings you stack up on top of one another, the worse the aerodynamic efficiency, so the triplanes did not really compete.

Q: When you were at Wright Field, a British de Havilland airplane was brought over to Dayton, where it was given to the Dayton-Wright people to put it into production. Were you involved at all in that?

A: No, I was not involved in the production of the DH-4; only in changes to adapt it to various uses.

Q: That's what they did mainly at McCook, then, wasn't it? They did the modification work and improvements on airplanes that were being used in the war?

A: Yes. For instance, we would install guns and cameras and things like that.

Q: Of course, they were expanding McCook all the time in 1918, weren't they?

A: Yes, they were adding to it. They added a material research division. They added a school (the Air Force Institute of Technology, located now at Wright-Patterson AFB) for officers destined for the engineering phase of aviation.

Q: Did you see much of Gen. Billy Mitchell? (*Note*: Mitchell is regarded by many as the father of the US Air Force.)

A: Occasionally, we would see General Mitchell. He came out once and flew in a glider that I had designed. He wanted to know something about gliding and soaring, which the Germans were more adept at than us.

Q: How did they get it off the ground? Did they tow it off the ground, similar to the way they do it now?

A: It was gotten off the ground with shock absorbers, a bungee catapult system. It didn't get much over 100 foot high. We also took it to some hills in the hope of getting some ascending currents. We got very little of that.

Q: Anybody crack up doing that?

A: No. There never were any crack-ups in the McCook Field glider.

Q: Well, that speaks pretty well for the design. Now, moving along to 1919—that's when I got there, in March 1919. Before I go ahead with that, I would like to ask you something about the helicopter. I know Col. Thurman Bane got very interested in helicopters. I remember Igor Sikorsky was the first man hired. Do you remember that?

A: Yes. I had quite a few contacts with both Sikorsky and de Bothezat.

Q: According to a story that I got from Mrs. Bane, Sikorsky was the first one there. He worked for several months at McCook but didn't seem to make enough progress. So, they let him go and hired de Bothezat.

A: That's true, but Sikorsky was never given enough rope to have anything built in the shops.

Q: Were you involved in his helicopter in any way?

A: No, I was more involved in the de Bothezat helicopter.

Q: What did you think of de Bothezat's helicopter?

A: It had some new ideas, some of which I furnished to de Bothezat. One was regarding the blades which were pivoted to find their own proper angle of attack.

Q: Was that actually the first helicopter to fly?

A: No. It was not the first helicopter to fly. It was one of the early ones, however.

Q: How high did the de Bothezat helicopter fly when he finally finished it? I think Colonel Bane was the first one to fly it.

A: It went up about 8 or 10 feet. Not high enough to be sure that we were out of the ground effect. He didn't go any higher because he was afraid of stability troubles causing a wreck.

Q: Then what finally happened to de Bothezat?

A: de Bothezat left working for the air service and found employment with an air-conditioning manufacturer in New Jersey, where he was designing fans for circulating air in mines and industrial plants. That was the end of de Bothezat for aviation, although he was the author of some very important papers on propeller theory.

Q: It must have been in 1919, you did some work with Maj. Edward L. Hoffman, who received the Collier Trophy in 1926 for his work on parachute development. You helped with some of the things that he was doing. He was in charge of the equipment section. What did you do with him?

A: I did two things with Major Hoffman. I helped with the installation of a parachute that was housed in the center section of a biplane. This was intended to let the entire airplane down if it got into any trouble of any kind. That thing was tested, and of course, the airplane was wrecked in the landing, but it did prove that the personnel could be saved in that way. The other project was the development of an airplane that would minimize injury in crashes. It was nicknamed "the flying mattress." It had safety belts attached to friction pulleys to decelerate the occupants. It had a pad full of springs and upholstery in front of the pilot and the passenger, which would collapse in the event that they hit anything very solid, thereby reducing the impact.

Q: Did you have something to do with that incline where they tested airplanes to find the cause of fire? They had an incline with a big concrete abutment there. They used to run airplanes full speed down this incline and crash into the wall. Hagemeyer made high-speed motion pictures. Weren't you involved with that?

A: No, that was not one of my projects. It was too destructive for my particular talents.

Q: I remember an airplane in about 1919 that was designed with armor plating on it. What do you know about that?

A: It was designed by Mac Laddon, with the idea that such an airplane could fly over trenches without being shot down by infantry fire. It was very heavy, so it did not have a very good performance. It was soon decided, after trying it out, that a faster airplane had a better chance of survival than a safe one that was heavy.

A very nice little airplane that I designed was the XB-1A. It was a takeoff of the Bristol Fighter but was more refined and with a monocoque fuselage, one of the first built in this country. I enlisted help from some factory in Grand Rapids that had developed a "blood glue." Henry Haskell was the inventor of that. His company today uses this glue for binding plywood. They built veneer panels that had the necessary curvature to make a fuselage.

Q: Around that time, they were fooling around with reversible propellers, weren't they?

A: Frank Caldwell was the developer of the reversible-pitch propeller. You can get that story from him.

I remember when Muir Fairchild cracked up an XB-1A in the middle of McCook Field. I ran out and complimented him on being safe. And he said to me, "Mr. Roche, this is hardly a time for congratulations. I'm very sorry I busted your airplane.

Q: And there were accidents . . .

A: I remember when Muir Fairchild cracked up an XB-1A in the middle of McCook Field. I ran out and complimented him on being safe. And he said to me, "Mr. Roche, this is hardly a time for congratulations. I'm very sorry I busted your airplane." That was one of the airplanes I designed. Forty of the XB-1A were produced by Dayton-Wright Aircraft Corporation.

Q: I used to fly that plane. It was a very nice airplane to fly.

A: They ended by burning those forty airplanes just to get rid of them because there was no servicing set up for them.

Q: That was a two-place job, was it?

A: Two place, observation airplane, equipped with guns, that could fight.

Q: There was one airplane I know from 1919 to 1920, when I was there—a plane that everyone seemed to want to fly. That was the Vought airplane.

A: Chance Vought designed the best of the training airplanes we ever had. He designed the VE-7, the first aircraft to be launched from a carrier, for the navy, and that airplane was really good.

Q: Yes, I remember the one at McCook Field.

A: They landed slowly. They could spin beautifully, recovering in a very short time. They had all the characteristics that you should have in a trainer.

Q: They had Hispano-Suiza engines in them. What about Theophile dePort . . . ?

A: He was one of the designers at McCook. He was educated in Paris as an engineer. He came to this country and wound up in Detroit and was associated with Alfred F. Verville. When Verville came to McCook Field, he brought along Mr. dePort. During a time when Verville was in France with his racing airplane, dePort was given the job of designing a very small messenger airplane that could fly from a dirigible balloon and vice versa.

Q: That is what it was originally built for—to take off and return to a dirigible balloon?

A: To fly between as a liaison between larger aircraft.

Q: You got to talk to Thurman Bane quite a bit, didn't you?

A: Not so very much.

Q: You probably worked under the chief engineers more, yes?

A: Yes. I was working under Clark and Martin. There was very little time for conversation. Virginius Clark was the first engineering officer in charge. He designed the "Clark Y airfoil" from data obtained during one of his trips to Germany. This was before World War I, before we were drawn into the war.

Q: What was your opinion of the German Fokker airplane?

A: We admired the Fokker airplane very much for its simplicity.

Q: I know I used to fly one in 1919 at McCook. The engine sounded like a can of nails.

A: It probably was a Mercedes-Benz engine, wasn't it?

Q: Yes.

A: And that was a very good engine. It was economical and powerful.

Q: They had some other airplanes there, Spads and the SE-5 and the Bristol. You people got a lot of good information from the test of those airplanes, yes?

A: Yes, a lot of good details, such as the streamlined wires and the fittings that went with them. That all came over from England.

Q: Were you involved in any of the racers that they were starting to build after 1920? Verville built the first racer, didn't he?

A: Verville built the first monoplane racer for the government. I was only involved in making modifications to our biplanes, to enter them in the races. That was one of the things that settled the question of biplane versus monoplane. I had been advocating the development of monoplanes but couldn't get anywhere until at the Cleveland Races a civilian monoplane called The Mystery Ship licked the pants off our best military biplane. It beat the Curtiss biplane by 50 miles per hour.

Q: I remember that very well. I would also like to ask you about when Doctor Moss came to McCook Field. I know he was there in 1919, possibly earlier. He developed the supercharger for the Liberty engine. That was first put in the LaPere, wasn't it?

A: That's right. That was put in the LaPere on a Liberty engine. Old Dr. Moss was working for General Electric. He came there very early.

CHAPTER 20
ALEXANDER N. P. DE SEVERSKY

INTERVIEWED MID-1960S
Alexander de Seversky went on to establish the New York Institute of Technology. Republic Aircraft modified his Seversky P-43 into the famous P-47 Thunderbolt, and nearly sixteen thousand were produced during World War II. This Russian/American immigrant was inducted into the National Aviation Hall of Fame in 1970 and died four years later at the age of eighty.

INTERVIEW CONDUCTED BY GEORGE W. GODDARD

Q: I knew you very well at old McCook Field, way back in the early 1920s. When you went there, Col. Thurman Bane asked you to develop a bombsight. That's right, isn't it?

A: No, Gen. Billy Mitchell asked me to develop a bombsight. When I arrived in this country after the Russian Revolution, I went to see General Kenly. I wanted to go immediately to Europe to join a combatant outfit, but General Kenly said to me, "We have a lot of young men who can fight, but we have very few people who know how to build airplanes." He asked me to go to Buffalo and take charge of inspection, testing, and production for the government of the SE-5 fighter plane. I was an electrical engineer, in charge of the inspection of planes, and a test pilot.

After the armistice occurred, I went back to New York. I had some money left, so I began to take English lessons from Ziegfeld Follies girls, but I found it very expensive. Very soon I discovered that I had run out of money but still hadn't learned English. Around that time, Horace Hicham—for whom Hicham Air Force Base, Honolulu, Hawaii, is named and who was the information officer of the Air Corps—came to me and told me we were going to Washington. I asked, "Why?" He said, "I'll tell you when we get there." On the way to Washington, he told me that General Mitchell was going to prove the superiority of the airplane over the battleship.

According to his intelligence report, I had a great deal of experience bombing the German navy, and I also saw German aircraft bombing the Russian navy. General Mitchell wanted me to be his consultant during this bombing test. He officially secured from the Secretary of War a position for me as a consultant for the War Department. I was with him many times at Langley Field. Everything went fine till we came to the 2,000-pound bombs. They were tested at Aberdeen but would not fuse properly. They were falling apart and would not explode properly. They also had some other problems.

Horace Hicham asked me, "What do you think we can do?" Then I told him a very interesting story. We had landed on a lake in the Gulf of Riga in the middle of World War I. A German airplane attacked one of our transports. His bomb missed the transport. He put his trail of bombs quite a way from the transport into the water. We kind of laughed about it, but all of a sudden we heard an SOS. The transport was sinking.

Then we realized what happened: The detonation and blast through the water had ripped open the bottom of that ship. I passed on this incident to Horace and told him, "I think if you really want to sink this battleship, you should try to put the bombs alongside the ship. Because of the shape of the bomb, the fuses probably will work, the bomb will detonate, and you will be able to sink the battleship that way."

That's what happened. General Mitchell was very happy. He asked me to come the next day. He said, "Now look, we have good pilots and good planes, but we haven't got a good device, a good bombsight. What's your experience?" So, I disclosed to General Mitchell my idea of a bombsight that I'd been using during the war. I also disclosed to him my ideas regarding inflight refueling.

He said to me, "I don't want to hear any more about it because we don't want to steal these inventions from you. But I'll tell you something . . ." He pressed a button and called in two assistants. He told them, "I want you to take Seversky and file his patents by tomorrow noon. Be in my office after lunch. I want to hear the rest of the story. And make him pay the filing fee so the government isn't on the patent." We worked overnight and filed those two patents on the bombsight and inflight refueling. General Mitchell then sent me to McCook Field.

Q: When did you get to McCook?

A: In 1921. Maj. Edward L. Hoffman was in charge of equipment. I gave him the inflight refueling system with all the details. General Mitchell wrote a letter saying he wanted this to be immediately developed. At the same time, I was authorized by General Mitchell to survey the industry. I selected Sperry Gyroscopic Company as the most suitable company to develop my gyroscopically synchronized control bombsight. That's how the thing started.

> But General Mitchell said, "Now, look here, I'd rather have one bomber that can hit something than a flock that can't hit anything. So, cancel one bomber and divert the money to a bombsight."

If it hadn't been for General Mitchell, it wouldn't have happened. Very few people know that it even started because of General Mitchell. He immediately realized the possibilities and directed the people at McCook Field to go ahead with development.

When I went to Sperry Gyroscopic, I asked how much it was going to cost to build a bombsight. I was told ten thousand dollars. The finance officer nearly fainted when I told him. He said, "My God, that's what we pay for a Martin Bomber." In those days, bombsights were being sold by the gross, and then all of a sudden it was ten thousand dollars!

But General Mitchell said, "Now, look here, I'd rather have one bomber that can hit something than a flock that can't hit anything. So, cancel one bomber and divert the money to a bombsight." He turned to me and said, "Look, Seversky, I'm going out on a limb with your bombsight. It had better be good or your life is not going to be worth a penny." That was right after the conclusion of the bombing test in 1923.

Q: How did you get into the Russian air service? How old were you then?

A: My father was an aviator. He purchased a Bleriot and a Farman, and he flew just for fun. He commuted between Saint Petersburg and our country place. So, we were around airplanes since we were kids. When Sikorsky built his four-engine bomber in 1912, he used me and my brother as ballast.

Q: Was he in Russia then?

A: Sikorsky started in Kiev. In fact, he graduated from the same naval academy that I graduated from. He went to Kiev and started designing gliders first and then airplanes. He was the first man in the world to build a four-engine bomber. During the war, I was a regular graduate of the Imperial Naval Academy. I got my naval wings and army wings because I went to both schools.

I started in the bomber force and lost my leg on my first bombing flight. That was in September 1915.

Q: Was that in a crack-up?

A: No, I was shot down by a German destroyer. It was at night over the Baltic Sea. Then, while still on crutches, I became the inspector of battle planes for the czar. I got some practical experience in the design of aircraft. Then when I got my wooden leg, I received special permission from the czar and was returned to combat duty. I then flew in the war for two more years with my artificial leg.

I found that not having my leg did not interfere with my flying. In fact, I found myself 25 percent less vulnerable because I was shot through my wooden leg several times and was able to keep on fighting, where my wingman had to go to the hospital. After the Communist revolution, I came to the United States by way of Siberia. I was assigned to McCook at that time as a civilian because I had to fly the airplanes to test my bombsight. I was assigned to the Flying Branch at McCook. I remember Ralph Lockwood, another civilian test pilot.

Q: How long did you stay at McCook Field?

A: I was actually working at McCook Field and at the Sperry Company as an employee of the government. I was developing a bombsight there. When the bombsight was finished, and since it was supposed to bomb moving targets, they gave us a really tough problem. They sent us to Langley Field. We were bombing the shadow of a dirigible that was moving at 60 miles per hour. It was all photographed by Hagemeyer. He took all the motion pictures of the test. One day General Mitchell came to inspect and was very much interested. We were very lucky that day. We had scored a bull's-eye every time.

I had built the first ballistic computer for the bombsight. It was very large, about 2 feet square, and weighed 60 pounds. In those days, that was a horrible weight. Today, a bombsight weighs 1 ton and costs millions of dollars. Anyway, I had to cut out the nose of the Martin Bomber. Still, there was not enough room. So, I took off my wooden leg, and then I slid in between the computer and the cockpit. I was then able to operate the bombsight. When we landed, General Mitchell greeted me. I started to apologize because I couldn't get out of the airplane because I had to put on my wooden leg.

I told the general not to worry because in production I was going to miniaturize the computer and bombsight. He said, "No, don't fool with that bombsight. It's perfect as it is. If we put it into service, the space problem will be solved very easily. The right leg of every bombardier will be amputated." He then shook my hand and left Langley.

Q: He was a great man, wasn't he? One of the greatest men ever to live in this aviation business.

A: Not only a tactical man, but he had uncanny technological vision—one of those minds. He was not an engineer, but he visualized technology far, far in advance. That's why he was able to translate that technology and build up future strategies and tactics on the technology of tomorrow. That's why his principles are still valid today. He was truly a great man in many ways. He started as my boss and then we became dear friends.

Q: In the Russian air force, did they have aerial cameras and do aerial photography?

A: Yes. I personally did some. On one bombing raid over a lake, which had a German seaplane base, after releasing my bombs, I took some shots leaning over the side of the aircraft. I brought some of those pictures back.

Q: Did you ever bail out of an airplane?

A: No. Several times I actually had my foot over the edge of the fuselage, but I didn't jump. I always tried to quickly analyze what was taking place. I tested a great many new airplanes that had never been flown before, but I was always able to resolve things, whether it was a flutter or a vibration or something. I did have quite a few narrow escapes. I always wanted to jump, but you see having a wooden leg, I always worried that I could get a big splinter in my body.

Q: Did you ever go back to Russia?

A: No, I never did.

Q: I would imagine that after the revolution, the new government confiscated all your family's property...

A: That's a natural thing. I never thought that chaos could last this long. I thought it would blow over in a few months. That's how far off I was on political aspects.

Q: When did you leave Seversky Aviation to form Republic Aviation?

A: In 1940, I decided I was going to leave the company. I knew the war was coming, so I began to work on my book, *Victory through Air Power*. I devoted all my time to writing the book—which, by the way, Walt Disney made into a picture. Here's an interesting story: The picture played an important part in the Quebec Conference in 1943. Did you know that? General Marshall and President Roosevelt on one side had reached an impasse with Churchill and the Royal Air Force and our Air Force on the other side. It was about how best to invade Europe. The airmen felt that we should not invade Europe unless we had command of the air over the channel. They could not convince General Marshall and President Roosevelt of this important condition. Then Churchill asked Roosevelt, "Did you see your American film called *Victory through Air Power*?" It had been released by Disney Studios in 1943. Roosevelt replied, "No, I haven't." Churchill said, "Well, I think you should see it."

They called Gen. Hap Arnold, and it was arranged to fly the film overnight to Quebec. Roosevelt, Churchill, Adm. King, Marshall, and all the rest of the Joint Chiefs of Staff viewed the animated cartoon. They then asked the Royal and US Air Forces what they wanted in order to accomplish command of the air. They said they wanted to choose their own target system. It was felt by the airmen that targets were not selected correctly by nonairmen. They said that if they had their own target system and were given top priority on logistics, there would be no interference by Germans in the air on June 6th. And that's what happened.

So, Walt Disney was very happy about it. He felt that his work had not been in vain.

CHAPTER 21
ALBERT WILLIAM STEVENS

A TRIBUTE

As readers of this book surely notice, the name of Albert Stevens recurs throughout the interviews, with fascinating anecdotes offered about him. Unfortunately, Stevens died in 1949 at the age of sixty-three, without having been publicly interviewed. This was a huge loss for aviation historians, because he was a man of superior intelligence—apparently bordering on genius—and was an extremely colorful character besides. Hereafter is a summary of his life and career.

Capt. Albert William Stevens was born in 1886 in Belfast, Maine. His mother died the year he was born, his father passed away when he was twelve, so he was eventually adopted. Stevens earned both bachelor's and master's of science degrees in electrical engineering from the University of Maine. Later in life, he would be honored with three doctor of science degrees.

Capt. Albert Stevens. *Army Air Service photo from the Thomas Harriman collection*

Prior to World War I, Stevens worked as a young man in Idaho, Montana, and Alaska. At the start of the war, he enlisted in the Army Air Service and was sent to the aerial photography school at Cornell University. Improving cameras and performing aerial photography would remain his passion for the remainder of his life.

Though he was never a rated pilot, his zeal to capture scenes from aloft would see him airborne at high altitudes more often than most pilots of the age. After being sent to France during the war, Stevens participated as an aerial photographer in the Chateau Thierry, Saint-Mihiel, and Meuse Argonne offensives.

Captain Stevens reported to McCook Field in March 1921. He remained attached to McCook till the engineering division was relocated to

Wright Field in 1927. He worked from Wright till 1930.

During those years, he was given temporary photography assignments throughout the United States and South America. He also developed an abiding interest in high-altitude parachute jumping and set several records, the highest jump being from 24,200 feet above the ground. He photographed from open cockpit aircraft at altitudes up to 39,000 feet.

In the early 1930s, Stevens took an assignment with the National Geographic Society to explore and photograph the upper stratosphere. In 1934, the society attempted during this exploration to establish an altitude record. "*Explorer I*" was the society's pressurized sphere, which was taken aloft by a gas-filled balloon. The three-man crew on the flight were William Kepner, Orvil Anderson, and Albert Stevens.

Captains St. Clair Streett and Albert Stevens preparing for a photo flight. *Photo courtesy of the US Air Force Museum*

At about 60,000 feet, the balloon ruptured and "*Explorer I*" began to free-fall. The decision to bail out was made. Capt. Anderson successfully exited the sphere first and deployed his parachute. Maj. Kepner exited next but decided to stand atop the plummeting sphere to ensure that Capt. Stevens also was able to safely leave the craft.

Stevens became stuck in the hatch. Seeing Stevens's dire situation, at an altitude below 5,000 feet, Kepner kicked Stevens in the chest, freeing him from the hatch. The cover of the January 1963 issue of *National Geographic* depicts this dramatic moment. All three men survived. Sixteen months later, "*Explorer II*" was launched, with just Anderson and Stevens aboard. This flight was a scientific success, setting an altitude record of 72,395 feet, a record that would stand for twenty-one years.

In April 1942, Captain Stevens was medically discharged from military service. He lived the rest of his life with his wife in California. However, he never forgot the Maine town where he was raised, returning there many times. Nor did the town forget him. Years after his death, the Capt. Albert W. Stevens Elementary School in Belfast, Maine, was established in his honor.

In the course of interviewing a colleague for his book, George W. Goddard shared a harrowing story about primitive early aviation experimentation. Stevens had a role in the story. The following is the general's telling of the incident:

In 1927, I was ordered to the Philippines, I wanted to give Albert Stevens his first flight on a night photo mission. I borrowed a Douglas transport, a single-engine transport, with a pilot and copilot. We built six bombs, which we loaded into the back end of the fuselage. We then cut a large hole in the bottom and installed a chute to slide the bombs out of the airplane. We had a little piece of cord that would pull the bomb fuse when the bomb was 100 feet from the airplane. The explosion would provide the flash for the night photo.

So, I took up Stevens and two other men from my lab. Gene Batten was flying the plane. Right over Wright Field, the bomb slid down the chute from the bottom of the fuselage, but it had either a defective fuse or a short cord. We estimate that the 60 pounds of powder exploded 25 feet below the aircraft, ripping out the lower-left longerons, taking off all the fabric. It broke all the ribs in the tail and even some of the ribs in the wing.

The explosion blew the three of us, Captain Stevens, Bill Oswalt, and me, into the structural brace wires and cross members. There we all hung, saying our prayers and trying to decide whether to join the Caterpillar Club membership, which requires that a parachute has been used to save your life. All we had to do was drop, for there was no floor beneath us. The pilot and copilot pulled hard to keep up the nose with full power.

It seemed like a long time before we returned to earth at Wright Field in total darkness. There were no landing lights on the runway or on the airplane. The plane hit very hard and bounced two or three times before we came to a stop. The fourth man that had gone up with us, by the way, was blown back into the tail of the aircraft and wound up with a wooden gusset around his neck. He was the only one in need of medical attention, but it was nothing serious.

A few days later, Douglas Aircraft and McCook Field engineers inspected the damage. They all agreed that we had made a great contribution by providing information about how to design future military aircraft so that they could withstand antiaircraft fire.

It was a memorable first night-photo mission for Albert Stevens.

CHAPTER 22
INSIGHTS FROM THE INTERVIEWS

This book is as much about people as it is about the advancement of aviation. In the course of conversations with selected people who contributed to aviation at McCook Field, I gained insight into them as individuals, as human beings, rather than as accomplished professionals. The following are a few accounts of these personal encounters and what they revealed to me.

GEN. JAMES DOOLITTLE

Because of Gen. James Doolittle's involvement at McCook, I felt his first-person account was essential for the book. However, Walter Boyne, director of Smithsonian Air & Space Museum, told me not to get my hopes too high about landing an interview. He said the general, though courteous, was weary of rehashing his life and accomplishments. I could well understand—that is, I could understand his being tired of being asked to go over and over the 1942 Tokyo raid.

However, I had little interest in discussing that raid. My interest centered around his involvement at McCook Field. His transcontinental flight, his being a student at McCook's engineering school, and his feat of performing an "outside loop"—all of this while stationed at McCook in the 1920s.

So, how could I get the general to sit down for an interview with someone who had no writing credentials whatsoever? I decided to contact him. I explained my background and my desire to limit my questioning to McCook Field topics, all in a letter that I mailed in September 1976.

A month later, I received a response. The general said he couldn't give a date at that moment, but that he would get back to me when he firmed up some plans. He also suggested I look up NACA Report No. 203, which covered the acceleration test he conducted at McCook

Lt. Gen. James H. Doolittle in his Los Angeles, California, office in 1977. *Photo by author*

in 1924 to meet a requirement for his master of aeronautical engineering degree from the Massachusetts Institute of Technology. I was elated by his response.

To prep for the interview, I visited several libraries (no internet in those days) and checked out every book and publication I could find regarding James Doolittle. I wanted to get a grasp of his entire life, not just his years at McCook. I didn't want to ask any question that would embarrass myself or the general. Also, there was no point in revisiting a topic that had been well covered in a previous publication.

One of my concerns was how much time I would be allowed for the interview. I wrote up a list of thirty-five questions, in descending order of importance, and massaged the list over and over. I prepped on the assumption I would be given only ten minutes, though I hoped for much more time than that.

By January of the following year, I realized that scheduling an interview weeks in advance would be impossible, given the general's busy schedule. I decided to put myself on twenty-four-hour standby. The only downside to that would be the extra expense of last-minute buying of an airline ticket from Indianapolis to LA.

Finally, on March 4, I received a call from the general's Los Angeles office, informing me that an interview could be conducted the following Monday morning at his office in the Mutual of Omaha building on Wilshire Boulevard. My response: "I'll be there." I took a day of leave from my job.

A health dilemma almost derailed everything. For months, I had periodically experienced a severe pain in my chest, usually in the middle of the night. Twice the pain had resulted in my wife driving me to a hospital emergency room. A pain-relieving shot would be administered, and I would be fine and return home. On the Friday before my scheduled interview, I had eaten out with friends—overeaten, actually—and later in the night had been visited by the pain in my chest. This time, the emergency personnel suggested that I check into the hospital, submit to some testing over the weekend, and talk with a surgeon on Monday.

I declined and asked for another shot of painkiller, telling them in no uncertain terms that I had a Monday appointment that I absolutely had to keep. They reluctantly agreed, and on Sunday, pain-free, I flew to Los Angeles as planned. (Two days after my return to Indianapolis, the pain recurred. A surgeon subsequently removed my gall bladder containing several stones, as well as my appendix. The surgery forever solved the problem.)

In Los Angeles, I was ushered into General Doolittle's seventh-floor office by his secretary. Dressed in a business suit, the general was seated at his desk and remained seated during the interview. He was businesslike, but very polite, answering all my questions and allowing me all the time I needed. As the interview ended, I asked him if I could take a photo, which was my routine request at all the interviews.

He agreed, and as I did so, he revealed an interesting side of his personality: He was inquisitive. My camera was an inexpensive Kodak 110, which was popular at that time. I had been using it in my flying for taking quick and easy aerial photographs. It was aim-and-shoot simplicity at its best. As I aimed it at the general, he asked me about the "palm of your hand" size of the camera, who manufactured it, the type and speed of film in it, how the film cartridge was loaded, its cost, and the quality of photos it produced.

I was impressed. This lifelong engineer and experimenter, whose mind had pushed past the envelope so many times during his career, was genuinely interested in my nine-dollar camera because it was new to him and he wanted to learn more.

GEN. GEORGE W. GODDARD

I traveled to Boca Raton, Florida, several times to consult with Gen. George Goddard. His expertise was aerial photography and he spent much of the 1920s doing just that at McCook Field. His experiments and advancements in the field were legion—from nighttime aerial photography to high-altitude image-making to inventing and perfecting cameras and equipment.

Talking with the eighty-nine-year-old was a rewarding experience. We spent many hours conversing about the early days of aviation in general and McCook Field characters in particular. He allowed me to copy tapes of his interviews with former associates, which he utilized in writing his autobiography, *Overview: A Lifelong Adventure in Aerial Photography*. Doubleday published it in 1969.

His tapes were important because he had interviewed several men who since had died, as well as one, John Macready, whom I was never allowed to interview. I was extremely grateful for the general's generosity. He seemed generous by nature. When we would take a lunch break from our conversations, he would insist on picking up the tab wherever we ate. Once I mentioned that I couldn't find a copy of his book at bookstores—there was no Amazon.com then. He said he would sell me a copy and sign it, adding, "It will be eight dollars ninety-five cents. I won't charge you any tax." What a memory. I cherish that book, the signed memoir of an accomplished gentleman who also was a businessman.

Gen. George Goddard at his Boca Raton, Florida, home in 1977. *Photo by author*

Then there was the time he insisted we ride in his new Mercedes Benz to the restaurant. I asked him what he thought of the car. He replied that he was pleased except for the starter, which kept going out. He was not happy about that. Then I heard him start the engine and realized that, even though the engine had engaged properly, the general reengaged the starter several times anyway. "See," he said, "the damned thing is not starting. I guess this starter is going out, too." It already had become clear to me that the general's hearing was beginning to fail. This episode was more evidence of that loss. I said nothing, however.

During one visit, I felt comfortable bringing up something that had puzzled me during interviews with several former McCook Field pilots: They each wore hearing aids in the left ear. General Goddard did, too. I asked about it. He said that many of the aircraft of that period had exhaust stacks running along the left side of the fuselage, with the exhaust opening positioned very near the open cockpit. Plus, the throttle usually was on the left side of the cockpit, so a pilot tended to lean in that direction—bringing the left ear even closer to a source of extreme noise.

I asked him why they didn't stuff cotton inside the leather skull helmets worn then, shielding the ear. He said some did that, but occasionally a spark from the exhaust would fly under the helmet and ignite the cotton. He leaned forward when telling me this and added, "Look, you can see the burn marks on my ear from back then."

GEN. HAROLD HARRIS

I journeyed twice to interview General Harris, finally succeeding on the second try. In 1977, the general lived in New Canaan, Connecticut. On my first attempt, I had flown into Boston late in the day and checked into a hotel, only to find a message that he could not meet with me the next day as planned, nor any day soon thereafter. His wife had fallen ill, and he had driven her somewhere for medical treatment. That trip was for naught.

Brig. Gen. Harold R. Harris at his Connecticut home in 1977. *Photo by author*

Months later, I succeeded in connecting with him, and when I arrived at his home, I was greeted cordially. He was quite willing to help me with my research project. To call him a gentleman is an understatement. While climbing stairs to his second-floor office/study, he took time to point out details of his eighteenth-century New England farmhouse. He noted its craftsmanship. I saw dates written on stairway walls from the pre–Revolutionary War era. Finally, settling in for the taped interview in his office, the general lit his pipe and began to recount his experiences. His sharp mind and clear voice belied his eighty-one years.

One moment of the interview stands out in my mind. We were discussing one of his most well-known adventures—the first emergency bailout of a pilot from a disabled aircraft using a backpack parachute. At one point, he reached across his desk to locate the logbook in which he had recorded the ill-fated flight. Test pilot logbooks of the 1920s had columns listed in this way: *Date, Type of Plane, Type of Engine, Type of Work Done, Duration, and Maximum Altitude.* Puffing on his pipe, the general thumbed through the timeworn pages till he located the entry.

He read aloud what he found: "Test in which a parachute proved very practical." He looked up and added, "Then someone put in brackets, 'Crashed.'" He looked up again and said to me, grinning, "Think of the troubles I would have avoided if I'd not had a parachute." He laughed.

GEN. LEIGH WADE

At his Washington, DC, home, General Wade very freely gave me his time. At the conclusion of the taped conversation, I asked him if I could photograph him. "Of course," he said, then asked me to wait a moment while he located something. He left the room and returned carrying a 12-by-15-inch framed photo of a falcon.

Maj. Gen. Leigh Wade proudly holding a framed picture of a falcon presented to him by Air Force Academy cadets a few weeks prior to my interview. *Photo by author*

The general said he recently had spoken to assembled cadets of the Air Force Academy in Colorado Springs, Colorado. Afterward, as a token of their gratitude and respect for his lifelong achievements and advancement of aviation, the cadets had presented him with the photograph of the academy's mascot. The general clearly had been moved by the gesture and had decided to include the falcon in any subsequent photo of himself.

GEN. HARRY A. JOHNSON

In 1978, I traveled to the general's home in San Antonio, Texas. There, a caregiver told me I would have only an hour for the interview. The general was receiving daily cobalt treatments for a cancerous tumor in his chest. When he walked into the interview room, he was stooped over. In the course of the interview, he quite clearly was weak and in pain. Despite all that, he did his utmost to help me with my research.

As the interview concluded, I asked if I might snap a photo of him. He granted my request, and what followed remains in my memory. I had assumed he would remain seated while I took his picture. Instead, he asked that I wait a moment. He then slowly stood, walked a few paces to one side, straightened his frame to its full 6-foot height, and said, "OK. Take the picture now."

The effort he took to stand upright surely was painful for him, but it demonstrated that his military bearing had not failed him, even as his health had diminished. Maj. Gen. Harry A. Johnson died three months after the interview.

GEN. HOWARD CALHOUN DAVIDSON

I made arrangements to meet with and tape-record General Davidson in Washington, DC. After arriving in the city the night before the appointment, I called his home and asked to speak with the general. I refreshed his memory about our appointment the next day and inquired when I should come by.

"Dinner will be at 6:00 p.m.," he said with military precision. I again asked when he would like me to interview him. "Dinner will be at 6:00 p.m.," he said again. Still uncertain when I should actually ask him questions, I inquired a third time. "And what time can I interview you?" His answer was the same, this time with a hint of irritation in his voice. Not really looking for a free meal but very much wanting to speak with him, I responded, "I will be there at 6:00 p.m." He said, "Fine. I will see you then."

At six o'clock the following evening, the housekeeper greeted me at the door. The general then came forward and led us into a dining room with a rather large and heavy table at its center. The table could easily seat ten people. The general sat at one end, and I sat at the other. Dinner then was served, one course at a time, and little conversation ensued except for the general thanking the housekeeper (and cook) for the excellent meal.

When dinner was finished, we adjourned to the living room and the interview began. The mood quickly shifted, becoming informal. I quickly learned that the general was especially proud of being a West Point cadet in his youth. After our conversation, he consented to be photographed and asked that it be taken in front of a large, well-lit painting of a much-younger General Davidson in full military dress.

The two-star general was depicted in the painting in a uniform with a shoulder patch showing that he was in the China-Burma-India theater of the war. Indeed, he was the commanding general of the Tenth Army Air Force from mid-1943 to the end of World War II. General Davidson clearly was proud of his service in uniform, and I thought the painting reflected the distinguished demeanor he exhibited during the entire evening.

GEN./REV. LESTER MAITLAND

Perhaps no one person in the history of McCook Field had more twists and turns in his life than Gen. Lester Maitland. World War I pilot. Test pilot. Racing pilot. Daring Pacific Ocean–crossing flier. Combat leader. Writer. Episcopal Church ecclesiastical leader. Many turns, indeed.

Though he retired from the US Air Force in 1943, while the war raged, in the late 1970s he was still very much alive, which suggested to me that his early retirement had little to do with physical health. There was a story there, I was sure, so he made my must-interview list.

My first contact with him occurred in the spring of 1977. I had written to him at an address in Red Bluff, California. His reply was on stationery labeled "St. Andrew's Episcopal Church." He responded by saying that he, indeed, had been at McCook "for just a few months in late 1918 and early 1919," but had worked on no projects there and therefore could be of little help to me. My reaction was that either he was being terribly modest or I had reached the wrong man. *Or*, I wondered, *had he merely decided not to talk about the past?*

Later that year, my curiosity piqued, and I drove to St. Andrew's in Red Bluff. I knocked on the door of the residence and a woman, without opening the door, asked what I wanted. I gave her my name and told her about my hope of speaking to Reverend Maitland about his time at McCook Field. She said she would inquire. Moments later, a man's voice spoke to me through the unopened door. "I told you I have nothing to say. You have the wrong person. Goodbye."

I was stunned. As I walked away, I began to wonder if I *had* reached the wrong person. I resolved to at least determine if the two people—the reverend and the aviator—were the same man and decided to start by visiting the local newspaper office. I was cordially greeted by the *Red Bluff Daily News* editor, who listened to my experience at the door of the church parsonage.

"Oh, you have the right man, all right," he said, smiling. "That indeed is famed pilot Lester Maitland." He said I was not the first to be turned away at the door and that the reverend, with few exceptions, distanced himself from his life as an aviator. While some local articles had been published about the former general, next to nothing had been contributed by the man himself. I thanked the editor and left.

Many years later, I confirmed through Internet research that Maitland had been dismissed from the military at the height of World War II because of a problem with alcohol consumption. Subsequent interviews with some of his peers confirmed it. To his credit, he led an exemplary life after leaving the military.

One more point about this man: In June 1927, he and Albert Hegenberger made a historic flight from Oakland, California, to Oahu, Hawaii—the first crossing of Pacific Ocean waters by a land-based aircraft. Their airplane was a Fokker trimotor named "*the Bird of Paradise.*" Many near disasters occurred during the flight.

Though this fight was just five weeks after Charles Lindbergh's crossing of the Atlantic Ocean, the Pacific venture was heralded and the two men were publicly saluted for the feat. In just one example of the acclaim they received, each pilot has a street named for him near Oakland International Airport.

What saddens me is that, in the years immediately following their flight, the men became estranged. Some speculated it was professional jealousy. Others offered different views about the split. In any event, apparently the two men never spoke to one another after the 1930s. People noted that in subsequent gatherings of military personnel, when it came time to pose for photos, Maitland and Hegenberger stood as far from one another as possible.

Imagine, if you will, two men bonding under pressure on a treacherous, long-distance flight and then walking away from each other without looking back. I find that very sad. Honestly, one of my underlying purposes in trying to interview Reverend Maitland was to establish a communication link between the two pioneering pilots, in hopes that one of them might eventually reach out to the other. However, General Hegenberger died in 1983, and Reverend Maitland passed away seven years later. A reconciliation never occurred, so far as anyone knows.

CHAPTER 23

THE PLANES AND PARACHUTES OF MCCOOK FIELD

In any recounting of a historic period, the men and women who lived through the era are of principal interest. We most closely identify with them as human beings rather than with the appurtenances of their existence (e.g., their clothes, housing, and tools). So it is that the people who drove or hitched a ride from their homes in Dayton to McCook Field day after day are the main story.

Nevertheless, the subplot of the McCook saga is filled with machinery. The courage demonstrated by helmeted fliers who climbed into untested aircraft and pushed the craft to their limits cannot be separated from the early generation machines they rode into the sky. The innovative engineers and tireless mechanics who systematically reinvented this new thing called aviation until they reached the plateau of tried and true did so in partnership with the aircraft they refined.

Hereafter are histories and descriptions of some of those aircraft—flying machines that made their way to McCook Field for testing and evaluation. The planes sometimes were of foreign design and manufacture, with McCook pilots and engineers tasked with gleaning information from them and applying it to other renditions of craft. Some airplanes and engines were wholly built at McCook, though that ended when Congress finally sided with aviation's private sector and got McCook out of manufacturing.

Some military planes given the McCook treatment were upgraded or modified to function in other airborne missions. They were transformed from warplanes to civilian craft for peacetime tasks, like spraying crops or delivering mail. Huge bombers were put through their paces. Smaller bombers were fitted with ship-sinking bombsights. An experimental helicopter model was painstakingly induced to leave the ground, if not actually fly. There even was a cycle craft.

Some of these planes made history in memorably long flights, with McCook personnel either preparing them for the flights or actually flying them. Some simply crashed and made history of another kind. A byproduct of all this flirting with disaster—that is, going aloft in new and still-unreliable aircraft—was the development of parachutes to preserve the lives of those whose aircraft let them down.

LIBERTY ENGINE

Gliders and sailplanes aside, no matter how great or innovative an aircraft design is, it will go nowhere without a power plant. Many times, the choice of engine will determine how successful a new aircraft will be. Looking at the famous 1903 Wright Brothers Flyer, the innovative structural design of the craft was a marvel for its day. But what happened on December 17, 1903, was the first successful *powered* flight of a heavier-than-air machine. Without that crude four-cylinder engine designed by the two brothers and largely handmade by their very able machinist, Charlie Taylor, they would not have enjoyed historical immortality. That engine propelled their craft into the air four times that day.

Some engines are more famous than others. The Curtiss OX-5, the Wright Whirlwind, and in modern aviation, the Pratt & Whitney PT-6A are a few examples of engines that powered aircraft to record-setting performances. Reading through this book, it is easy to notice how many times the Liberty engine is mentioned in conversation. Some referred to its reliability. Others found it unreliable. It generally was considered a good engine for its day. The Liberty engine powered many aircraft during the McCook Field era and its development deserves more than a footnote.

The United States declared war on Germany in April 1917. In order to be an effective wager of war, America needed many tools that it did not have. One of the tools it lacked was an aircraft industry that could manufacture both combat aircraft and engines. The belligerent powers that had been fighting in Europe since August 1914 had well-established aircraft companies and engine manufacturers. Had it been a race, America would have been in last place.

To address this shortfall in aviation products, several federal task forces were established. One created in May of 1917 was the Aircraft Production Board. It looked to the nation's existing industrial leaders to start the armament ball rolling. This board called upon two established and successful automobile engine designers, Jesse G. Vincent and Elbert J. Hall, to quickly design an aircraft engine. Vincent was with the Packard Motor Car Company and Hall with Hall-Scott Motor Company. In a Washington hotel meeting, they were asked to design an aircraft engine that could perform as well or better than any engine the European powers had. Two huge requirements given them were that the engine had to be mass-produced and it had to come into production quickly. Delay was not an option.

The story is told that the two engine designers were ordered to remain in the hotel till they adopted a design. In five days, they completed the task. The Liberty engine was born. A few weeks later, an eight-cylinder prototype had been assembled at Packard Motor Car's Detroit facility. It was sent to Washington, DC, where it was tested extensively. In the next month, after more testing, four additional cylinders were added and the iconic Liberty L-12 engine was complete.

The engine was rated at 400 hp. According to *Jane's All the World's Aircraft, 1919*, it was a twelve-cylinder, liquid-cooled, V-piston engine with a 5-inch bore, a stroke of 7 inches, a displacement of 1,649 inches, a length of slightly over 67 inches, a height of 41.5

inches, and a dry weight of 844 pounds. Its compression ratio was 5.4:1, and all importantly, its power-to-weight ratio was .53 hp/pound.

Within a month of this improved variant, the US military contracted with six automobile manufactures to produce more than twenty-two thousand engines. Those well-known manufacturers included the Packard, Ford, Lincoln, Marmon, Cadillac, and Buick automobile companies. With the exception of Marmon, which was based in Indianapolis, Liberty production definitely was a Detroit operation.

Ford Motor Company was given the task of producing the cylinders. By innovating their production process, Ford was able eventually to increase its mass production rate twelve times what it was at the beginning. In the end, Ford built 430,000 cylinders and 4,000 engines, one-fifth of all the Liberty engines produced. Lincoln Motor Company, by investing in a new plant, produced 15 percent of the 13,500 Liberty engines built by war's end. Production by the manufacturers did not end with the Armistice between Germany and the Allied powers. It continued, and almost 21,000 Liberty engines finally were built.

Despite the vast amount of money spent to build the Liberty, few of the engines manufactured prior to the end of hostilities made it into combat. The exception was the Airco DH-4, which saw combat over France.

At the war's end, the large stockpile of Liberty engines was distributed and installed in a variety of aircraft. Besides the British-designed, American-built DH-4, the engine powered several Douglas aircraft, notably the 1924 World Cruisers. It was used on the US Navy Curtiss NC-4 flying boat, which became the first aircraft to cross the Atlantic in 1919. Six Liberty engines were used to power the massive Army Air Service Barling Bomber in the early 1920s. France, England, and Italy utilized the Liberty to power some of their postwar designs. A few Liberty engines were installed in automobiles with land speed records in mind. During World War I, the engine showed potential use in tanks. Several American-designed, Liberty-powered tanks were built.

Over the ensuing years, the engine was tweaked into many variations. It was inverted in some aircraft and adapted to being air-cooled. The engine was redesigned as a six-cylinder, the L-6, and as an eight-cylinder, the L-8. In later years, a British car company named Nuffield installed a variant of the Liberty in tanks that saw combat during World War II. There also is a history of the Liberty engine powering various watercraft, competing in races and setting speed records in the process.

A handful of Liberty engines today are on static display in museums. An operable Liberty type V-12 is on a test stand at Old Rhinebeck Aerodrome near Albany, New York. On scheduled weekend air shows, it is fired up. This author can attest that the sound of the historic engine is worth the price of admission.

CURTISS JN-4

The Jenny. That's what this beloved aircraft was called in its heyday and still is referred to more than a hundred years after it first took to the air. Like the Phoenix of Greek mythology, it was reborn numerous times in useful and memorable roles, from military pilot trainer to military weapon of war to airmail carrier to civilian pilot trainer and, finally, as a favorite aircraft of barnstormers, the 1920s air show pilots and their wing-walking partners.

Curtiss JN-6HG-1 "Jenny" with a detachable target glider mounted on the top wing. One of many roles the JN series performed during its long life. *Army Air Service photo from the American Aviation Historical Society archives*

The first Jenny models were JN-1 through JN-3. They were designed by Benjamin Thomas and were built by the Curtiss Aeroplane Company of Hammondsport, New York. The first "JN"—from which "Jenny" was derived—made its maiden flight in 1915. All JN models were designed as two-seat tandem biplanes and marketed as a state-of-the-art military trainer. The company eventually built, or subbed out for other manufacturers to build, more than 6,800 JN models from the JN-1 to the JN-6HP.

The company was founded by Glenn H. Curtiss (1878–1930). Curtiss was a renowned motorcycle racer. In 1907, he set an unofficial world motorcycle speed record of 136 mph, a mark that stood for twenty-three years. He also was a gasoline engine designer and aircraft manufacturer. Among his many engine designs was the iconic OX-5, a V-8 liquid-cooled aircraft engine that became the first American-designed engine produced in volume.

Curtiss was a fierce competitor on the racetrack, in the business world, and in the courts. His civil court actions were highlighted by legal tussles between himself and the Wright brothers. It involved litigation over aircraft patent lawsuits. The civil court battles between the two parties bordered on hatred.

In an effort to discredit the claim of Wilbur and Orville Wright to have been the first to fly a powered heavier-than-air aircraft, Curtiss tried to show that Samuel Langley accomplished the feat several months prior to the successful Kitty Hawk flight. These lawsuits began in 1909 and still were unresolved when the United States entered World War I in 1917. America needed aircraft production from both companies at that point, and the litigation proved a hindrance and was allowed to die. Considering the heat generated in the bitter lawsuits, it is surprising that a merger of the two companies and ten smaller firms in 1929 successfully formed the Curtiss-Wright Corporation.

The Jenny began life as a training aircraft, but one year after it made its maiden flight, eight JN-3s were pressed into service by the US Army as observation planes in a quest to capture Mexican revolutionary general and bandit Pancho Villa. He had been crossing into the United States, raiding villages and crossing back into Mexico. After a deadly raid on the New Mexico town of Columbus, the president of the United States ordered Gen. John J. Pershing to go after Villa.

The JN-3s mainly were used as observation platforms in that venture, but mechanical problems developed in the harsh Mexican desert climate. Still, this was the first time the United States used aircraft in an authentic military role and much experience was gleaned from the Army Air Service deployment. The experience led Curtiss to develop the much more successful JN-4.

As a trainer, the JN-4's role in World War I was critical. It is estimated that 95 percent of US pilots who trained for this conflict received some basic training in the JN-4. This model was equipped with a Curtiss 90 hp OX-5 V-8 engine. The underperforming engine was perfect for a novice pilot. With a top speed of 75 mph and a ceiling slightly above 6,000 feet, it was a near-perfect trainer. Several JN-4s were modified into single-stretcher ambulance planes. Though some of the trainer aircraft had machine guns mounted and racks for bombs affixed, none were used in combat in the European war. In 1919, a highly modified US Marine Corp JN-4 made what is believed to be the first successful dive-bombing attack. It occurred during an assault on rebel forces in Haiti.

After the war, the government sold thousands of these craft in the civilian market. Some were in "crate from the factory" condition and sold for less than one hundred dollars. One of them was purchased in mid-1923 by twenty-one-year-old Charles Lindbergh. In the JN-4, he is said to have taught himself how to fly and to have soloed. On May 15, 1918, six converted JN-4s flown by US Army Air Service pilots made the first scheduled airmail flights. The pilots were under the command of Maj. Reuben H. Fleet, who later would become the contracting officer at McCook Field and, eventually, an aircraft industry entrepreneur.

Numerous black-and-white film clips from the 1920s capture the Jenny in its most memorable role—as a barnstorming aircraft. Nomadic pilots of varying degrees of expertise roamed the country in those days trying to forge a living from performing impromptu air shows. Because it was inexpensive, the Jenny was the perfect airplane for these flying showmen. Typically, the JN-4 pilot would fly over a small town, perform some aerobatics to create attention, and then land in a nearby pasture. He would pass the hat or offer to sell rides. If lucky, he would clear enough to buy a meal and a few gallons of fuel before flying to the next venue.

The highlight of any performance would be the wing-walking act, especially if the walker was a young and pretty female. A walker seldom wore a parachute. After he or she crawled onto an upper wing, a quick loop would follow and observers on the ground would hold their breath. It was not work for the faint of heart.

Nineteen Jenny aircraft of different models were based at McCook Field. These were primarily in the beginning years of the facility (1917–19) and served engineers in a variety of missions, including as transports and in vital research.

DH-4

A de Havilland DH-4B3 based at McCook Field. *Army Air Service photo from the American Aviation Historical Society archives*

In the course of an interview with Gen. James Doolittle, the general noted that the United States in World War I did not have a US-designed aircraft that could readily be used in combat by American pilots. It was decided in 1917 at the offset of America's participation in this European conflict—which already had been waged for three years—to take a combat-proven foreign design and mass produce it in the United States. Thus the DH-4 became the country's mainstay military aircraft.

This proved to be both a blessing and a curse. The blessing was that the design could be built in great numbers for quick use in Europe by a young and shamefully small US Air Service. But at the end of hostilities, a large number of the planes remained in government inventory, and it became a victim of its own quick production success: no thought was given to creating successor aircraft.

The thinking at the conclusion of the Great War was that this conflict was truly "the war to end all wars" and there was little need to waste lean government funds on developing planes that were likely never to be needed. The thinking was that with all these DH-4s on hand, the United States was well armed in the air for many years to come. Many in Congress saw little need to approve appropriations for either development or production of advanced aircraft designs, so long as these war surplus craft existed. Consequently, pilots and their commanding officers, who wanted modern state-of-the-art aircraft, felt that new designs would only come about if the large number of DH-4 craft disappeared—by any means possible. Attrition was their ally.

In the end, the DH-4 became the workhorse for a multitude of missions, mostly military but some civilian as well, such as carrying of airmail on that venture's infant and primitive air routes. The primitive and dangerous routes paved the way for airline routes. One airmail pilot, Charles Lindbergh, flew the DH-4 several years prior to becoming a household name following his nonstop New York–Paris flight. Some DH-4s were even used by fledgling airlines in the United States and around the world. During the course of its life, the plane underwent numerous modifications to better meet specific missions.

The first DH-4—the Airco DH-4—was created by famed and prolific British aircraft designer Geoffrey de Havilland (1882–1965). It made its maiden flight in August 1916 and entered military service with the British Royal Flying Corps seven months later. It was a two-seat tandem biplane built of wood and fabric. This configuration was unchanged for its entire production life, but substantial upgrades were made in engine performance during the aircraft's evolution. The original British production model was powered by a 160 hp Beardmore Halford Pullinger engine. Several other engines followed, perhaps the best of the British choices being the 375 hp Rolls-Royce Eagle.

Then came the American DH-4. At the start of United States involvement in the war in 1917, the Bolling Commission was dispatched to Europe to examine state-of-the-art combat aircraft the allies were flying. The idea was to select the most desirable aircraft for mass production in the United States. The commission recommended the Bristol F.2 Fighter, the Royal Aircraft Factory S.E. 5, French SPAD S.XIII, and the DH-4. In July 1917, a single DH-4 was sent to the United States to reverse-engineer and produce. Several companies, including Dayton-Wright Aircraft Company, Boeing Airplane Company, and Standard Aircraft Corporation, received contracts to build this aircraft. These companies made more than a thousand modifications to the original British design.

The US government ordered more than nine thousand DH-4s from these manufacturers. Only a fifth of the ordered planes ever reached France during the war. The first one didn't exit a production line till 1918. In the end, 4,800 planes were built in the United

States before production was halted. The aircraft was equipped with the US-designed-and-built Liberty engine. This twelve-cylinder, 400 hp engine was built by automobile manufacturers Packard, Ford, Lincoln, Marmon, and Buick. The planes were flown by US pilots and served with distinction in their combat role during the war.

A de Havilland DH-4 modified at McCook Field into an air ambulance. *Army Air Service photo from the American Aviation Historical Society archives*

It is hard to believe in this modern era of a huge US aviation defense industry with cutting-edge technology that US aircraft played such a small role in World War I. America's aviation contribution in that conflict was a combat aircraft of foreign design built in the United States and powered by an engine designed and built in this country. The Liberty engine was produced in such great quantities that it powered a legion of aircraft for a generation after the war.

Following the war, the young Boeing Aircraft Corporation and several other manufacturers were awarded contracts to turn surplus DH-4s into the safer and improved DH-4B. The Army Air Service, Navy, and Marine Corps flew various models of the DH-4 till they were retired in 1932. The aircraft served the military in multiple roles with more than sixty mission modifications. These included air-to-air refueling experiments, which led to an endurance record of keeping a plane aloft for a day and a half. Several DH-4s were modified into stretcher ambulance aircraft. The plane was used for several coast-to-coast flights. In 1927, a Marine Corps DH-4 was deployed to combat rebels in Nicaragua.

Some who flew the plane nicknamed it the "Flying Coffin" or "Widow-Maker." Were the labels deserved? For its day, it was a safe aircraft in good flying conditions. It was not an all-weather aircraft. It did not perform well when its fabric wings were covered with ice. The biggest criticism was the location of the fuel tank, which was situated directly in front of the forward pilot. A crash, even a relatively minor one, could lead to rupture of the fuel tank and fire, trapping the pilot. It should be noted that many aircraft of that era had similar design faults and were given similar nicknames.

At McCook Field, the DH-4 was the plane most commonly used by the Engineering Division. A listing of aircraft stationed at McCook in May 1921 shows forty-seven DH-4s of one model or another. The German Fokker D7 was the second most numerous with eight. One of the many research experiments conducted at McCook was in regard to the postcrash fire problem. In one slow-motion filmed experiment, the fuselage of a DH-4 was mounted on a slide at a 30-degree angle. The fully fueled fuselage, with the engine running, then slid down the slide into a concrete barrier. The film captured the exact point of fuel flash during a crash. These tests led to design changes to the fuel tank and fuel line for safer operation.

Today, the DH-4 is a rare bird. Worldwide, there are nine original examples on static display in museums, including the prototype US-built aircraft at the National Air and Space Museum in Washington, DC. None are in airworthy condition, though one is undergoing restoration in Florida. One replica of the plane is routinely flown in New Zealand.

FOKKER PW-7

A Fokker PW-7 based at McCook Field. *Army Air Service photo from the American Aviation Historical Society archives*

When I first contacted Gen. James Doolittle, he suggested I locate Report 203 of the National Advisory Committee for Aeronautics, predecessor to today's NASA, and become familiar with its contents before interviewing him. He said I would have a clearer understanding of some of the groundbreaking research and flight testing conducted at McCook Field. The report, *Acceleration in Flight,* was written by the general when a young lieutenant in 1924 after a comprehensive set of airborne tests took an aircraft to its failure point. During my interview, the general referred to this report briefly but with pride.

The aircraft used by Doolittle for the tests was the Fokker PW-7, which first was named D-XI. Designed by Reinhold Platz for Anthony Fokker's Dutch aircraft company, it had a 300 hp Hispano-Suiza engine. The Spanish-Swiss company had proved itself in manufacturing a multitude of reliable aircraft engines during World War I. The D-XI fabric-covered steel tube fuselage design had several other distinguishing characteristics. This single-seat craft was 11.5-feet high. Its wing placement was known as sesquiplane, which meant the plywood-covered lower wing was far smaller in area than the upper wing. In addition, the water-cooled engine had two radiators, each situated on an opposite side of the engine.

The D-XI made its maiden flight in 1923. It was designed for the Dutch government, but because of financial woes, Fokker explored foreign markets. Eventually, 117 were sold to foreign countries, according to a 1989 entry in *Jane's Encyclopedia of Aviation*, including air forces in Romania, Switzerland, Spain, and Argentina. The overwhelming number were sold to the five-year-old USSR. In 1924, the US Air Service became interested and bought three for McCook Field engineers to evaluate. These three D-XI's were modified, incorporating a 440 hp, V-1150 Curtiss D-12 engine. The engine had been used in several racing planes. This modified version was renamed the Fokker PW-7.

It was one of these PW-7s that then lieutenant Doolittle used to compile his NACA Report 203 and earn a master's degree from MIT. The report in its entirety is seventeen pages long, with several small photographs and technical graphs. Here are some excerpts:

Introduction

This work on accelerometry was done at McCook Field in March 1924 for the purpose of continuing the work done by other investigators and obtaining the accelerations which occur when a modern high-speed pursuit airplane is subjected to the more common maneuvers. The results are presented in this form for publication as a technical report of the National Advisory Committee for Aeronautics.

The airplane used was the Fokker PW-7. The airplane mounts the Curtiss D-12 engine, and all control surfaces are balanced. This airplane has the following characteristics:

> Total weight as flown ~(approx.) 3,200 pounds
> Engine power ~420 at 2,100 rpm
> High speed at ground ~156 mph

The accelerometer used is similar to the one designed by Mr. F. H. Norton for the National Advisory Committee for Aeronautics, and was built by the Emerson Instrument Co. The National Advisory Committee for Aeronautics accelerometer designed by Mr. Norton is described in Technical Report No. 100.

The instrument was calibrated by attaching it to the flywheel of a steam engine capable of maintaining constant speed for a given throttle setting. Since the wheel revolved in a vertical plane, the instrument traced out a sine curve of amplitude 2 g. Three runs were made with the instrument in the position to give negative accelerations. Eight points on the calibration curve were obtained from those runs. Three additional points were obtained by removing the instrument from the wheel and holding it erect, on its side, and inverted, corresponding to 1 g, 0 g, and −1 g.

Mounting of the Instrument

The accelerometer was placed at the c.g. of the airplane and was so oriented that the accelerations recorded were those perpendicular to the plane of the wings. Considerable difficulty was encountered in designing a suitable mounting for the instrument, but it was found that excellent results could be obtained by supporting it on rubber sponges. The instrument was carried in a box which allowed a clearance of about three-quarters of an inch on all sides. Four sponges were placed under the instrument, with two on top. This mounting absorbed all vibration except when the airplane was held in a power spin and a tight spiral with power.

In the case of the spin, the amplitude appears to be dependent upon the engine speed, while the period is probably dependent upon the airplane itself. The principal cause of the vibration in this maneuver appears to have been propeller flutter. In the case of the power spiral, the fact that the acceleration is fairly large and of considerable duration caused the sponges to be compressed, thus decreasing their elasticity and allowing the effect of the vibration on the records to be much more marked.

The accelerations were taken for the following maneuvers:

> loops at various speeds
> single and multiple barrel rolls
> power spirals
> tailspins, power on and off
> half loop and half roll, and "Immelman turn"
> inverted flight
> pulling out of a dive at various air speeds
> flying airplane level and straight with considerable bank angle
> flying in "bumpy air"

Summary of the Results

The accelerations in suddenly pulling out of a dive are greater than those due to any maneuver started at the same speed.

The accelerations obtained in suddenly pulling out of a dive with a modern high-speed pursuit airplane equipped with well-balanced elevators are shown to be within 3 or 4 percent of the theoretically possible accelerations. How close this agreement would be in the case of a similar airplane equipped with unbalanced elevators would be determined by additional experiments.

Accelerations in flying the airplane in average "rough air" do not exceed 2.5 g.

Effect on the Pilot of Large Accelerations

The maximum acceleration which a pilot can withstand depends upon the length of time the acceleration is continued. It is shown that the pilot experiences no difficulty under the instantaneous accelerations as high as 7.8 g, but that under accelerations in excess of 4.5 g, continued for several seconds, the pilot quickly loses his faculties. This loss of faculties is due to the fact that the blood is driven from the head, thus depriving the brain tissues of the necessary oxygen. To the pilot, it seemed that sight was the only faculty that was lost. The flight surgeons at McCook Field are of the opinion that sight is the last faculty to be lost under these conditions, even though the pilot may be under the impression that he retains all the others. This opinion is based on the observation of men undergoing rebreather tests.

The acceleration which an individual can withstand for any length of time depends upon his blood pressure, the person with the higher blood pressure being able to withstand the higher acceleration. Upon the condition of the heart depends on the ability of the individual to recover quickly from the effect of prolonged acceleration. If the heart is in good condition, there is no danger in undergoing such a strain unless the acceleration is continued for a period in excess of ten or twelve seconds, after which death will result. While this is disconcerting to the pilot, it is not necessarily dangerous for one in good physical condition. The same is true of the rebreather test; unconsciousness will result from the deprivation of oxygen and death will result if this is continued for the same length of time.

Author's note: A few years after this report was filed, Doolittle would become a household name because of his air racing triumphs. Then, in early 1942, "Doolittle's Raiders" made the front page when they executed the first bombing of Tokyo, Japan, at a time when Americans sorely needed a hero. Because of this, Doolittle was thought of as a daredevil. Nothing could be further from the truth. Doolittle had a PhD in engineering, and as one can see in this 1924 report, he was meticulous in compiling details. He carefully calculated risk, which perhaps is why he lived to age ninety-six.

FOKKER D.VII AND FOKKER D.VIII FIGHTERS

Example of a Fokker VII used by German aviators with great effect during World War I. *Photo from the Bill Larkin collection in the American Aviation Historical Society archive*

McCook Field was the home of the US Army Air Service's Engineering Division, whose sole mission was research and development. This differed from the standard Air Service airfield, where pilots either were being trained to fly or were poised for immediate air combat duty in the event the country was threatened with attack. While a test pilot might have in his resume some combat experience, the mission of the Engineering Division was research, flight testing, and most important, detailed reports of findings. Fokker fighters were among the aircraft closely evaluated by McCook's aviation engineers.

During World War I, it always was deemed a plus when an ally commandeered an important piece of enemy armament for analysis, particularly if the armament appeared to outperform Allied equipment. After the conflict, enemy armament was appropriated for further scrutiny. Through studying and testing, one could learn much. Sometimes the equipment would be reverse-engineered and developed into a new aircraft.

One plane of special interest to Allies was the German Fokker D.VII. Germany deployed the aircraft during the final six months of the war. It appeared to be superior to the Allied aircraft it encountered in the air. A measure of the respect given to this aircraft can be found in the Armistice document that ended the war in November 1918. In clauses relating to "the Western Front" was a demand that Germany surrender all Fokker D.VIIs to the Allies. The US Army and Navy received 142 of these aircraft.

On a listing of aircraft based at McCook Field, one finds no fewer than eleven Fokker D.VIIs and two Fokker D.VIIIs, with project numbers painted on their vertical stabilizers. No doubt about it, the Allies and the US Army Air Service wanted these formidable enemy aircraft scrutinized, and McCook Field was the place to do it. Just one example of experimentation with the Fokker planes involved replacing the original German-made engine with the US-built Liberty L-6 engine. The performance of the plane with each engine was then compared.

Always looking for a better fighter aircraft, the German Empire's aviation bureau had sponsored a competition in January 1918. Reinhold Platz, a designer with the Dutch aircraft company founded by Anthony Fokker, had months earlier designed a plane that featured a cantilevered wing with a thick and rounded leading edge. The wing design proved to have better lift and stall characteristics than the wing designs used previously. During flight testing, Manfred Von Richthofen, also known as the Red Baron, flew the craft and reported some in-flight concerns. Structural changes by Platz followed and in later test flights, Richthofen and other frontline combat pilots were satisfied with the craft's performance.

This aircraft was designated the D.VII. It had a wingspan of 29 feet and a length of 22 feet. At maximum load, it weighed in slightly less than 2,000 pounds. The plane was powered by either a six-cylinder, water-cooled Mercedes or a six-cylinder, water-cooled BMW (Bavarian Motor Works) engine. With the BMW IIIa engine, the craft had a maximum speed of 124 mph.

Fokker was immediately given a contract for four hundred of the aircraft. Because of the urgency stemming from the late stage of the war, Germany wanted to get these aircraft to the front as soon as possible. Therefore, the German aviation bureau divided manufacturing among Fokker and other aircraft firms. Though the decision to contract with multiple manufacturers caused some construction problems, in the last five months of the war, some 3,300 Fokker D.VII's were built. The aircraft soon became the favorite of German combat pilots. Some pilots flying the plane became household names in Germany and abroad because of their high number of victories in air battles. Though Richthofen was killed prior to the D.VII's arrival to frontline squadrons, Hermann Goring scored twenty-two victories and Ernst Udet had sixty-two victories by war's end, some of them recorded flying the D.VII. Both of these air combat veterans had high praise for the D.VII's maneuverability, climb, and spin characteristics.

With the end of World War I, the D.VII was used in combat roles in other nations. Just as the Armistice halted hostilities in France, a nine-month war developed between Hungary and Romania with Hungarians deploying the D.VII. The Polish air force and some Polish American volunteers flew fifty of these aircraft in their 1919–1920 war with Russia. In all, the Fokker D.VII flew under the auspices of twenty countries. Today, some D.VII models are on display in museums around the world, and replicas have been built through the years. Several years ago, this author witnessed a replica of the Fokker D.VII flying at the Old Rhinebeck Aerodrome in upstate New York.

In the last few months of the war, Fokker unveiled another fighter designed by Reinhold Platz. This aircraft was the last Fokker to join the German air forces in the field and became the last aircraft to score an air victory in that war. This craft was distinctive because it was a parasol-monoplane. Starting life as the Fokker E.V, it had several accidents involving wing failure.

After modifications, it was redesignated the Fokker D.VIII. This plane had a wingspan of 27 feet and a length of 19 feet. Fully loaded, it weighed 1,334 pounds. Power was supplied by a nine-cylinder, air-cooled rotary engine that churned out 110 hp, which was enough to give the craft a competitive speed and climb rate. Like the Fokker D.VII, its ceiling was 20,000 feet.

This Fokker design made its debut at the front just twenty-five days prior to the Armistice. Of the 380 planes manufactured, fewer than one hundred made it to the front. Despite its short war exposure, the airplane gained a favorable reputation from pilots for being very maneuverable and easy to fly. The single-parasol wing design, which at first glance gave the illusion of the wing not being connected to the fuselage, earned the aircraft the nickname "Flying Razor."

Though the terms of surrender that ended the war required the scraping of most German airplanes, including the D.VIII, a few were not destroyed and became prizes of Allied victors—including the two that made their way to McCook Field for testing. Airmen in six countries flew this aircraft during the war and after. An original wingless fuselage of the plane is on display at a museum in Italy and a full replica is in a Canadian museum.

FOKKER T-2

Fokker T-2 transport with Oakley Kelly (*center*) and John Macready, at right with hands in pockets. *Army Air Service photo from the American Aviation Historical Society archives*

Seldom in the 1920s was a US Army Air Service aircraft purchased and modified with a single mission in mind, especially when the plane was as large and costly as the Fokker T-2. But the aircraft's singular mission warranted the inordinate expenditure and assignment of manpower. The mission was to fly from one end of the United States to the other, nonstop.

This flight would make history and McCook Field played a pivotal role in it. The nonstop transcontinental trip was accomplished May 2–3, 1923. At that time, the previous longest nonstop flight in the United States was from Omaha, Nebraska, to Philadelphia, Pennsylvania. Commanding that flight was World War I ace Capt. Eddie Rickenbacker.

A previous transcontinental trip across the United States with many stops was accomplished in 1911 by Calbraith Perry Rodgers, grandnephew of famed US Navy commodore Mathew C. Perry. The plane used was a Wright brothers Model EX named the Vin Fiz. The manufacturer of a popular soft drink by that name sponsored the forty-nine-day, seventy-five-stop flight, which included sixteen crashes.

After the concept of a nonstop flight was accepted by the US Air Service, a suitable aircraft had to be selected. At the time, the best aircraft available was deemed to be the German-built Junkers JL-6 powered by a 185 hp BMW engine. However, that craft would need to be extensively modified. Furthermore, it not only was the product of a foreign manufacturer; it was of German manufacture. This was close enough after the end of World War I that feelings toward Germany still ran high. Thus the search continued and finally settled on the Fokker F-IV. It, too, was of foreign design. It was built in the Netherlands by aircraft legend Anthony Fokker, who had built many innovative combat aircraft for the Germans. However, with some American modifications and the installation of the iconic American Liberty engine—a 400 hp type V-12 power plant—it would pass as an American aircraft.

As in all taxpayer-financed projects, a justification for the costly mission was needed. According to Louis Casey, who in 1964 authored a ninety-page booklet entitled *Smithsonian Annals of Flight*, Volume 1, Number 1, "The First Nonstop Coast-to-Coast Flight and the Historic T-2 Airplane," the flight was promoted by the Air Service this way: "In summary, the purpose of the flight was to test the new Army transport model T-2 monoplane, to test the Liberty motor and ascertain the longest time it could run in actual service, and, further, to test the endurance of pilots. Finally, it was hoped that a successful flight would be positive proof that the airplane, for purposes of commerce as well as war, had come to stay."

A year prior to the flight, a Fokker F-IV from Europe arrived in a shipping crate at McCook Field to begin its transformation. The first engineering was on the unassembled wing section to determine what load the wing could carry and the aircraft's possible ceiling. This was vital because the aircraft had to carry an unusually large load of fuel and would cross high mountains along its journey. After these tests proved successful, numerous modifications were made. Some of these were substantial. For example, the original F-IV had single pilot controls. Because the nonstop flight would require two pilots, a second set of controls had to be added.

In the wing was installed a 410-gallon fuel tank. Also, 185-gallon and 40-gallon fuel tanks were installed in the fuselage. Numerous other items were added or refitted. They ranged from adding a 10-gallon water tank and improved Goodyear tires to re-covering the entire fuselage. One of the biggest modifications, of course, was the replacement of its original power plant with the 400 hp Liberty engine.

Most of these modifications and test analyses were overseen at McCook Field by Lt. Earnest W. Dichman. He was to be the copilot on the flight, along with Oakley Kelly. However, Dichman was sidelined after a near-fatal aircraft accident. His replacement was McCook Field's record-setting high-altitude pilot John Macready. The two pilots, by the way, would make their way across the United States by following Rand McNally roadmaps, the standard manuals for all cross-country flights.

The redesignated T-2 (Transport 2) now had an impressive gross weight of 10,850 pounds, of which 687 gallons of fuel constituted 40 percent. Its wingspan was just under 80 feet, and its overall length was 49 feet. Fuel selection was interesting. According to Casey in his 1964 booklet, tests on fuel samples at McCook Field "indicated that natural California fuels had an antiknock characteristic equivalent to twenty percent benzyl added to the fuels refined in the East. This was an early application of what we now familiarly refer to as the octane rating of fuel." After this was discovered in the McCook Field laboratory, the flight crew insisted that fuel for the flight come from California.

In order to take advantage of the prevailing westerly winds that exist above the United States, the nonstop attempt was started from San Diego. This west-to-east direction would give favorable tail winds but would require crossing mountains in the early stages of the flight before fuel had been burned off. To avoid the high terrain when fully loaded, the plane would have to be flown an additional 360 miles. On a first attempt out of San Diego, a return was made because of low fog. Prior to landing back in San Diego, it was decided to salvage something from the failed attempt by setting a local endurance record for time aloft. This they did at just over thirty-five hours. This record-making flight also proved the airworthiness of the T-2.

A month later, the weather forecast appeared favorable for a second west-to-east attempt. The weather cooperated for this attempt, but the engine did not. The flight had to be terminated near Indianapolis. After replacing the engine, it was decided to change the direction of the flight. The next attempt would be made from east to west, starting in New York. By reversing direction, the craft would weigh less upon reaching the western mountains and a higher altitude could be attained. This would allow a more direct route for the flight.

Prior to the third cross-country nonstop attempt, the T-2 set another endurance record out of McCook Field. This time the time aloft was pushed to more than thirty-six hours. The official observer for this endurance flight was Orville Wright, who frequently was called to McCook as an official observer.

The third and successful attempt departed Roosevelt Field, New York, on May 2, 1923. The flight lasted just under twenty-seven hours, landing at Rockwell Field, San Diego, California, on May 3. The highest altitude reached was 10,500 feet. The average ground speed was 92 mph. The T-2 was flown back to McCook Field before being flown farther east to Washington, DC, to be placed on permanent display at the National Air Museum on the Washington Mall.

FRENCH NIEUPORT

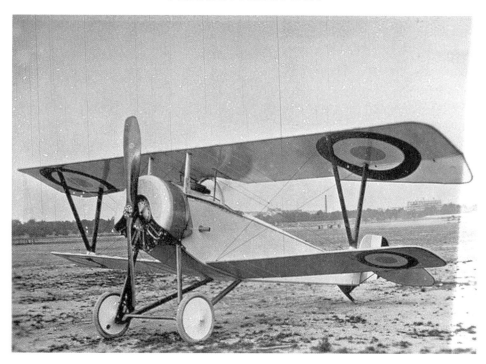

A French Nieuport fighter. *Photo from the Bob Williams collection in the American Aviation Historical Society archives*

Each aircraft based at McCook Field during the ten years it operated was assigned a project number. The total was 465 aircraft—including five Nieuports. The project number or "P" number was painted on each plane's vertical stabilizer. Today, an aviation historian looking at old military aircraft photographs can easily identify any aircraft assigned to the Air Service Engineering Division, McCook Field.

For example, the list published in the October 1956 issue of the *American Aviation Historical Journal* shows that P-1 was a Curtiss JN-4B and P-145 was a German Junker JL-6. During World War I, many Allied aircraft were shipped to McCook Field to be tested for speed, rate of climb, stability, and maneuverability. After the Armistice, many aircraft flown by the Germans and other defeated powers found their way to McCook Field for similar evaluation.

The journal list shows that of the five French Nieuports shipped to McCook and flight tested, P-10 was a Nieuport 16 that was wrecked in March 1918. The P-11 was also a model 16, and after being tested, it was sent to salvage in 1921. P-38 was a Nieuport 28 that was wrecked in May 1920 while being flown by Louis Meister, one of several civilian test pilots employed at McCook. P-153 was a model 27 that eventually was retired and shipped to a museum. P-155 was another Model 28, scrapped in 1924.

These Nieuports were products of a French company founded by Edouard Nieuport in 1908. It remained in business till 1937. In 1909, the first of many models took to the air. But it was the design of their second model, which made its first flight later in the year, that marked a new era in aircraft design. That model featured new comfort for pilots of the era: While a pilot still sat in an open cockpit, the fuselage was enclosed. This shielded an aviator from most of the elements, at least from the chest down.

Manufacturing difficulties soon arose for Nieuport in the form of underperforming engines. In response, the company decided to manufacture its own. A year after its first plane was unveiled, the company started producing a two-cylinder, 28 hp engine. It proved successful. It eventually was mated with the Nieuport II, which was produced for a few years. Considering the minimal horsepower of this engine, the plane remarkably set a speed record in 1910 of just under 75 mph. A year later, two Nieuport IIs were fitted with engines that increased horsepower to 70 and 100, respectively, and won several air races.

The Nieuport II had a design innovation. It was equipped with what might be called a joystick. The stick gave the pilot control of the plane's yaw and pitch. Foot pedals controlled wing warping, which was used to roll the aircraft. This is unlike today's aircraft with a joystick, which gives a pilot control of roll and pitch along with rudder pedals for controlling yaw. This might seem odd to a modern pilot, but wing warping for roll was a major part of the Wright brothers' very broad patent granted in 1906. Several years later, the aileron—a French word for "little wing"—was introduced for roll. The introduction of the aileron was partly to get around the Wright brothers' patent, which was contested in court till 1917.

In 1911, three years after founding the company that bears his name, Nieuport was killed in an aircraft accident. Sixteen months later, his brother, who had carried on the work, was killed in another aircraft accident. The company's leadership was taken over in 1914 by Gustave Delage, who began work on a racing biplane of sesquiplane design. That wing design marked all Nieuport variants through Model 27. Model 28 was redesigned to have two wings of equal chord and also replaced the earlier version's "V" wing struts with two solid-looking, wide wing struts. It was this model, the 28, that was used by the US Air Service upon its arrival in France during the war. According to the not-for-profit Warbird Heritage Foundation of Waukegan, Illinois, the US purchased 297 model 28s. America's top ace, Capt. Eddie Rickenbacker, and Canada's premier ace, Billy Bishop, both flew Nieuport fighters in some of their first kills. It also is worth noting that Quentin Roosevelt, son of our twenty-sixth president, was killed while flying a Nieuport 28.

During World War I, numerous Nieuport variations were flown in combat by French and American pilots and fliers from some other Allied countries. Most wartime Nieuport models were powered by a rotary engine. In such an engine, the crankshaft remains stationary when in operation with the entire crankcase and attached cylinders rotating as a single unit. The goal behind the design was enhanced cylinder cooling. Until the mid-1930s, engine cooling was a constant problem, and many clever solutions were attempted.

Several authentic Nieuport aircraft are on static display in aero museums, but none are in flying condition. One full-sized replica of the Nieuport 17 can be flown, and several organizations are in the process of building and flying other replicas.

DOUGLAS WORLD CRUISER

One of five Douglas World Cruisers with seven of the eight flight crew members. Leigh Wade is third from right, wearing goggles. *Army Air Service photo from the American Aviation Historical Society archives*

There are many significant firsts in aviation history. The first to cross the Atlantic, the first to cross the Pacific from mainland United States to Australia, the first to fly over the poles, and numerous other benchmark flights. They each are special accomplishments and required courage, planning, and hard work. A feat that might qualify as extra special was the first flight to circumnavigate the globe—an "around the world" flight.

The flight was accomplished by the US Air Service, and much of the meticulous planning and preparation occurred at McCook Field. McCook also loaned several of its pilots as well as several skilled mechanics to the effort for the better part of a year. The aircraft chosen for this record flight in 1924 was the Douglas World Cruiser.

Though some books refer to four Cruisers being involved in the flight, the count actually came to five. Because the undertaking was to be an "America did it first" moment, the aircraft were named after major American cities—the "Seattle," "Chicago," "New Orleans," and "Boston," with a backup plane tagged the "Boston II."

In 1923, the Air Service announced it was interested in purchasing five aircraft to attempt an around-the-world flight. One of the craft would be used for testing and flight training at McCook Field prior to the flight. The remaining four would actually make the flight. The thinking behind the multiple-plane approach was that, while not all might survive, at least one would make history by completing the journey. Several aircraft manufactures showed interest in developing an aircraft for the long flight.

However, a two-year-old aircraft manufacturer in Santa Monica, California, headed by Donald Douglas, proposed using an airplane his company already had in production and could be modified for the mission. By using a proven design, the timeline would be shortened. That fact was not lost on the Air Service, because other countries were considering sponsoring an around-the-world flight. Time was of the essence if the US hoped to be first.

The proposed plane was the Douglas DT. This aircraft was a two-place biplane designed and operated as a torpedo bomber. Douglas Aircraft sold dozens of the model to the US Navy, as well as to several foreign navies. Ninety DTs were built during its production life, which ceased in 1929. After a contract was agreed upon, five Douglas DTs were taken directly from the production line. The work began to modify each into a Douglas World Cruiser, or DWC.

One modification was the installation of a 420 hp Liberty L-12A engine. Another was revamping of the fuel system. The system was redesigned by a young Jack Northrup, who later would head his own aircraft company that produced innovative military test and production aircraft. Northrup's fuel tank modification involved using six fuel tanks, which increased the fuel capacity to 644 gallons, nearly 2 tons of fuel. The entire fuselage of the DT was strengthened, and a modified wing was incorporated, along with a larger rudder.

The one component that did not have to be redesigned to a large degree was the DWC undercarriage. Because the flight would require landing on both land and water, several conversions from wheels to floats and back to wheels were required. The DT already had this capability because of its naval operations. The World Cruiser had a wingspan of 50 feet, a length of 39 feet, and a height of 15 feet with floats attached. Its gross weight was 8,000 pounds with floats attached, the floats adding 800 pounds. With floats in place, the top speed was 100 mph.

The prototype DWC was delivered for tests to McCook Field in November 1923. After successful testing, the Air Service ordered readying of the remaining four Cruisers. The last of the modified craft was delivered in March of the following year. For four weeks, the crew of each plane—a pilot and copilot/mechanic—practiced at McCook Field in the prototype and eventual flight training aircraft.

The first week of April 1924, the four World Cruisers departed the Seattle area westward on the ultimate adventure. Three weeks later, the lead Cruiser, the "Seattle," struck a mountain covered in dense fog on the Aleutian Peninsula. After ten days of hiking down the mountain, the two crew members found safety in an Alaskan fishing village. The other World Cruisers continued westward. In the course of their journey, the crews experienced time-consuming political receptions during stopovers, constant maintenance issues including multiple engine replacements, and several near-death flying experiences.

On the final leg of the journey, near the Faroe Islands, the "Boston" was lost when it was forced by engine problems to land on rough seas. It took on water while being towed behind a naval vessel and sank. Both crew members were saved. The two remaining Cruisers flew on to the eastern coast of North America, landing in Nova Scotia. After some hurried modifications at McCook Field, the prototype DWC was christened "Boston II" and flown east to join up with the two surviving original Douglas World Cruisers. The three planes then continued west to the starting point of Seattle, where the six-month adventure culminated in success. The 24,000-mile flight logged 371 hours in the air, with an average speed of just under 70 mph. All eight crew members who participated in any part of the circumnavigation feat were awarded the Distinguished Service Cross.

After completion of this flight, the Air Service contracted with Douglas for six additional World Cruisers, minus the extra fuel capacity and with two machine guns mounted in the rear cockpit. These six aircraft were initially designated the Douglas Observation Seaplane or DOS. All in all, the success of the world flight made Douglas a household name. The company did not waste the opportunity. It adopted the motto "First Around the World—First the World Around." Douglas Aircraft, of course, went on to produce such venerable craft as the DC-3 transport and the DC-8 jet airliner.

The DWC "Chicago" is on permanent static display in the National Air and Space Museum in Washington, DC. The "New Orleans" is on permanent static display in the Museum of Flying at the Santa Monica, California, airport, very near to where it was born. The "Boston II" was disassembled for unknown reasons. A few of its parts, including its data plate, are in a private collection, and a piece of its fabric is in an aviation museum in Illinois.

Author's note: Shortly after the conclusion of the renowned flight, world adventurer, writer, and radio personality Lowell Thomas contracted to write the complete saga of the adventure, *The First World Flight*, as published by the Houghton Mifflin Company in 1925.

BARLING BOMBER

The Barling Bomber in flight. *Army Air Service photo from the American Aviation Historical archives*

The wingspan of the huge plane was 120 feet, and its length was 65 feet. It stood almost three stories high and weighed just over 21 tons. It was powered by a half-dozen Liberty L-12A engines, each producing 420 hp. The plane had three wings, four rudders, and ten wheels. When in full military operation, it carried a crew of two pilots and five gunners manning 30-caliber weaponry. In the mid-1920s, it was described as "massive," "gigantic," "colossal," and a "monster." When the giant craft flew, it was the largest aircraft in the world. Its final cost, after a series of overruns, came in at slightly more than a half-million dollars. The flamboyant Gen. Billy Mitchell, who generally got his way, pushed for the plane to be built, so it was. But, in the end, only one of the aircraft was constructed.

The official Air Service name for this airplane was the Witteman-Lewis XNBL-1 (Experimental Night Bomber, Long Range), but everyone called it simply "the Barling Bomber."

It was General Mitchell who approached British aircraft designer Walter H. Barling with an appeal for a heavy bomber capable of carrying a large load of bombs, enough bombs to sink a battleship. That was General Mitchell's specific intended use for the weapon. Barling had in his resume another huge bomber he had designed for the Royal Aircraft Establishment in 1919. That bomber, the Tarrant Tabor, crashed on its maiden flight, killing the crew. Post accident analysis determined the Tabor was too heavy and imbalanced. Because the Tabor nosed over on its fatal takeoff roll, the flight crew of the Barling Bomber insisted it be fitted in the nose with two high-off-the-ground wheels.

Gen. Billy Mitchell leaning against the nose gear of the Barling Bomber. Aircraft designer Walter Barling is to the right. *Army Air Service photo from the American Aviation Historical Society archives*

In 1920, General Mitchell approved specifications for two prototypes of the bomber. Barling then resided in the United States, and the Witteman-Lewis Company of Teterboro,

New Jersey, was awarded the contract to supply the aircraft's components. Assembly was in Dayton, Ohio, under the direction of the Air Service Engineering Division at McCook Field. Therefore, all components were shipped by rail to McCook Field. As assembly began, it was discovered that some parts did not fit. After rainy days, rainwater became trapped in the wood and fabric wings. Finally, it was decided to move all components to a larger Dayton-area airfield, the old Wilbur Wright Field in Riverside, Ohio. There, a large hangar was constructed at immense cost to facilitate assembly.

As construction of the first bomber progressed, so did the cost. In late 1921, Congress started looking at what some then termed "Mitchell's Folly." Some of the plane's performance statistics were not impressive. Yes, it could carry a bomb load of 5,000 lbs., but its cruising speed was barely more than 60 mph. It had a maximum range of 170 miles. The plane could only reach an altitude of 7,500 feet, and that was if all six of its marginally reliable Liberty engines were fully functioning. In the end, funding for the second prototype was cut.

After the construction of the lone Barling Bomber, flight testing followed. This assignment was delegated to two veteran McCook Field test pilots, Harold R. Harris and Muir S. Fairchild. Barling did join the flight crew on its first flight. The date was August 22, 1923. The massive craft rolled 960 feet in thirteen seconds before lifting off Wright Field's grass runway.

This is how Walter Barling later recorded his reaction to the flight, as reported by C. V. Glines in a History Net article:

> You can perhaps imagine after these many years of intense study, repeated discouragement, worry, nervous tension, and hopeful expectation, my response to hearing the cheery call of Lieutenant Harris, "Let's go!"
>
> I was not anxious about the ship's ability to fly. It has been observed that the engine mounts were absolutely rigid even at low engine speed, which tests this feature better than higher speeds. We knew, too, from previous tests that the wing structure and fuselage could be relied upon for strength and rigidity. With these points in its favor, the only uncertainty lay in the controls and landing gear. As for the latter, I had great faith in the oleo legs.
>
> I stationed myself in the rear upper gun cockpit. From here I could see each of the engines, the wings, fuselage and tail. We made the turn at the takeoff point. I could not but marvel at the ease with which the great ship made the turn. She can turn on the ground on an axis inside of a wingtip and almost on one undercarriage. I was a bit worried, however, that the abrupt turn would injure the skid.
>
> From my lofty aerie, I surveyed the structure of my gigantic plane and was glad that I had been given this part to write in the romantic manuscript of human accomplishment.

There were further test flights, and the plane set several records for time aloft with record amounts of load carried to attitudes above 5,000 feet. It also amazed crowds when it flew west to St. Louis, Missouri, for the International Air Meets of 1923 and 1924. It was during the preparation for flying the Barling east—that is, across the Appalachian Mountains to Washington, DC—that its undeniable shortcomings hove fully into view. A planned flight to Washington's Bolling Field to show off the plane was delayed when concern arose about the bomber's ability to hold altitude over the West Virginia mountains if one or more of its engines failed.

Walter Barling was impressed with his namesake bomber, but in short order, the aircraft lost favor with the Air Service. It made its last flight in 1925. For all its promise, all its cost and man-hours of development, it flew for less than two years. The plane was dismantled and its components put in storage at Dayton's Fairfield depot. In 1929, Maj. Henry "Hap" Arnold became Fairfield Depot's commanding officer. In discovering the bomber's components in a warehouse, he ordered them burned. The airplane's lack of success was an embarrassment to the Air Service. Today, one of the few remaining components, two wheels from its complex oleo landing gear, can be seen at the US Air Force Museum at Wright-Patterson Air Force Base, in Ohio.

MARTIN BOMBERS

A Martin Bomber over Washington, DC. *Army Air Service photo from the American Aviation Historical Society archives*

Over the last hundred years, the United States has produced a long line of bombers. These bombers have proven superior in terms of their technology and durability. Aircraft such as the Boeing model 17 and model 29 heavy bombers helped stop the Axis powers in World War II. Later, heavy bombers like the Convair B-36, appropriately nicknamed the "Peacemaker," and the Boeing model 52 helped deter belligerent countries from threatening the United States and its allies. Today, North American Rockwell B1-B and Northrop B-2 bombers continue in that role. Where did this line begin? Let's look at the first of the American-designed and American-built bombers—the Martin bombers.

When the United States joined other Allied powers in World War I in Europe, the US Army Air Service had neither bombers nor aviation weaponry. Though some DH-4s and a few other single-engine aircraft were modified to drop a bomb or two—with some pilots hand-dropping small bombs from the open cockpit—they were not designed to carry and drop a heavy load. US ally Great Britain had the Handley Page Type O bomber, which was a large plane for its day. Another ally, Italy, had a variety of Caproni heavy bombers. On the other side of the battle line, Germany had the Gotha. That heavy bomber carried a load much greater than anything the allies could put in the air. The Germans used this bomber to execute nighttime bombing raids on London, with considerable loss of life. Twenty-two years later, such German bombing recurred.

The US Army Air Service wanted an American-built aircraft designed for no other purpose than bombing. Toward the end of World War I, the Glenn L. Martin Company of Santa Ana, California, offered its design, the GMB (Glenn Martin Bomber) or MB-1. This biplane had a crew of three in open cockpits. It featured twin vertical rear stabilizers with attached rudders and four-wheel landing gear. The wingspan was an impressive 71 feet. Its maximum payload (crew, fuel, and bombs) was 3,500 pounds. The MB-1 had a cruise speed of 92 mph and a range of slightly less than 400 miles.

Powering the craft were two of the standard engines of the day, the 400 hp liquid-cooled Liberty. Air Service brass liked what they saw on paper and issued a contract to Martin for six of the planes. The first was delivered one month before the end of the war. Three more were delivered before hostilities ended, and contracts for the remaining two bombers were canceled.

A ten-passenger conversion of the Martin Bomber. *Army Air Service photo from the American Aviation Historical Society archives*

After the cancellation, three more eventually were delivered, though modified for different missions, according to a July 1995 issue of *Skyways*. The GMT (Glenn Martin

Transcontinental) was modified for an increased range of 1,500 miles, a long distance for that era of flight. The GMC (Glenn Martin Cannon) sported a 37 mm cannon in the nose. The GMP (Glenn Martin Passenger) was a ten-passenger enclosed transport. This aircraft was later given the designation T-1. The six surviving MB-1s were modified and operated by the Postal Service. In all, twenty MB-1s were built, including ten for the US Navy.

In the fall of 1920, the Martin Company introduced a somewhat improved version of the MB-1. The Air Service designated it the NBS-1 (Night Bomber-Short Range), but it's commonly called the MB-2. This bomber had a larger payload by 1,500 pounds but also had a slower top air speed. The MB-2 required a crew of four, utilized Liberty engines that produced an additional 20 horsepower, and rode on two wheels. An outstanding feature of the MB-2 was its folding wings that made storage in tight hangers easier. Some 130 MB-2s were produced, the first twenty by Martin and the remainder by three manufacturers that won low-bidder contracts: Curtiss, LWF Engineering, and Aeromarine Plane and Motor Company.

The last twenty of the fifty that Curtiss bid on and built were powered by engines equipped with General Electric turbo superchargers. Though problematic at times, the superchargers allowed the MB-2 to reach altitudes in excess of 25,000 feet. In June and July 1921, the MB-2 took part in bombing exercises off of the Virginia Capes. These well-publicized exercises were part of General Billy Mitchell's staging to show that battleships—the pride of every fleet—could be sunk from the air.

Numerous McCook Field pilots took part in these exercises—some as pilots of the Martin bombers, others transporting material to airfields supporting the joint US Navy-Army mission. In addition, McCook Field research and development was conducted on the MB-2s based there, in an effort to improve its delivery of bombs. The bombing exercise was a huge success for Mitchell's cause, especially after his bombers sank the heavy battleship *Ostfriesland*, a former German man-of-war surrendered to the United States at the end of the war. In all, four former German warships were sunk. The exercises showed the United States and the world the critical need for bombers in an air arsenal, as explained in some detail on the Naval History and Heritage Command website.

The MB-2 remained the frontline bomber of the Army Air Service for nine years. Today, a surviving MB-2 is on static display at the National Museum of the United States Air Force at Wright-Patterson Air Force Base.

S.E.5 AND S.E.5A FIGHTER

It is commonplace for allies to share technology during times of war, when they are fighting a common enemy, and later during peacetime. The thinking is that though one country may be sharing a coveted advancement with another country, the sharing ultimately may occur both ways. During World War I and after the conflict, several allies, notably Great Britain, France, and Italy, shared their aircraft technology with the United States. After the war—and after the United States started producing advanced technological aircraft itself—the flow of information started reversing itself.

The foreign aircraft shared with the US Army Air Service were test-flown and evaluated. Some of what was gleaned from the evaluations was engineered into later American designs. A listing of aircraft based at McCook Field shows that over several years, no fewer than nine British S.E.5 fighter aircraft of various models were evaluated in depth by the field's test pilots and engineers. Two of those S.E.5s were at McCook at the height of US involvement in the war.

The S.E.5—Scout Experimental 5—was a wartime product of the Royal Aircraft Factory, a British research establishment. That organization-built aircraft of its own design under the support of the UK Ministry of Defense. This was similar to the relationship between McCook Field and the US Department of War, today's US Department of Defense. During the early years, the Engineering Division at McCook Field designed and manufactured military aircraft. This was very unpopular with the established military aircraft manufacturers of the day. They felt it would force them out of business. Several congressional hearings were held in the early 1920s, and it was decided that having a strong private aircraft industry was beneficial to the country's security. At that point, the US military got out of the aircraft building business but continued its research and development activities.

Great Britain had been at war for more than two years when, in November 1916, the first prototype of the S.E.5 took to the air. The first two prototype craft were involved in accidents, one resulting in a fatality. An investigation determined the aircraft's wing design was faulty. After modifications, full production began. Following the production of seventy-seven S.E.5s, an advanced model, the S.E.5a, was produced with an improved engine. Its water-cooled French-built Hispano-Suiza V-8 power plant produced 200 hp. However, this engine proved problematic and later models were powered by a 200 hp Wolseley Viper. Seven aircraft manufacturers were contracted to build this aircraft. A one-thousand-plane contract was awarded to the Curtiss Aeroplane and Motor Company, located in Buffalo, New York. However, the war ended. Of the planes ordered, only one was constructed.

The S.E.5 and S.E.5a had several unique physical characteristics that are obvious in a profile view. The upper wing had a very pronounced dihedral. But even with this low bend in the middle of the upper wing, the pilot had difficulty seeing over the elevated wing. Because of this design, the pilot seat in the open cockpit had to be raised. Because one fix often leads to other issues, the pilot's head was subject to the craft's slipstream, so a higher-than-usual windscreen was installed. Another issue resulted from the cockpit's placement midway along the length of the fuselage. This positioning resulted in a vision problem while taxiing. A pilot couldn't see over the engine cowling.

Also, placed above the upper wing was either a single .303 Vickers or a .303 Lewis machine gun, which was synchronized to fire through two-bladed or four-bladed propellers. When not to be utilized as a fighter, the airplane's fuselage had attachments so it could carry up to four 25-pound bombs. In the spring of 1918, one S.E.5 was extensively modified, and that plane was given the designation S.E.5b. By the end of production, 5,200 S.E.5s of all variations were built.

The Royal Aircraft Factory S.E.5a biplane proved itself one of the fastest airplanes in World War I, with a top speed of 138 mph. It earned a repetition among pilots as a stable and very maneuverable aircraft in combat. Aviation author Robert Jackson has written that this aircraft has been described as "the Spitfire of World War I." That is a huge compliment indeed.

During World War I, several US Army and Navy units were supplied the S.E.5a for combat. At the war's conclusion, the Royal Air Force replaced the S.E.5a fleet that had served them so well. Canadian pilot Billy Bishop recorded seventy-two victories flying the plane, South African pilot Andrew Beauchamp-Proctor scored fifty-four victories with the S.E.5a, and British pilot Edward Mannock downed sixty-one enemy aircraft flying one, before he himself was killed over France in July 1918. After the war, surplus S.E.5a airplanes saw further service in multiple air forces around the world, including several in South America.

At least one original S.E.5a is known to be in airworthy condition today. Several original planes are in museums around the world. Flyable reproductions are more plentiful today and have been utilized, sometimes not with historical accuracy, in motion pictures.

PACKARD-LE PERE LUSAC-11

To say the United States was not prepared for its late entry into World War I in April 1917 would be an understatement. A total lack of military armament was most evident in its combat-ready aircraft. None of the fifty-plus aircraft that the Signal Corps had on hand could be shipped to France for military missions.

To remedy this dire situation, the French sent a contingent of engineers to the United States to assist in the development of combat aircraft and their quick construction. Aeronautical engineer Capt. Georges LePere of the French air service was a member of that commission. He was given the important task of working along with McCook Field's Engineering Division to design a two-seat escort fighter. The result was the LUSAC—LePere United States Army Combat—aircraft. The LUSAC-11 stagger-wing biplane of wood and fabric construction weighed in at 3,745 pounds when fully loaded. It utilized a 420 hp, water-cooled Liberty L-12 engine.

A distinguishing feature of this craft was a radiator fared into the upper wing. Designed as a combat aircraft, it had two synchronized machine guns. One was fired through the propeller by the pilot, and two more were operated by the observer from the rear cockpit. Its maximum speed at sea level was 133 mph. In mid-May 1918, the prototype of this new design made its inaugural flight at McCook Field.

Though this first flight had a slight glitch because of human error, resulting in a forced landing, further test flights proved successful and the US military was impressed. The brass were so impressed that several thousand of the craft were initially ordered by the government from Packard, Brewster, and Fisher Body Corporation. Then the Armistice was signed. This brought about peace but also resulted in the cancellation of most military contracts, including those for the LePere. Only thirty of the aircraft were built, twenty-seven of them delivered by Packard. The other three were built with a 420 hp Bugatti-16 engine and were designated the LUSAC-21.

In fact, the cancellation of contracts for this aircraft might have occurred anyway for another reason. Just prior to the end of the war, two LUSAC-11s were sent to France for evaluation as combat aircraft. An aircraft performing well stateside did not necessarily translate into similar performance in the field. The plane's evaluation in France was not favorable, and the aircraft was never used in combat.

A supercharger installed on the side of an aircraft. *Army Air Service photo from the American Aviation Historical Society archives*

After the European war concluded, the Le Pere LUSAC-11 had much more success setting altitude records. Dr. Sanford Alexander Moss (1872–1946) of the General Electric Company designed and tested the first turbosupercharger. With this device attached to a Liberty-type V-12 engine, Moss did his initial testing at ground level—at the top of Pikes Peak in Colorado. Experiencing success, Moss decided it was time to attach the device to an aircraft for high altitude evaluation. The plane chosen was the LUSAC-11, and the launch site was McCook Field.

Maj. Rudolf Schroeder and later Lt. John Macready both used this aircraft for high-altitude research and, in so doing, established several altitude records. Mating the LePere aircraft with the General Electric turbosupercharger proved beneficial. In September 1921, this turbosupercharger-modified LePere flew to an altitude of more than 34,000 feet, nearly twice the ceiling of the LePere as originally designed. For his development work on the turbosupercharger, Moss was awarded the Collier trophy in 1940.

Today, only one LePere exists. It is on static display at the National Museum of the Air Force at Wright-Patterson Air Force base, just a few miles from where it was initially tested and where several altitude records were set.

SOPWITH CAMEL

British-designed-and-manufactured Sopwith Camel. *Photo from the Gerald Balzer collection in the American Aviation Historical Society archives*

Snoopy wears his goggles and flowing white scarf. He's perched high atop his doghouse. In his vivid imagination, the year is 1918. He's a British fighter pilot in France during World War I, and he's on the prowl for his archenemy. Suddenly, he and his foe tangle in an intense dogfight. Twists and turns ensue, and the end is always the same: Snoopy meets his doom at the hands of the Red Baron. One can only wonder what Baron Manfred von Richthofen, the real "Red Baron," would have thought about having his exploits portrayed in a comic strip called *Peanuts*.

Cartoonist Charles M. Schulz (1922–2000) always portrayed Snoopy flying, in his mind, a Sopwith Camel. The Camel was not an imaginary aircraft, of course. It was a famed British fighter and one of the most famous of all aircraft flown in the war. Nearly 5,500 were constructed by the British manufacturer Sopwith Aviation Company. Camel pilots scored more victories, almost 1,300, in this aircraft than any other fighter used by the allies. Though it was not the easiest plane to control, in the hands of an experienced aviator, it was deadly.

In the October 1956 *Journal of the American Aviation Historical Society*, three Sopwith aircraft were listed as being based at McCook Field for evaluation. Each plane was assigned a "P," or project number, meaning they were in some sort of testing program. Project number 75, for example, was a Sopwith Salamander. Project number 149 was a Sopwith Snipe. Project number 99 was the only Sopwith Camel at McCook. Records indicate that a Sargeant Maden was killed flying this plane at McCook in October 1920.

The Camel was designed to replace two aircraft used in combat by the RAF. The first was the Sopwith Pup, which proved inferior in battling German aircraft. The second plane replaced by the Camel was the French Nieuport 17, also shown to be inadequate against German fighters. In early 1914, Herbert Smith joined Sopwith and became chief designer by the end of the year. He was asked to design a faster plane that could support heavier armament. The resulting aircraft flew just before Christmas 1916, and five months later, Sopwith contracted to mass-produce the plane.

The Camel originally was powered by a 130 hp, Clerget 9B, nine-cylinder, air-cooled, rotary piston engine. As production ensued, other engines of comparable horsepower were utilized. The Camel had a top speed of 113 mph and weighed 1,453 pounds, giving it a useful load (pilot, fuel, and armament) of 523 pounds. It could fly 300 miles without refueling and could reach an altitude of 19,000 feet. The plane carried two .303 Vickers machine guns that fired through the craft's two-bladed wooden propeller. Beneath the fuselage, the Camel could carry four 20-pound bombs.

"Camel" was never the aircraft's official name. Pilots and ground crews named it such. Because the aircraft was designed to replace the Sopwith Pup, personnel first called it the Big Pup. Later, a metal fairing was placed over the Vickers machine gun breeches to prevent freezing at high altitudes. In profile view, this fairing gave the plane a hump, which led wags to christen the plane a "camel," and the Sopwith Camel is what unofficially the aircraft will ever be known.

Another physical characteristic of this plane was two wings of different dihedral. To simplify construction, a Sopwith factory worker suggested having no dihedral in the upper wing and 5 degrees of dihedral in the lower wing. This was very evident when viewing the Camel from the front.

Because of design idiosyncrasies and wicked center-of-gravity issues, a two-seat Camel was required for training new pilots in the craft. Lt. Col. L. A. Strange helped train pilots. In his book *Recollections of an Airman*, he wrote about the difficulty young pilots experienced controlling the plane. "In spite of the care we took, Camels continually spun out of control when flown by pupils on their first solos. At length, with the assistance of Lt. Morgan, who managed our workshops, I took the main tank out of several Camels and replaced it with a smaller one, which enabled us to fit in dual controls." This modification helped reduce the casualty rate during advanced fighter training.

The Camel became a favorite combat plane. Maj. Billy Barker was the most decorated serviceman in Canadian history, including earning the Victoria Cross—equivalent to the US Medal of Honor. Barker scored most of his forty-six aircraft and balloon victories flying a Camel. The victories occurred in a one-year period, ending in September 1918. During the war, a joke went around that in a dogfight, the Camel offered pilots a choice of "a wooden cross, the Red Cross or a Victoria Cross."

The Camel was adapted to various missions. Several naval squadrons were equipped with Camels, which were launched from platforms mounted on capital ships. Some were flown from the earliest British aircraft carriers. One of the more interesting experiments conducted in mid-1918 was the use of a Camel as a parasitic fighter: the plane would be flown to and attach itself to a trapeze dangling from the underside of a dirigible. When London was being bombed at night by German Gotha Bombers, the Camel served well as a home defense night fighter. However, as the war drew on, the Camel was not able to keep up with the latest German aircraft. At that point, it was given a new role of attacking ground troops.

During World War I, fifty Royal Air Force squadrons, along with nine Royal Naval Air Service squadrons, were equipped with Camels. Five US Army Air Service squadrons and the US Navy also flew the Camel. In all, the Sopwith Camel was utilized by fourteen nations. After the 1918 armistice, Great Britain and several other allies—the United States was not among them—continued fighting well into early 1920 in the Russian civil war. The British RAF deployed the Camel to that country.

As of this writing, there are possibly eight original Camels in existence. All are on static display, except for one in New Zealand that has been restored to airworthy condition. Two are on static display in the United States; one at the National Air and Space Museum Udvar-Hazy Center in Chantilly, Virginia, and one at the National Naval Aviation Museum in Pensacola, Florida. Replicas in flying condition are common.

During the Great War, Thomas Octave Murdoch Sopwith's company built more than 16,000 aircraft. Subcontractors also built the plane. Murdoch lived an exciting and full life, in and out of aviation, and passed away in 1989 at the age of 101.

MB-3 AND MB-3A

The Thomas-Morse MB-3. *Boeing Aircraft Corporation photo from the American Aviation Historical Society archives*

For a period of three years in the early 1920s, the primary fighter aircraft of the US Air Service was the Thomas-Morse MB-3 and the Boeing MB-3A. By 1925, both were considered obsolete, and a phaseout from active service began. A total of 265 of these aircraft were built.

The MB-3 was a single-seat biplane and with a wingspan of 26 feet and a length of 20 feet. Its maximum gross weight was 2,539 pounds, and its top speed was 140 mph. It was powered by a single Wright-Hispano H water-cooled engine rated at 300 hp. Being a fighter-type aircraft, it did not carry bombs but featured forward-firing, propeller-synchronized guns of either .30 or .50 caliber. According to a comprehensive study published in the *American Aviation Historical Society Journal* in October 1956, nine MB-3s and MB-3As were based at McCook Field. However, because the craft was the primary fighter in the Air Service arsenal for three years and filled out squadron fleets at military airfields in surrounding states, many visiting MB-3s frequented McCook.

In the aforementioned AAHS study, the aircraft that carried project number P-313 is of interest. This was a Thomas-Morse trainer of unknown model. Being a trainer, it more than likely was a two-seat version. The report indicated the aircraft was shipped to Brooks Field, Texas, in January 1924, where it was "not accepted by the government." That suggests that it was tested by McCook Field test pilots and found to not meet Air Service standards. The P-313 notation illustrates the day-to-day work that military and civilian test pilots were doing at McCook—all the ordinary testing that didn't make newspaper headlines.

During World War I, the French-built Spad XIII was a favorite of Allied pilots, and many American air aces racked up victories in the aircraft, including celebrated pilots like Eddie Rickenbacker and Frank Luke, "The Arizona Balloon Buster." Nearly 8,500 were produced. The US Air Service purchased nine hundred, and of the sixteen operational pursuit squadrons active in Europe at the time of the November 1918 Armistice, nearly all were equipped with the Spad XIII. At the end of hostilities in France, the Spad XIII was carried to America to form the backbone of the nation's pursuit fleet.

A French-designed-and-built "Spad" fighter. *Army Air Service photo from the American Aviation Historical Society archives*

Yet, many months prior to the armistice, US military leaders were looking for the Spad's replacement. A callout for design proposals was made to several American aircraft manufacturers. One stipulation was that the new design had to use the Wright-Hispano engine. B. Douglas Thomas, the chief engineer and corporate partner of the Thomas-Morse Aircraft Corporation of Ithaca, New York, submitted his design for the MB-3. Two months prior to the Armistice, his company was awarded a contract for four prototypes. Seven months later, the first MB-3 made its inaugural flight.

Tests of these prototypes did reveal minor design flaws. However, after sixteen months of further refinements, the military was overall impressed with the plane's performance, and in mid-1920 awarded a contract to Thomas-Morse for fifty additional planes. Further testing at McCook Field produced more refinements and the MB-3A resulted. This model was easily identifiable because it featured a radiator mounted on each side of the fuselage instead of a single radiator mounted in the upper wing.

The Air Service wanted two hundred of the MB-3A versions and called for competing bids from Thomas-Morse and rival aircraft manufacturers, as noted in the September–October 2007 issue of *Pelletier*, *Air Enthusiast*. As it turned out in the world of government bidding, the Boeing Company won the low bid. Thomas-Morse was not totally shut out of MB-3 production business, however, and supplied the military with several other versions of the aircraft. Two versions were designed for racing—the MB-6 and the MB-7—and in a third modification, the company replaced the biplane configuration with a parasol wing.

Military missions and performance specifications are always in a state of flux. Consequently, military hardware goes beyond its prime and must be replaced by a new generation. For the Thomas-Morse MB-3A, the new kids on the block were the Curtiss PW-8 and Boeing PW-9 pursuit aircraft.

Many retired MB-3A aircraft were refitted as MB-3Ms and used as advanced trainers till the end of the decade. There are no known original MB-3 or MB-3As flying today. However, detailed plans are marketed for anyone caring to build a replica.

VOUGHT VE-7 AND VE-7S

An aircraft that was flight-tested and evaluated first at the US Army Air Service Engineering Division at McCook Field during World War I later catapulted itself into a more significant role with the US Army's rival service, the US Navy. In fact, because of the success of this aircraft, the company that built it established itself as one of two leading manufacturing contractors of fighter aircraft for the navy—the other being Grumman Aircraft. This company was Lewis and Vought Corporation and the aircraft that started that multidecade relationship was the single-engine biplane VE-7.

The aircraft's historical distinction is that it was the first fighter aircraft the navy had in its fleet. In 1922, the VE-7 also made the first takeoff from a US Navy aircraft carrier. Five years prior to that noteworthy event, the US Army at McCook Field tested and evaluated the plane's performance as a two-seat training aircraft. At least one VE-7 two-seat trainer was built at McCook prior to testing.

The United States entered World War I in April 1917 totally unprepared materially, especially for an air war. A few months later, sensing a prime business opportunity, Birdseye Lewis and Chance M. Vought formed a company named Lewis and Vought Corporation. Vought had been chief engineer of the Wright Company, a commercial aviation firm created by Wilbur and Orville Wright in 1909. The partners' objective was to secure military aircraft contracts.

The VE-7 trainer was their first attempt at an Army Air Service contract. It made its maiden flight in 1917. Alluding to himself, Lewis called the aircraft "Bluebird." The design incorporated several features from European designs and used the Wright Hispano-Suiza engine. This gave the airplane a maximum speed of 106 mph, which was faster than the average training aircraft of the day. After Lewis and Vought presented an improved design redesignated the VE-8, the army awarded the company a thousand-plane contract. Then the war ended and the contract was terminated.

That's not the end of the story, however. The US Navy, which appears to have had at least one liaison officer based at McCook during the testing phase, a Lieutenant Price, now showed an interest in the VE-7. The aircraft was purchased, and in mid-1920, Navy brass received their first VE-7 to flight test. Shortly after this acquisition, production began, but not as the two-seat trainer that McCook Field had been evaluating. It was decided to modify the design and build it as a single-seat fighter—the US Navy's first fighter. The designation for the aircraft was the VE-7S.

Production work, as was US Navy policy during that time, was carried out at the Naval Aircraft Factory in Philadelphia, Pennsylvania. A total of 128 VE-7s of all variations were built. One model is of particular interest: The VE-7SF was created with the thought of enhancing chances of survival for pilots of the airplane who were forced down at sea. Stowed away in the fuselage were inflatable bags meant to keep the craft afloat.

Later, when the US Navy organized its first two fighter squadrons, they were outfitted with the VE-7S. In 1922, an improved version of the VE-7 designated the VE-9 was produced. Of the twenty-one aircraft of that model that were delivered for operational use, four were modified for deployment as observation seaplanes, which could also be catapulted from battleships. Between 1918 and 1927, thirteen different models derived from the original VE-7 were built. By 1928, the navy was phasing out all of these aircraft. There are no original VE-7 or VE-7S aircraft that were preserved. A replica of the "Bluebird" was completed in 2007.

The historic takeoff from a naval carrier occurred on October 17, 1922, on the western side of Chesapeake Bay in Maryland. Lt. Cmdr. Virgil Griffin Jr. performed the feat. The vessel was the newly commissioned USS *Langley* (CV-1), which was the Navy's first aircraft carrier. This carrier actually was a retired cargo ship that had transported coal for the energy needs of the fleet. Modifications were made to it, and a flat top was added. Lieutenant Griffin's plane was the Chance Vought Corporation VE-7. Lewis had retired and the corporation name reflected that change.

After 1928, the corporation was taken over by United Aircraft and Transportation

Corporation, but Vought continued designing naval aircraft. Even after Vought's unexpected death of natural causes in July 1930, the company continued designing aircraft for its biggest customer, the US Navy. Over the years, the company has been sold, bought, merged, resold, and renamed several times. Today, it is called Triumph Aerostructures—Vought Aircraft Division. The company, under whatever name, has produced a multitude of successful US Navy aircraft designs.

An outstanding example was the famous gull-wing F-4U. The company built 12,571 of that land- or carrier-based aircraft from 1940 till 1953. It saw tremendous utilization during World War II in the Pacific theater and later during the Korean War. Today, the still-competitive F-4U is a favorite at air races. Designing into the jet age, the company produced the tailless F-7U Cutlass that exhibited creativity in aircraft design. Several years later, the F-8U Crusader and A-7 Corsair II supersonic, carrier-based aircraft served with distinction in the Vietnam War.

LOENING PW-2

Sometimes an aircraft is remembered not because of its performance or for how many were produced or for the air battles it fought, but because it was part of a historic event. A Loening PW-2A was such a plane, and its history-making event was that it crashed.

About the plane: the PW-2 was designed and built by the Loening Aeronautical Engineering Corporation. Grover Cleveland Loening (1888–1976), the founder of the company in 1917, had the distinction of being the first person to earn a degree in aeronautical engineering from Columbia University. Prior to starting his aviation company, Loening managed the Wright Company factory in Dayton, Ohio. Though Loening designs were considered to be innovative for the day, few of his planes were mass-produced. After World War I ended, there were few dollars available for mass production. In 1920, his company designed the Loening S-1 Flying Yacht, which targeted the high-end civilian market. Of the sixteen built, nine were purchased by the US Army Air Service. This floatplane could carry four passengers plus a pilot and was propelled by a pusher engine. For this design, Loening received the prestigious Collier Trophy in 1921.

The corporation's biggest seller was the two-seat Loening OL, an amphibious observation aircraft that made its first flight in 1923. In twenty variations, 165 of these aircraft were produced and sold to the US Navy and US Army Air Service. The profile of the plane was very distinctive: its huge, single fuselage-centered pontoon protruded well in front of the propeller. In 1928, some of the company's key engineers, including Leroy Grumman, departed the Loening Corporation to form Grumman Aircraft. Loening ceased operating that year. Grover Loening subsequently formed another company and later experimented with innovative design projects.

There were seven PW-2s produced in three variations. Three were PW-2s. Four were designated PW-2A, and one of those later was modified and designated a PW-2B. Six of the seven planes made were based at McCook Field and evaluated by the

Engineering Division. The original contract called for several more to be built, but that was amended after the P-233 crash (*see below*). The power plant for the PW-2 and PW-2A was the 140 hp Wright-Hispano-8 engine. The single PW-2B was powered by a 350 hp Packard engine.

About the crash: The particular Loening plane was a high-wing monoplane assigned to McCook Field and given the project number 233. P-233 was painted on its vertical stabilizer. This aircraft was not considered a great design. On October 20, 1922, the plane designated P-233 had its rendezvous with destiny. On that date, the PW-2A came apart in midair over a residential area of Dayton, Ohio, and crashed into the backyard of a home. Such crack-ups were not unheard of, unfortunately. Aircraft being tested at McCook Field rather frequently fell to the earth, oftentimes resulting in the death of the pilot as well as a crew member or two.

On this day, however, the flight-test pilot of the stricken aircraft bailed out and landed in an arbor, where he was entangled with vines, scratched and bruised but still quite alive. Lt. Harold R. Harris survived because he had strapped on a backpack parachute before going aloft.

It was novel for any pilot to wear a chute in that era. Even when they had the option, few pilots chose to wear them. The parachute Harris wore that day enabled him to jump well clear of his disabled craft. Once a safe distance away, he pulled the ripcord and the silk chute deployed without becoming entangled in the falling plane, as sometimes occurred when nonbackpack chutes were called upon. So, Harris became the first pilot to survive a crash by deploying a backpack chute and riding it safely to earth. Because the flight test world in the early 1920s was small, word of this death-defying escape via parachute spread quickly.

The backpack parachute had been around for several years but wearing one was not mandatory. So, few pilots did. Why? Two reasons. First, some pilots felt that wearing a chute was a sign of fear or lack of confidence about bringing a plane safely back to earth. No pilot in that new era of flight wanted to look like he had an ounce of fear. It was a "devil be damned" attitude. Pilots in the 1920s had heard stories of famous World War I fighter pilots who jumped from burning planes without even having a primitive chute, rather than suffer the agony of going down in a burning aircraft. A tough breed.

The second reason had more to do with comfort in open cockpit airplanes. The cockpit cavity was designed to accommodate the pilot, his clothing, and not much more. The pilot's seat typically was at a height that would keep the pilot out of the elements as much as possible. The pilot's leather-helmeted head might protrude from the cockpit, but a small windscreen kept him out of the sometimes bitter-cold slipstream. Whereas if the pilot wore the backpack parachute—that is, was sitting on it—his face would be raised to where the windscreen couldn't protect him from the cold air.

Lieutenant Harris, who was taller than many of the pilots of his day, incidentally, made the fateful decision that October day to wear a backpack chute and accept the discomfort of the wind in his face. Attitudes changed after his story made the rounds.

Lives were saved as a result and before long the wearing of a backpack chute was made mandatory for military pilots.

PARACHUTES

Man invented what could be termed a parachute centuries before the airplane. The first attempt to float down safely from a high place occurred in the fifteenth century. Louis-Sebastien Lenormand, a French man, is given credit for making the first modern parachute and making the first recorded jump with it. This occurred several years before the French Revolution. It was Lenormand who later coined the term "parachute." About the same time, another Frenchman, Jean-Pierre Blanchard, took flight in a hot-air balloon and jumped out of the basket while wearing a harness attached to his unfolded parachute. Silk material seemed to be the answer for making a light parachute, but how to make it compact continued to elude experimenters.

In the early twentieth century, attempts were made to fold a silk canopy and shroud lines into a bag and attach the bag to a jumper's back. A rope connected the chute in the bag to a hot-air balloon or the newly invented airplane. It was hoped a jumper's weight would properly deploy the chute, but this method did not always work. In 1911, Grant Morton made the first successful jump from an airplane. His platform was a two-seat Wright Model B airplane, high above Venice Beach, California. On this jump, Grant, who sat next to the pilot, had an attached chute wadded up in his arms. He simply leapt from the plane. Fortunately for him, the silk canopy properly opened.

During World War I, a parachute was widely used by observers in ground-tethered highly explosive hydrogen balloons. The silk canopy was loosely attached to the bottom or side of the basket and a rope connected the chute and the observer. Because there was no forward motion and resulting air current, this worked fairly well. Moving aircraft still were a problem. Many times, shroud lines would snag a disabled aircraft and drag the pilot down to his death. A cockpit also afforded little room for a parachute. Consequently, an opened chute sometimes was tacked with thin tread to the exterior of a fuselage so that the weight of a jumper would safely pull the chute free. Again, the canopy or its shroud lines often would become entangled on the tail of the craft with devastating results.

The role that the Engineering Division at McCook field played in developing the "backpack parachute" cannot be overstated. David Gold, longtime engineer with the Irving Parachute Company and an aviation historian, wrote at length about McCook's contribution to the parachute's development.

The following long excerpt of Gold's account is taken from the Spring 1979 quarterly publication of the *SAFE Journal*:

> In the closing months of World War 1, the start of one of the most important milestones in the development of life-saving parachutes took place at McCook Field, Dayton, Ohio. Realizing that parachutes could indeed save fighter aviators from

burning in critically disabled aircraft, the United States Army Air service formed a parachute section at Wilbur Wright Field in Dayton; the work was soon transferred to McCook Field, which had superior facilities for parachute development and testing.

Because Army Air service people knew of his advanced thinking regarding parachute ideas and his wide experience in aircraft as a pilot, J. Floyd Smith was transferred in October 1918 from his job in aircraft production engineering to head the newly formed Parachute Section. Soon at his side was Guy M. Ball, well known to Smith for his aircraft work. The Section grew with the addition of men like James "Jimmy" Russell and Sgt. Ralph W. Bottreil, already a famed parachutist. At the beginning of 1919, energetic Maj. E. L. Hoffman was put in charge of this parachute development team.

Parachutes from all over the world were drop-tested. It was soon evident that none of these met the stringent requirements set up by the Parachute Section. Tested parachutes proved too weak and failed structurally even at moderate drop velocities. It also was soon realized that the static-line mode of operation was not suitable at all. Smith had advocated for some time the concept of a pack-on-the-back aviator type of parachute, which would be operated by a free-falling man manually pulling a ripcord. It was decided to follow this concept and Smith developed his basic ideas with much help from Ball.

A prototype Model A parachute was designed, built and subjected to a vigorous test program under all conditions, including drops from airplanes in spins. The canopy was 30 feet in diameter, made of 1.6 per ounce per square yard Habotai silk, and comprised forty gores. Braided silk suspension lines were used, 250 lbs. in breaking strength, as they proved more suitable than any other cordage previously used, such as hemp. The parachute pack used flaps which were released by the pull of a ripcord; elastics pulled these flaps back and allowed a spring-loaded pilot parachute to burst into the airflow and deploy the parachute canopy from the pack.

It finally was decided that the Model A was ready for a live jump test! Maj. Hoffman chose Leslie L. Irvin to make this leap because of his vast experience as a jumper and his background in the aeronautical field. Irvin was one of many to respond to McCook Field's invitation for parachute ideas. He had submitted a parachute design, but it was rejected because it was static-line operated. He was an immediate convert to the concept of a manually operated parachute and made numerous trips between McCook Field and Buffalo, where he had a small parachute business with George Waite, a silk merchant.

Waite joined Irvin in making parachutes for testing at McCook when Irvin was informed that only silk parachutes would be tested. (Irvin's original submission was a cotton canopy.) During these trips, Irvin offered suggestions for improvements. On April 28, 1919, "Sky-Hi" Irvin, a name he had acquired because of his numerous activities in aeronautics, climbed into the turret cockpit of a USD-9 airplane piloted by Smith. He was wearing a prototype Model A parachute which had been drop-tested successfully eleven times by Smith and Ball. At an altitude of 1,500 feet at 80 miles per hour, Irvin jumped, yanked his ripcord, and the parachute streamed out and opened in one and two-fifths seconds!

Upon landing, Irvin broke his ankle when a gust of wind swung him into the ground. In the hospital, he was told a few days later that he was being given the initial order for a quantity of three hundred parachutes, standardized Model A in design, which had a twenty-eight-foot diameter canopy. This was the start of the Irving Air Chute Company's growth. On May 14, 1919, Floyd Smith made a jump, deliberately not pulling the ripcord until he fell an estimated 500 feet. On the same day, Jimmy Russell, Sgt. Bottreil, and Jimmy Higgins made their first jumps with the manually operated parachute.

A series of interesting designs followed the acceptance of the Model A backpack parachute. It led to the creation of the Model S parachute, which formed the basis of parachutes to be built for years to come. In fact, the C-9 parachute canopy widely used today (1979) is a carbon copy of the twenty-eight-foot model S canopy.

In 1926, Maj. E. L. Hoffman was awarded the Collier Trophy for his leadership in developing a practical parachute.

One idea about as old as the airplane itself was having an entire disabled aircraft parachuted to the ground. Just ten years after the Wright Brothers achieved success with their 1903 Wright Flyer, French engineer Capt. M. Couade proposed such a plane parachute. In Captain Couade's design, a small pilot chute would deploy, dragging the main chute into the air. By placing the parachute in the rear of a fuselage, ground impact would occur nose-first. Bodily injury would be avoided by having the pilot exit the craft and climb onto the shroud lines away from the plane itself. Alas, World War I began and Couade's ideas were shelved.

The idea of parachuting entire planes persisted. At McCook Field, research and development engineers explored the idea. They dropped the idea eventually. Technology and materials were not yet available to bring the idea to reality.

Today, several general aviation aircraft offer the feature and pilots have been saved. The most popular examples are the SR 20 and SR22 of the Cirrus Aircraft Company. Its system, called "CAPS" for Cirrus Airframe Parachute System, has the parachute stowed in the top of the fuselage. When a pilot pulls a stiff cord that hangs from the cockpit ceiling, an explosive device rips the top of the fuselage and the parachute is deployed. The entire aircraft containing the pilot and passengers then floats to the surface.

It should be noted that the use of this safety system generally causes major damage to an airplane, in most cases rendering it beyond repair. However, occupants of a plane usually survive. Several other light-sport aircraft manufacturers have similar parachute systems. One is by Flight Design, a German manufacturer. The company employs the system in its CT series of aircraft.

F. W. GERHARDT CYCLEPLANE

The William F. Gerhardt "cycleplane." *Photos from the February, 1924 issue of* The Slipstream

In a February 1924 issue of the McCook Field newsletter, *The Slipstream*, the editor wrote:

> It would no doubt be judged presumptuous for Slipstream to announce that a new epoch in flying has been ushered in with the recent debut of the Gerhardt Cycleplane, but even with the presence of the popular ridicule which followed the unspectacular "initial flights" of the strange craft there must be a certain trend of seriousness attached to the fact that the machine did actually leave the ground on several occasions and remained in the air a brief period solely by the propulsive power furnished by the pilot. We must also attach a certain amount of significance to the idea since it must be admitted that the man who conceived it, did so upon scientific calculations, and with no hope of accomplishing a complete success at this time. It is believed, therefore, that our readers will be interested in the true facts concerning the Cycleplane as written by the inventor, F. W. Gerhardt.

In a comprehensive article, Gerhardt himself then went on to write about the problem of human-powered flight, which had challenged adventurous minds for thousands of years. He noted that, in modern times, man attempted to solve the problem by various means, including attaching wings to a bicycle. Alas, the small wing area could not lift the bike on the strength of the biker's pedaling.

Gerhardt's personal effort dated back to 1920, when he was employed under George de Bothezat. Along with a Mr. Pratt, another McCook Field aeronautical engineer, Gerhardt elaborately calculated the feasibility of designing a craft for human-powered flight. His mathematical findings showed that the craft required wings spanning 40 feet—multiple wings 18 feet high. Construction with private funds began in February 1923.

Gerhardt wrote: "The first fuselage and propulsive mechanism were built for the pilot, in a prone position, operating a very simple pedal mechanism with a pusher propeller at the rear. When completed, this apparatus was pushed out the loft door, the propeller attached and an attempt made to turn over the propeller at its designed revolutions." The method of using a pilot in a prone position could not produce the required propeller revolutions. After this dismal attempt, it was decided that the bicycle pedal system would produce the best power: "We secured an old double-geared bicycle and, after dissecting it, put it together in such a way as to drive the propeller as a tractor."

Next was the search for an adequate flight-testing site. "Through the kind cooperation of the Engineering Division" at McCook Field, a tented shelter was secured and assembly of the unique seven-winged craft began. Gerhardt continued:

> The more of it that was assembled, the more discouraged we became of ever making such a flimsy looking structure hold together long enough to be wheeled outside the hanger, let alone take the air with a load of 250 pounds."
>
> One quiet (calm wind) night in July, on Friday the thirteenth, to be exact, the craft was brought out. Lt. Harris acted as chief pallbearer while Mrs. Harris lighted the way with the trusty family bus. The date lived up to its reputation, for despite the most violent efforts on the part of the cycleplane operator, the craft refused to budge an inch. A little push by bystanders only caused a portion of the tail to fall off and the whole rear end to sway violently about the tail skid and axis. Needless to say, the test was not considered an unqualified success.
>
> Four days later, the apparatus was pushed out with a towing wire attached after the fashion of a kite string. An automobile was employed to furnish the towing power. At first the machine was towed without a passenger and we were pleased to see it leave the ground at a much[-]lower speed than one would be led to expect by computation from existing data. We then immediately attempted to do the same thing with a passenger and, much to our astonishment, Mr. Pratt was able with considerable exertion to keep the machine aloft for a considerable period of time without further towing power from the automobile. This in itself, as we later realized, was actual flight by manpower, the only difference being that the efficiency of the towing rope is 1.0 whereas that of the propeller is around .8.

Some structural weaknesses were discovered during this test and after several modifications were made, further testing continued. After three more flights of marginal success and more modifications to the propeller pitch, a flight was made where "the apparatus was off the ground for several inches over a distance of twenty feet." Though during this flight, the craft was attached by wire to the automobile, a spring balance indicator showed that the automobile was not towing the craft. Gerhardt declared:

> This naturally is the proof that steady level flight was accomplished. It must be

admitted that quite a thrill was derived from the result, as it meant that the theoretical calculations were confirmed.

It was in October that the craft was again wheeled out when it was expected to obtain some moving picture records and then disassemble the craft until a later date. Lieutenants Alex Pearson and Mac Macready arrived on the scene in time to direct the comedy settings. Everything was put in readiness and the operator took his position for the take off. The towing tug moved forward and the operator began to pump the pedals, but no sooner had the craft cleared the ground than something essential to the rigidity of the structure gave way and the fuselage gently folded in two and the seven wings collapsed backward.

Naturally the question arises as to what were the technical results of the trials. They were: (1) Scientific demonstration of the predicated possibility to fly level with the normal power a man can produce; (2) The accumulation of certain data for further and more interesting developments suggested by it.

Dr. Gerhardt concluded the article this way: "It seems highly probable that, in the future, man will be able to take advantage of the currents as do the birds, and soar indefinitely, going from one favorable current to another by means of his own effort."

Author's note: That future day arrived on August 23, 1977, at Shafter-Minter Field near Bakersfield, California, when a pedal-powered craft, "the Gossamer Condor," flew the first-ever figure-eight course. Nearly two years later, on June 12, 1979, another craft, "the Gossamer Albatross," flew across the English Channel.

ENGINEERING DIVISION HELICOPTER

The following excerpts are from an article printed in the January 1923 issue of the McCook Field bimonthly newspaper, *The Slipstream*. They concern the testing of an early vertical-lift aircraft designed by Dr. George de Bothezat.

The editors wrote:

The Engineering Division Helicopter—the first to make a successful flight—is equipped with a le Rohne engine rated at one hundred eighty hp but developing under the conditions one hundred seventy hp. Its weight with pilot and gas included is about three thousand six hundred pounds. The lift of the helicopter is derived from four six-bladed propellers, each being eight meters in diameter, set in motion by a special gearing system connecting the motor to the propellers.

When a person speaks of a "helicopter" to one not familiar with aeronautics, he is talking in an unknown language. It is, in fact, a comparatively new word and represents a vehicle of the air that up until the present day has been nothing more than an object of experimentation, or a phantastic dream of the aeronautical engineer and amateur inventor.

Attempts, even prior to the development of airplanes, were made to develop a machine capable of lifting itself vertically into the air. In the current twentieth century, it is interesting to note that one hundred years ago, many who were, "authoritative in aeronautical questions' declared that 'aerial navigation will never reach a stage of absolute practicability and perfection until the problem of vertical flight is solved. When the helicopter is developed, it will mean that this problem is solved.

Col. Bane and the de Bothezat Helicopter. *Photo courtesy of Mrs. Thurman H. Bane*

The de Bothezat Helicopter hovers a few feet above the ground at McCook Field. *Photo from the January, 1923 issue of* The Slipstream

The article continued:

> For some time, the Engineering Division, Air Service, at McCook Field, has been carrying on exhaustive experimentation in a type of helicopter designed by Dr. George de Bothezat. Publicity on the development of the machine has been carefully restricted and up until the present period not an inkling of what was being accomplished has been given to the press. However, since the helicopter has been completed and tested, through the forbearance of the press and a request from the chief of the Air Service, an account of the first flight has been given out.
>
> The hangar housing the helicopter has been for many months closed to all employees except those actually employed in the construction or otherwise in higher authority in the Engineering Division. The Special Research Section has therefore been more or less a place of mystery, and what the machine looked like or how it operated was a puzzle except to the few mentioned.
>
> It was the morning of December 18, 1922, at McCook Field that the first flight in public was made, the helicopter piloted by Maj. Thurman Bane. Calmly taking his place in the pilot's seat, Maj. Bane primed the motor and it started. The four great propeller wings or screws began to rotate like giant pinwheels. The helpers then stood clear of the machine while the pilot gradually increased the speed of the motor. The propellers rotated faster and faster, without the familiar drone, however, that is common with the airplane propeller and with the six blades plainly visible on each of the four propellers as they spun around.
>
> She lifted herself lightly, an inch, two, three, up—up, up until she stood about 3 feet clear of the ground and remained at an altitude between 2 to 6 feet for one minute and forty-two seconds.
>
> While in the air, the machine was remarkably steady, merely the slightest oscillations being observed. Hovering at the height mentioned, the helicopter drifted along possibly 300 feet with the wind.

The report continued:

> Drifting close to the fence, Maj. Bane was forced to make a landing, which was brought about under complete control. By observing the wheel marks in the light snow, which covered the ground at the place of landing, it could be seen that the machine landed on a spot not more than 3 feet in length.

The article concluded:

> This feature is significant in the fact that the helicopter has recorded the first successful landing of this kind in the history of aeronautics. The layman can at once surmise what it will mean when machines are perfected with the ability to take off

and land in so small a space. It will mean that the smallest city lot, street block, or top of building may be used for an aerial station. An ideal dream, you say, yet remember we are just relating the first flight of this kind—a short one to be true, but let us recall that the first airplane flight of the Wright Brothers some twenty years ago lasted less than half a minute.

The first flight of the helicopter is regarded as highly gratifying both by the inventor and by the officials of the Engineering Division. It is a great step toward the final goal to perfection and, if we can hope for advancement as rapid as has been wrought in airplanes, it is no idle dream to picture common helicopter flights within the next fifteen years.

Author's note: Contrary to what was written in this 1923 article, most aviation experts feel that because this craft did not rise above "ground effect"—the litmus test for aeronautical engineers judging whether an aircraft indeed has flown—one cannot really give the "First Flight" title to the de Bothezat design. That honor is generally bestowed upon Igor Sikorsky for his 1939 helicopter, a flight that did rise above ground effect. That being said, certainly the de Bothezat craft helped move the ball forward in the quest to develop a helicopter. After all, the mission of the Engineering Division at McCook Field was not unlike that of today's Edwards Air Force Base in California's high desert. That is, the goal was not always to achieve final success but to research and develop craft with an eye toward future successes.

CHAPTER 24
LIFE AT MCCOOK FIELD

An alumna of McCook Field whom the author had the good fortune to interview was Darlene Gerhardt. One time when the tape recorder was not playing, I asked her about social customs at McCook. This was in the mid-1970s during the so-called sexual revolution, when social norms were being tested. In that era, one had several ways to get to know people of the opposite sex. So, I asked Darlene how a person in the 1920s went about meeting new friends. What was dating like back then? Her paraphrased answer was, "Well, from what I see on TV, it was very different than today, that's for sure."

For one thing, Friday nights were not the end of the workweek. Social gatherings did not happen till Saturday night because Saturday was either a half day of work or a full day. The social gatherings usually were in someone's home. The person planning the event invited with great care, to ensure a good mix of the sexes and a cross-section of talents.

A sure way of being invited, Darlene said, was to have a skill or talent that would add to the party atmosphere. Always in demand were people who could play the piano or the harp, sing, or perhaps read poetry with feeling. McCook Field was a military post, and many college-educated single officers were present. Invited guests were expected to fit into such a milieu. On occasion, dances were held in the post cafeteria or at summertime picnics. However, the house party was the prime ticket. An evening date for two usually would be dinner at one of Dayton's downtown hotel restaurants.

Two stress-free McCook Field pilots enjoying the annual picnic in Dayton's Miami River. *Photo courtesy of Darlene Gerhardt*

So, while McCook was a place of technical achievements and aircraft development, with various exotic machines the focus of attention, more than anything else the story of McCook Field was about people. One of the best remaining records about the culture of McCook comes from the post newspaper, *The Slipstream*.

The bimonthly publication first published in August 1919 mirrored what was going on there. This ranged from aviation advancements, cafeteria announcements, notices of upcoming family picnics, and post-sponsored sporting events to workplace gossip and topical humor. The following are some of those accounts:

Knowing how primitive roads were in 1920, a story printed in one issue, authored by McCook's commanding officer Maj. Thurman Bane, is of particular interest. Maj. Thurman Bane reported on a road trip he and his wife took. After arriving in San Francisco (probably by train), he purchased a Ford automobile. They then drove around and through Northern California mountains, including the High Sierra country up to Lake Tahoe. He described driving through 15 inches of snow. After returning from weeks of this, Bane commented, "Feel fine, had a helluva good time, now bring on the work."

A 1921 issue of *The Slipstream* had a personals column. This was one of the notices: "Carl V. Johnson suffered the loss of his baby last month. His many friends offer their sympathy." No details were provided about the baby or its mother.

Because these were Prohibition years, this gibe appeared: "Whatever else may happen, now that the country's dry, the sailor will have his port, the farmer will have his rye, the cotton still will have its gin, the seacoast its bar. And each of us will have a bier, no matter where we are."

McCook was an inventive place, and one particular page of *The Slipstream* listed 110 inventions that were submitted to the McCook's Patent Section in a single month! McCook offered its employees aviation-related courses taught by leading engineers and test pilots based at the field. No fewer than forty-three courses were listed, ranging from wind tunnel operation to electrical equipment installation.

The December 1919 issue had a full-page article regarding the new management of the cafeteria. The article talks of the health dangers under the former management and how the facility was improved. "The cafeteria building was first thoroughly fumigated and all cooking utensils, dishes and silverware were scoured. The post surgeon inspects the cafeteria daily, which makes it absolutely necessary that it be kept in a strictly sanitary condition at all times. All employees in the cafeteria must pass a physical examination given by the post surgeon." This was at a time when the Spanish flu was a scourge. The article also noted that thirty-four loaves of bread were found in the trash can after lunch and that diners now were limited to two slices of bread per meal.

Ladies had special cafeteria seating arrangements. "The first five tables on the east side of the main dining room have been reserved for ladies; the first two tables have been equipped with chairs and the other three tables will be equipped with chairs as soon as a sufficient number can be obtained. Men are requested not to occupy these tables." The article noted that "a dining room with tables seating four each has been opened in the south end of the building for those desiring waiter service. The prices charged in this room are the same with one exception, an additional charge of ten cents is made to everyone." So, what were the food prices? Meat orders were fifteen cents and a slice of pie was a nickel. This was at a time when the average weekly pay was sixty-two dollars before federal tax deduction.

The August 1921 issue included more "Personals." Here's one: "The collection of chiggers some of us accumulated at the picnic may have been a bit annoying, but ask any of the girls of the general files what they think of the comparative efficiency of the chiggers as to that of the festive and elusive flea. Since moving into their new quarters, they have been obliged to interrupt daily tasks at numerous and frequently recurring intervals because of fleas."

Another personal notice was also in this issue: "Mr. and Mrs. J. W. Vanden of Jackson, Tennessee, the uncle and aunt of Albert G. Pendleton, whose death was caused by the recent crash of a plane from this field, sends the following card of appreciation to the friends of Mr. Pendleton." The following appeared in the same issue: "Lt. Fairchild (who later would earn the rank of general) has been granted a thirty-day leave and will return to duty about June 10. The heartfelt sympathy of the entire Field is extended to the lieutenant, whose wife was called by the Grim Reaper during the past month. Funeral services were conducted at her home, to which place the body was shipped from Dayton."

And then there was this classic:

Mariana McKnight just loves taxis. Ask her if she doesn't. The Wednesday morning that it rained so hard, she decided that she was flush enough to take a taxi to the field. Everything went lovely till they reached the south end of the field when the engine failed and they were stuck. She was patient though and didn't complain while the chauffeur attempted to get the taxi going. Then he beat it up the road to the main entrance and left her sitting there alone. So, she decided it was time to act. She didn't realize she was alone till said chauffer had been gone some time but when she did find it out she "hot-footed" it through the dampness to the entrance and finding the chauffeur there, she unlimbered her vocabulary and told in forcible though lady-like English exactly what she thought of him. The ride cost her a dollar plus and then she didn't even get here! She'll just love to tell you about it. Ask her.

Still another read: "There is a new addition to the Timekeeping Department in the way of new equipment, consisting of a wristwatch Mr. Jache wears on his right arm. It is a Sears-Roebuck model and has all the qualities of a Big Ben. Mr. Jache says all timekeepers and taxi drivers should have one."

The July 1920 issue has two pages about an upcoming picnic. The picnic events would include swimming, track, baseball, and dancing. The music was to be provided by Miss Ehrstine: "Boys, you know her. She's the one who plays the piano at the cafeteria during lunch."

In the April 1920 issue was a piece documenting the everyday life of the McCook employee:

"The Things We Enjoy Most on Our Trolley Rides to and from the Field."
1. The heavy woman of the "I-Won't-Wash" type, who drops down on your lap for a trip around the world on two seats for a nickel, and when you reach your station you have to knock her on the back to remind her that you are still under there and would like to get out.
2. The Jane, hanging on the strap in front of you, who drains her umbrella in the lap of your freshly pressed suit.
3. The officer, who insists upon wearing spurs and jabs them into your best silk hose every time the car jolts.
4. The man sitting next to you, who crowds you into the corner and deliberately coughs in your face during the entire ride.
5. The party who must read the Morning Journal, regardless of the small amount of space, and pokes you in the ribs every time he turns a page.

The September 1923 issue described how eleven records for speed, duration aloft, and distance were set in eleven days by six McCook Field pilots. At a ceremony, trophies were presented by Dayton Mayor James M. Cox.

In the January 1923 issue was a two-page story, "From Sea to Sea by Airplane." Written by Lt. James Doolittle, it includes his account of his two months of physical training to condition his mind and body for the cross-country flight: "It was just such training as the pugilist or the athlete would put himself through for an important contest, with regular hours, daily exercise, practice and total abstinence from all injurious habits as a part of my routine program."

Finally, a little romantic story was featured in the February 1921 issue. It seems Perry Sacksteder, a draftsman in the Ordnance Department, had been called to serve in the US Army during World War I. He was posted in Paris. One day on a Parisian boulevard, he met a "pretty dark-eyed mademoiselle." When the war ended, unlike many other US servicemen who came home after finding true love in Paris, Sacksteder was determined to bring his love back to America. It took several years of paperwork, but she finally arrived in New York City's harbor and marriage followed.

EPILOGUE

My personal journey to explore the history of McCook Field and to document it through voices of people who worked there was long and winding. I never envisioned the passage of so many years between the moment I started learning about the storied place and the publication of this volume. But that's the way of history; a significant moment usually is shorter than the subsequent telling of it.

I am glad for the trek back in time. Listening to men and women talk about their McCook experiences transported me to a period in the history of flight when far more about aviation was unknown than was known and discovery seemed an everyday occurrence. Trial and error was the way forward, with failures common and progress incremental. People of vision, talent, conviction and grit were the catalyst for progress and credit should be given leaders in Washington and in uniform for gathering such people in one place and giving them the freedom to fail.

It is easy to view this early era in aviation as quaint, with clever people doing rudimentary things that we now take for granted. Pioneers never receive full measure of respect from succeeding generations. Today's risk-averse young people—many of whom can't imagine riding in an automobile without a seatbelt or pedaling a bike without a helmet—would deem it crazy to fly to 20,000 feet in an untested aircraft whose wings might or might not stay attached, let alone do so without the insurance of a parachute. This is called courage.

The 1920s era in aviation was a period of daredevil pilots as well as gutsy engineers and some visionary administrators who fended off bureaucrats so the work of advancement could proceed. All of them had a lot of fun in the doing. Fifty years later, the pride they felt in their aeronautical accomplishments was evident in the matter-of-fact interviews contained in this book.

As a long-time aviator, I am humbly indebted to the men and women who were instrumental in advancing the science of aviation to where I can routinely leave mother Earth, play among clouds and safely touchdown miles and miles away. Flight today is an ordinary and yet exhilarating experience and I am happy to have known, if briefly, some of the people who made it so.

BIBLIOGRAPHY

Note: All publications directly sourced are attributed in the text of the book. The following are additional sources from which I have accumulated general knowledge of the subject matter.

Aldrin, Edwin E., Jr. *Return to Earth*. New York: Random House, 1973.

Berg, A. Scott. *Lindbergh*. New York: G. P. Putnam's Sons, 1998.

Casey, Louis S. *Smithsonian Annals of Flight*, Vol. 1, no. 1. Washington, DC: Smithsonian, 1964.

Dierikx, Marc. *Anthony Fokker*. Washington, DC: Smithsonian Books, 2018.

Doolittle, James H. *I Could Never Be So Lucky Again*. New York: Bantam, 1991.

Glines, Carroll V. *Jimmy Doolittle*. New York: Macmillan, 1972.

Glines, Carroll V. *The First Flight around the World*. Missoula, MT: Pictorial Histories Publishing, 2000.

Goddard, George W. *Overview: A Lifelong Adventure in Aerial Photography*. Garden City, NY: Doubleday, 1969.

Gregory, H. F. *The Helicopter*. Cranbury, NJ: A. S. Barnes, 1976.

Grosser, Morton. *Gossamer Odyssey*. Boston, MA: Houghton Mifflin, 1981.

Hoppes, Jonna Doolittle. *Calculated Risk*. Solana Beach, CA: Santa Monica, 2005.

Bibliography

Johnson, Mary Ann. *McCook Field*. Dayton, OH: Landfall Press, 2002.

Keisel, Kenneth M. *Dayton Aviation*. Charleston, SC: Arcadia, 2012.

Kelly, Fred C. *Miracle at Kitty Hawk*. Boston, MA: Da Capo, 1996.

Roseberry, C. R. *Glenn Curtiss: Pioneer of Flight*. Garden City, NY: Doubleday, 1972.

Thomas, Lowell. *Doolittle: A Biography*. Garden City, NY: Doubleday, 1976.

Thomas, Lowell. *Famous First Flights That Changed History*. Guilford, CT: Lyons, 2004.

Thomas, Lowell. *The First World Flight*. New York: Houghton Mifflin, 1924.

Wagner, William. *Reuben Fleet and the Story of Consolidated Aircraft*. Fallbrook, CA: Aero, 1976.

Wallace, Sally Macready. *John Macready: Aviation Pioneer*. Manhattan, KS: Sunflower University, 1998.

Waller, Douglas. *A Question of Loyalty*. New York: HarperCollins, 2004.

Williams, Robert E. *American Aviation Historical Society*, Vol. 44, no. 3, Fall 1999.

INDEX

Aeronca C-2, 111
Air Force Institute of Technology, 12, 113
Air Service Engineering School, 12
Aircraft Production Board, 135
Akeley camera, 86, 87
Aldrin, Edwin E., Sr., 12, 41–42, 65, 100
Aldrin, Edwin E., Jr. "Buzz," 12, 41
Allen, Bryan, 83
Allen, Edmund T., 62
American Aviation Historical Society, 11
Amis, William N., 110
Anderson, Bob, 62
Anderson, Orvil, 124
Arnold, Henry H. "Hap," 15–16, 23, 103, 122, 158
Atlantic-Fokker C-2, the Bird of Paradise, 14, 22, 133

Bagley, James W., 42
Ball, Guy M., 173
Bane, Bessie Louise, 10, 18, 43, 114
Bane, Thurman H., 6, 13, 18, 24, 42, 43, 50, 55, 60, 65, 69, 84, 94, 98, 101, 114, 116, 118, 179, 182
Barker, William "Billy," 165
Barksdale, Eugene Hoy, 14, 63–64, 110
Barling Bomber (Witteman-Lewis XNBL-1), 59, 64, 71, 75, 92, 136, 155–158
Barling, Walter H., 37, 59, 75, 156–157
Batten, Eugene C., 110, 125
Beech Mystery Ship, 17, 53, 117
Beech, Walter, 53
Bell, Larry, 73
Bendix Trophy, 54
Berger, A. L., 109
Bergh, Diane Goddard, 11
Beauchamp-Proctor, Andrew, 162

Bishop, William "Billy," 152
Blood Glue, 115
BMW "Bavarian Motor Works," 21, 68, 147
Boeing Aircraft Company, 101, 140, 141
Boeing, Bill, 101
Boeing MB-3A, 166
Boeing, Wilhelm, 102
Boeing B-17, 158
Boeing B-29, 158
Boeing B-52, 158
Bolling Commission, 140
Bolling Field, 29, 35, 58, 69
The "Bonehead" trophy, 50
Boulton, B. C., 90, 111
"Boston," 36, 64, 153–154
"Boston II," 37, 153–155
Boyd, Albert, 77
Boyne, Walter J., 11, 126
Bristol Fighter, 69, 115, 117, 140
Brookley, Wendell Holsworth, 76, 79
Breuets Aircraft, 100
Bruner, Donald, 13, 62
Burka, Doc, 57

Caldwell, Frank, 115
Callizo, Jean, 109
Captain Albert W. Stevens Elementary School, 125
Carroll, Franklin O., 115
Caterpillar Club, 125
Chance-Vought F4-U, 170
Chance-Vought VE-7, 116, 168–170
Chance-Vought VE-7S, 169
"Chicago," 153–155
Christiansen, Hester, 72–74

Index

Churchill, Winston, 122
Cirrus Aircraft Company, 174
Clark, Virginius Evans, 108, 113, 116
Cloud Flying Instrument Board, 41
Cloud Seeding, 13
Collier Trophy, 12, 19, 22, 57, 115, 163, 170, 174
Consolidated Aircraft Corporation, 101, 102
Consolidated B-24 Liberators, 101, 111
Consolidated B-36 Peacemaker, 111, 158
Consolidated PBY Catalina, 101, 111
Consolidated PT-3, 103
Coolidge, Calvin, 31
"Cup of Good Beginnings and Bad Endings," 61
Curry, John Francis, 24, 45, 65
Curtiss Aeroplane and Motor Company, 101, 137, 161
Curtiss, Glenn H., 137
Curtiss JN-4 "Jenny," 76, 136–139
Curtiss NC-4, 136
Curtiss OX-5, 135, 137–138
Curtiss-Wright Corporation, 138

Daland, Elliot, 61
Davidson, Howard Calhoun, 67–71, 131–132
Dayton-Wright Aircraft Corporation, 116, 140
de Bothezat, George, 28, 37, 69, 73, 114, 175
de Bothezat helicopter, 13, 28, 55, 64, 88, 91, 110, 114, 177–180
Deeds, Edward Andrew, 82, 86, 105, 106
de Havilland, Geoffrey, 140
Delage, Gustave, 152
de Port, Theophile, 116
de Seversky, Alexander N. P., 29, 73 118–122
DH-4, 16, 38, 48, 58, 66, 76, 86, 88, 99, 100, 113, 136, 139–142
Dichman, Ernest W., 61, 93, 150
Disney, Walt, 122
The Dole Prize, 50
Doolittle, James H. "Jimmy," 6–7, 21, 43, 44–54, 79, 110, 126–128, 139, 184
Doolittle, James H. "Jimmy" III, 6–7
Douglas, Donald, 14, 78, 154
Douglas Torpedo Plane "DT," 154
Douglas World Cruiser "DWC," 14, 136, 153–155

Edwards Air Force Base, 7, 180
Eubank, Eugene Lowry, 28, 110
Explorer l, 124
Explorer ll, 124

Fairchild, Florence, 60
Fairchild, Muir Sandy, 39, 50, 60, 74, 75, 76, 93, 157
Fairfield Depot, 68, 158
"the Fighting McCooks," 12
The First World Flight, 155
Fleet, Reuben H., 18, 21, 65, 101–103, 138
Flight Design Aircraft Corporation, 174
"the Flying Ass" trophy, 51 61
"the Flying Coffin," 48, 141
"the Flying Mattress," 115
"flying razor," 148
Fokker, Anthony, 73, 149
Fokker D-7, 142
Fokker D.VII, 146–148
Fokker D.VIII, 146–148
Fokker F-IV, 149
Fokker PW-7, 142–145
Fokker T-2, 93, 148–150
Ford Motor Company, 42, 136
French Nieuport, 68, 151–152

Gallaudet Aircraft Company, 102
Gallaudet, Edson, 102
General Electric Company16, 108–109, 117
General Motors, 15, 86
Gerhardt Cycleplane, 75, 77, 81–83, 175–177
Gerhardt, Darlene E., epigraph, 13, 77–83, 181
Gerhardt, William Frederick, 10, 75, 77, 81, 175–177
Glacier National Park, 107
Goddard, George, 11, 14, 32, 125, 128–129
Gold, David, 172
Goring, Hermann, 147
Gossamer Albatross, 83, 177
Gossamer Condor, 83, 177
Gotha bomber, 25, 159, 166
Griffin, Virgil Jr., Lt. Cmdr., 169
Grosvenor, Gilbert, 108
Grumann, Leroy, 170
Guardian Angel Parachute, 84

189

Index

Hagemeyer, Louis, 84–88, 115, 121
Haizlap, Jimmy, 53
Hall, Elbert J., 135
Hallett, George E. A., 15–21, 101
Hamilton, Charles K., 20
Hamilton, Hayden, 11
Handley Page Type O bomber, 159
Harding, Jack, 14, 36, 37, 85
Harriman, Thomas, 27–30
Harris, Harold R., 13, 17, 28, 37, 43, 49, 52, 55–66, 75, 76, 81, 92, 104, 110, 129–130, 157, 171, 176
Hart, Schaffner and Marx, 52
Haskell, Henry, 115
Hegenberger, Albert Francis, 12, 13, 14, 22–26, 42, 133
Heron, Sam, 19
Hicham, Horace, 118–119
Hispano-Suiza engine, 116, 143, 161
Hitler, Adolf, 53
Hobley, Alfred H., 71, 85
Hoffman, Edward L., 12, 57, 84, 115, 119, 173–174
"honeymoon special," 60
Hoppes, Jonna Doolittle, 6–7
Huff, Thomas, 61
Hutchinson, James Troy, 46, 48

Irvin, Leslie L., 12, 173
Irving Air Chute Company, 12, 172

JN-4 "Jenny," 76, 136–139
Johnson, Harry Anton, 31–32, 74, 131
Jones Barany Chair, 25
Jones, E. T., 16–17

Kelly, Oakley, 13, 43, 60, 93–97, 105, 150
Kenney, George C., 98–100
Kepner, William, 124
Kerber, L. V., 78, 90, 111
"Kettering Bug," 86, 112
Kettering, Charles F., 15, 82, 86, 112
Keyes, C. M., 101
Kilner, Walter Glenn "Mike," 36
Kodak 110 camera, 127

L-6 engine, 136, 146
L-8 engine, 136
Laddon, I. Mac, 62, 66, 78, 90–91, 111, 115
Laird, Matty, 54
"Laird Super Solution," 54
Lambertson, Giles, 11
Langham, Roy, 38, 110
Langley Field, 35, 58, 118, 120
Langley, Samuel, 112, 138
Lawrance, Charles L., 19, 64
Lenormand, Sebastien, 172
LePere aircraft, 13, 16, 37, 66, 70, 117
LePere, Georges, 162
Lewis, Birdseye, 169
Liberty Engine, 16, 37, 48, 68, 90, 117, 135–136, 141
Liberty L12, 135, 149, 154, 156, 162
Lindbergh, Charles, 13, 19, 24, 42, 138, 140
Lockwood, Ralph, 51, 110, 113, 120
Loening, Grover Cleveland, 73, 170
Loening PW-2, 57, 170–172
Luke, Frank, 167

MacCready, Dr. Paul B., 83
Mackey Trophy, 104
Macready, John A., 13, 14, 17, 34, 56, 96, 97, 104–110, 128, 150, 163
Maitland, Lester, 14, 22–23, 132-133
"the Manchu Law," 21
Mannock, Edward, 162
Marshall, George, C., 122
Martin B-10, 111
Martin Bombers, 16, 59, 120, 121, 158–160
Martin, Frederick, L., 36–37
Martin, Glenn L., 73, 78, 159
Mather, Stephen, 105–107
Maughan, Russell L., 14
McCook, Anson, 90
McDoudall, Harry, 107
McFarland, Ross, 56
Meade, George J., 16
Mercedes-Benz, 117
Miester, Louis, 51, 110, 151
Mitchel Field, 29, 34, 94
Mitchel, John Purroy, 94

190

Index

Mitchell, William "Billy," 13, 44, 58, 60, 65, 72, 73, 80–81, 86, 97–99, 113–114, 118–121, 156, 160
Monosoupape, 43
Monteith, Charles Norton, 77
Moriarity, Louis P., 113
Morse, Alan, 75–76
Morton, Grant, 172
Moseley, Corliss C., 64
Moss, Dr. Stanford Alexander, 108–109, 117, 163
Murdoch, Thomas Octave, 166
Museum of Flying, 155

NACA, National Advisory Committee for Aeronautics, 58
NACA Report 203, *Acceleration in Flight*, 127, 142–145
Napier, 73
NASA, National Air and Space Administration, 58
National Air and Space Museum, 142
National Air and Space Museum, Udvar-Hazy Center, 166
National Archives, 10
National Air Museum, 150, 155
National Aviation Hall of Fame, 33, 44, 98, 101, 104, 118
National Geographic Society, 108, 124
National Museum of the United States Air Force, 10, 158, 160, 164
National Naval Aviation Museum, 166
Nelson, Erik, 14, 36–37
"New Orleans," 153
Newell, Joseph S., 51
Niedermeyer, Frederick W., 110
Nieuport, Edouard, 151
Niles, Alfred S., 51
Northrop Grumman B-2, 158
Northrop, Jack, 154
Norton Bombsight, 70

Ogden, Henry, 36
Old Rhinebeck Aerodrome, 136, 147
"Operation Paperclip," 77
The Orteig Prize, 50
Ostfriesland, 59, 160

Oswalt, Bill, 125
Overview: A Lifelong Adventure in Aerial Photography, 11

Pachard-Le Pere LUSAC-11, 162–164
Packard Motor Car Company, 89, 135–136
Pan American Airways, 55, 105
Parachutes, 49–50, 84, 92, 124, 172–174
Patrick, Mason, 36-37, 42, 46, 59, 103
Patterson, Lt. Frank S., 12
Pearson, Alexander Jr., 28, 79, 92, 110
Pershing, John J., 73, 138
Platz, Reinhold, 143, 147
Pratt, E. L., 13, 175
Pratt & Whitney PT-6A, 135
PT8, 29
Pulitzer Race, 64

Quebec Conference 1943, 122

Reagan, Ronald, 10
Recollections of An Airman, 165
Republic Aircraft Corporation, 122
Republic P-47 "Thunderbolt," 118
Richthofen, Baron Manfred von, "The Red Baron," 110, 147, 164
Rickenbacker, Edward, 149, 152, 167
Roche, Jean Alfred, 29, 78, 90, 109, 111–117
Rockwell B-1B, 158
Rockwell Field, 150
Rodgers, Calbraith Perry, 149
Roma, 27
Roosevelt Field, 94, 150
Roosevelt, Franklin, 122
Roosevelt, Quentin, 94, 152
Royal Aircraft Factory SE-5, 16, 43, 111, 117, 118, 140, 160–162

Sadi-Lecointe, Joseph, 109
Scheider Trophy, 52
Schroeder, Rudolph "Shorty," 12, 18, 25, 34–35, 61, 64 70, 71, 86, 108–109, 163
Schulz, Charles, 164
"Seattle," 153–154

191

Index

Seversky P-43, 118
Shafter-Minter Field, 83, 177
Sikorsky, 55, 73, 114, 120
Slipstream newspaper, 175, 182–184
Smith, Art Roy, 51, 55, 87, 110, 113
Smith, Herbert, 165
Smith, J. Floyd, 173–174
Smithsonian Air and Space Museum, 10, 126
"Snoopy," 164
Sopwith Camel, 68, 164–166
Sopwith, Thomas Octave Murdoch, 166
Spad, 68, 111, 117, 167–168
Spad XIII, 140
Sperry Gyroscopic Company, 119, 120
Sperry, Lawrence, 25, 73
Spirit of St. Louis, 19
St. Andrews Episcopal Church, 132
Standard Aircraft Corporation, 140
Stevens, Albert William, 13, 29–30, 31, 38, 51, 88, 105–108, 123–125
Stinson, Jack Beavers, 78
Stout, Bill, 82
Strange, L. A., 165
Strategic Air Command, 98
Streett, St. Clair "Bill," 28, 36–37
Sutton, Harry, 92

Tarrant Tabor, 156
Taylor, Charlie, 135
"The Flying Bathtub," 111
This Field is Small screenplay, 11
Thomas, B. Douglas, 168
Thomas, Lowell, 11, 155
Thomas-Morse MB-3, 76, 166–168,

Udet, Ernst, 147
USS *Langley* (CV-1), 169

Van Zandt, J. Parker, 40–43
Verville, A. V., 78, 90 111, 116, 117
Verville Racer, 64, 117
Victory Through Air Power, 122
Vin Fiz, 149
Vincent, Jesse G., 16 89, 135
Vought, Chance M., 29, 73, 116, 169

Wade, Leigh, 14, 33–39, 64, 85, 110, 130–131
Warner, Eddie P., 58
Western Air Express, 64
Westinghouse, George, 19
Whitman, Ray, 78
Wickam, Shelby, 10
"widow maker," 141
Wilbur Wright Field, 157, 173
Williams, Al, 46
Wright Aeronautical Corporation, 112
Wright brothers, 152
Wright brothers 1903 Flyer, 135
Wright Field, 63, 88, 124
Wright, Orville, 14, 73, 96, 109, 111–112, 138, 150
Wright-Patterson Air Force Base, 12, 53, 135
Wright Whirlwind engine, 19, 53, 135
Wright, Wilbur, 14, 138

XB-1A, 115, 116
XCO-5, 108–109
XCO-6, 90

Yonkers Aircraft, 93